~ MINTER BAY ~

Land, Lore, Loss, and Lucre

in the

South Salish Sea

Jay Miller, PhD

Minter Bay at low tide

Contents

MINTER BAY

Land, Lore, Loss, and Lucre

Contents

Acknowledgments

Thanks are as on-going as the unfolding and unraveling of the truth about native Minters. Friends at Puyallup, Skokomish, Swinomish, Sauk, and elsewhere among both Lushootseeds have urged me on. As keepers of the notebooks and allies in research, I commend Carla Rickerson, Karyl Winn, Janet Ness, Sandra Kroupa, Diana Shenk, Lisa Scharnhorst, Avril Madison, Jennifer Evans, Linda DiBiase, Steve Eichner, Andrew Popochock, John Medlin, Dr Louis Hieb, and, most especially, Gary Lundell. Other helpful archivists have been Elaine Miller, Lynette Miller, Joy Werlink, Sherrie Maljkovic, Valerie-Anne Lutz, Marilyn Graf, and Gary Fuller Reese. Gary Lundell not only handed me the notebooks for the first time, but he listened to my findings as they unfolded, suggested relevant archival materials, read drafts of this book, and, willingly, spent ten hours in a car touring the Key Peninsula once I was ready to finish off this project (for that moment). Reference Specialist is a title he has richly earned, along with great gratitude from anyone needing help at UW – SC [former MSCUA].

For technical and emotional support, I am grateful to Warren Caldwell, Herb and Natalie Shippen, Tom Steinburn, Ellen Lowe, Astrida Blukis Onat, Lona, Jim, and Claude Wilbur, Brent Galloway, Celia Celffalo, Sarah Campbell, Carolyn Marr, Marge Coale, Ann Chi'en, Coll-Peter Thrush (mostly), Alexandra (Sasha) Harmon, Alan Stay, Catherine Schrup, Harry Chesnin, David Secord, Amy Adams, Charles Roth, Barbara Efrat, Barbara and Robert Lane, James Hirabayashi, John Bower, Jeff Schuster, Laurel Sercombe, Janet Pollak, William Seaburg, Dale Kinkade, Harvey Markowitz, Pamela Amoss, Sam and Janet Stanley, Wayne and Shirley Suttles, Sara Steel, Lucy Steelman, Denis Popochock, Jorge Villarreal, Rahmi Aiken, Bill Holm, Roger Ernesti, Jay Ellis Ransom, Marilyn Richen, Tammy Jackson, John and Marcia Winterhouse, both Bruce Millers, and Vi Hilbert. As a prior book benefited from three mother-son teams, Minter was aided by Popochock father and son of a reading family.

Gratefully, Ann Richel Schuh gave the first draft a thorough reading, heavily marked for coherence. Kurt Reidinger both edited drafts, found edata, particularly for things fishy, and paddled ahead in quest of truth. We were abetted by Patt O'Flaherty. Geoff Keyes, a blacksmith and computer geek working at both ends of the tech scale, saved the day several times.

Closer to home, Mary Laya, Julian Baumel, John Adams, Sally Anderson, Robert Keyes-Bach, and Monday Nite listened well during my incremental enlightenment. In particular, the full recognition of Laura Belle Downey Bartlett's career taught me an important lesson in the limitations of public documents in lieu of seeking out a person in her former home and context.

Lastly, the first identification of the scribe of the Minter notebooks was found in a reprint given to me decades before by either Erna Gunther or Viola Garfield, who both knew Arthur Ballard. All of the permissions for access to and then the slog through archives only served to reveal the obvious once I saw his name in my own Salish files in my own house. Most appropriately, it was his brief autobiography still in native keeping that provided full details. Unlike those who belonged at Minter until burned out, I can indeed say, with Dorothy, there is no place like home.

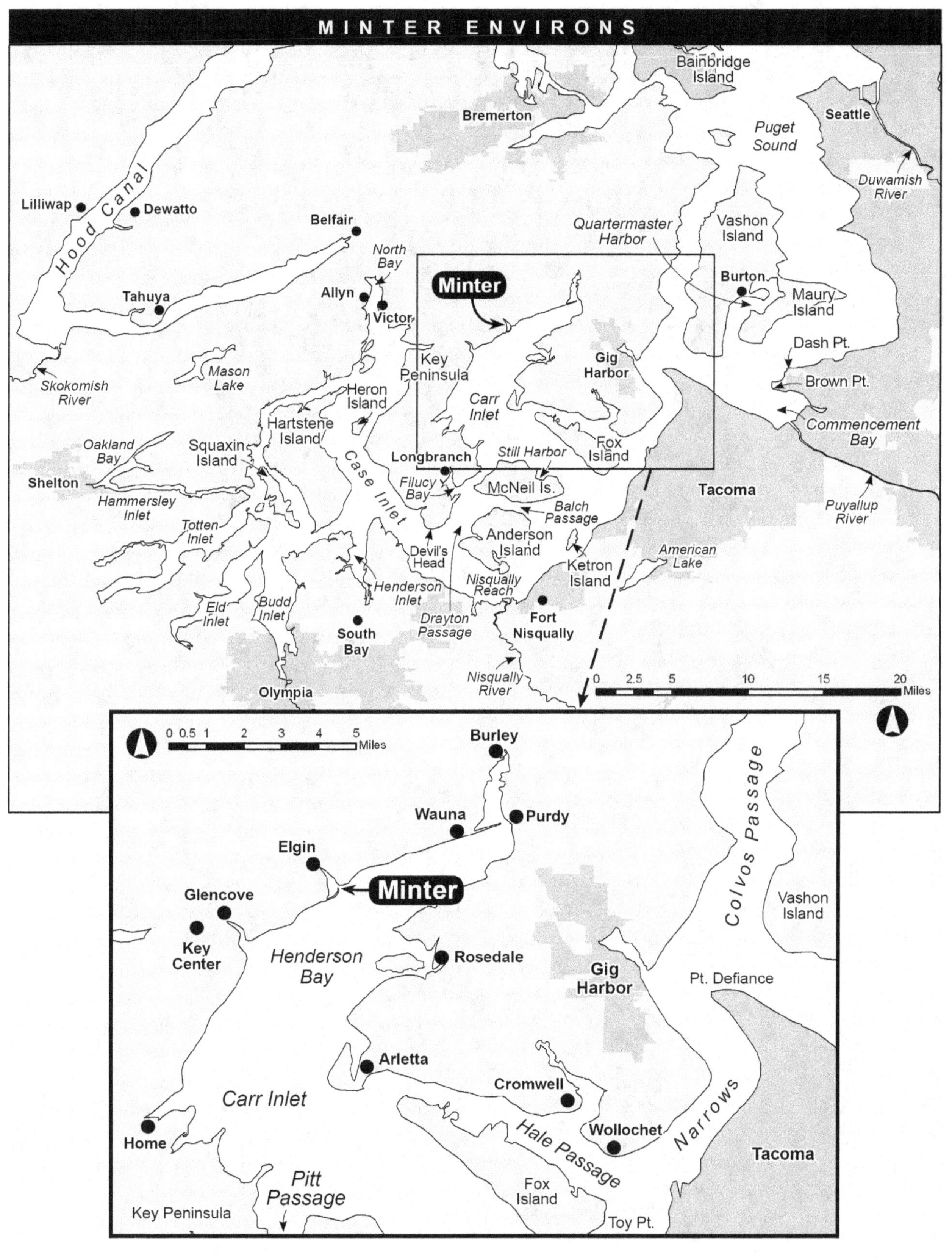
MINTER ENVIRONS
Bainbridge Island
Bremerton
Seattle
Puget Sound
Duwamish River
Lilliwap
Dewatto
Hood Canal
Belfair
Quartermaster Harbor
Vashon Island
North Bay
Minter
Burton
Maury Island
Tahuya
Allyn
Victor
Dash Pt.
Key Peninsula
Gig Harbor
Brown Pt.
Mason Lake
Skokomish River
Heron Island
Carr Inlet
Commencement Bay
Hartstene Island
Oakland Bay
Squaxin Island
Case Inlet
Longbranch
Still Harbor
Fox Island
Shelton
Filucy Bay
McNeil Is.
Tacoma
Hammersley Inlet
Balch Passage
Puyallup River
Totten Inlet
Anderson Island
Devil's Head
American Lake
Ketron Island
Nisqually Reach
Henderson Inlet
Eld Inlet
Budd Inlet
Drayton Passage
Fort Nisqually
South Bay
Nisqually River
Olympia
0 2.5 5 10 15 20 Miles
0 0.5 1 2 3 4 5 Miles
Burley
Purdy
Wauna
Elgin
Glencove
Minter
Key Center
Colvos Passage
Vashon Island
Henderson Bay
Rosedale
Gig Harbor
Pt. Defiance
Arletta
Cromwell
Carr Inlet
Hale Passage
Wollochet
Narrows
Home
Tacoma
Pitt Passage
Fox Island
Key Peninsula
Toy Pt.

Maps

Minter Bay from the Air

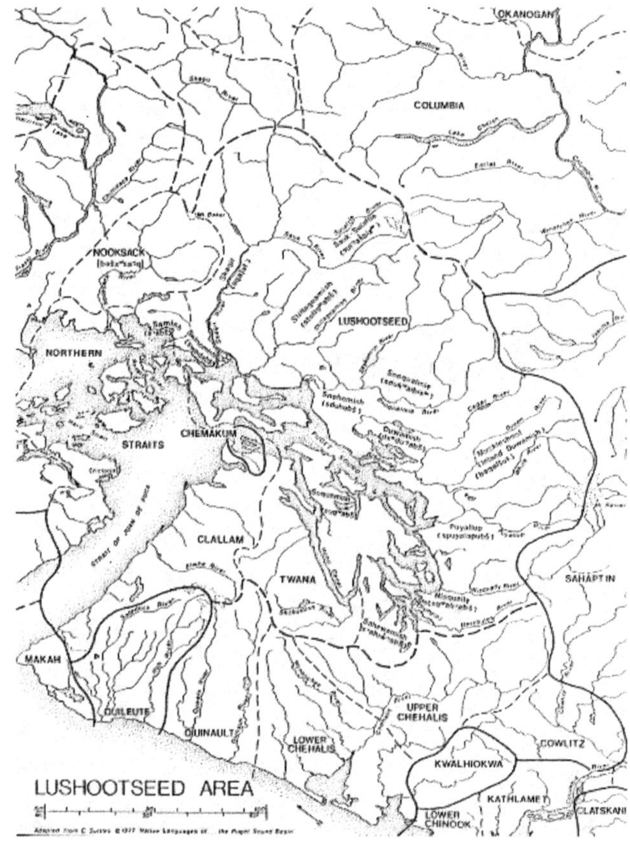

INTRODUCTION

On 8 March 2000 I first looked at three remarkable notebooks filled with handwritten fieldnotes describing a once-thriving native community, known today in English as Minter ~ Minter Bay, near the Narrows at Tacoma in southern Puget Sound, but the scribe neglected to affix his or her name.[1] Intrigued, I have been entangled, ensnared, and immersed in studying the Narrows and Minter environs ever since.

The title refers to both these notebooks and to the dynamics of this native community, always prominent but for a varied reason. Aboriginal Minters were enmeshed in vast indigenous kinship networks, webbed across landscapes, and intergrading cultures, before they became ensnarled and dispossessed of their land and resources by locals working for global forces.

Given my understanding of this native Puget Sound culture as an "anchored radiance" rippling throughout an enmeshing web of rings and rays, these notebooks record details, unique for the region, about this elite community that were impressive and compelling enough to test our academic understanding of published ethnography, including my own. Hooked, I then gave myself one year to identify this unknown ethnographer and untangle the mysteries of the people who lived there, especially those who were personally named in their own native language (Lushootseed)[2] on the diagram of the prime resident household <A13>.[3]

Filled with terms from the Puyallup language (a southern dialect of Lushootseed Puget Salish, transcribed adequately for that time), these notes showed a dynamic, resourceful, prominent town coping with social trauma, arson, and tragic land loss by transforming into their final identity as the competitive eaters ("biters" [sx̣əƛ̓əbabš] or "chompions" [sx̣əƛ̓alikʷabš]) who are mentioned in recent ethnography and federal court cases.[4] During earlier identities, they had

---

1 In a sense, these notebooks found me. A delay in gaining access to the Melville Jacobs collection found me in UW Special Collections the same week as three academic colleagues had asked what I knew of these three notebooks. Since I then knew nothing of them, I decided to have a look. This book is one result.

2 Appendix B provides an overview of this language and guide to the pronunciation of its distinctive sounds.

3 Conventions for quoting pages and text from these notebooks include A, B, C to refer to the three separate notebooks, [ ] mark added clarifications, { } quote direct peculiarities of the original text, and <#> locate the actual pages in the notebooks. Smith internally referred to them as 1, 2, 3, though the covers are marked I, II, III in blue ink.

4 Also [sx̣oƛ̓əbabš, sx̣oƛ̓babš, sx̣oƛ̓alikʷabš, Sot'lbabc]. Linguistic analysis and spelling indicates that the root x̣o'tl̓ [modernized as x̣əƛ̓] means "to bite into, nip, champ, savor at first eating, and, by extension, to gorge," while the rest of the name includes -bš "tribe." Other forms correlated with this root are x̣aƛ̓ "like, want"; x̣əč "mind, thoughts, emotions, sense"; and a compound word for "converse," literally meaning to nibble each other's faces. The name sometimes has the form sx̣o'tl̓alikʷabš with the addition of -alikʷ- to indicate a repetitive activity with a definite finesse and outcome. Insisting that the English translation better conform to the Lushootseed word, with a bit of tweaking, provides "chompions" as the best match. There is, moreover, an implication that nobles in this community were also "swells"

hosted a training (or "finishing") academy (culture camp) for youngsters of the nobility, as well as defended themselves with special powers derived from natural features of their land base.[5]

< §4 Jerry Meeker >

Of particular note, according to Jerry Meeker, the clearly named native elder whose knowledge is recorded and archived between these pages, their homes had been "burned out" by settlers. This occurred before "official local history" when, until the recent past, "the authentic history of Puget Sound is to be read for the most part, in the vellum pages of the unglamorous but unvanquishable Anglo-Saxon."[6] Prominent in later history, Jerry Meeker is famous as a Tacoma booster, real estate tycoon, stalwart Presbyterian, and controversial reservation reformer or "sell-out." Like many others, he is implicated in the "Violence over the Land" that defines the history of America (Blackhawk 2006).

Since these notes had never been properly attributed,[7] they had not entered the court or public record for Lushootseeds. In Washington State, the on-going defense of treaty rights to hunt, fish, and clam gave further incentive to review these notes, allied documents, and the published records. Maps and local histories easily locate the place that is now called Minter, an east-shore notch in the Key Peninsula across the (Puget Sound) Narrows from modern Tacoma, but they do not mention the misnamed "homesteaders" who burned out native homes, both at Minter and their next refuge down the shore at Glencove,[8] in order to log off the land, cash in, and let it revert for taxes in lieu of putting down roots and entering written history. Only decades

---

(LD: 28, 258, 260,263, 264, 292). [***LD*** is the *Lushootseed Dictionary* by Dawn Bates, Thom Hess, and Vi Hilbert, 1994].

[5] By hosting this academy at Minter, the leading family asserted a very high social rank, personally exemplied by Damasq, my term for their head woman. Only a handful of such "queens" as known by name from the region. These include Ki-kai-si-mi-loot, (nicknamed "Queen" by William Tolmie at Fort Nisqually), who aided the 1841 Wilkes US Exploring Expedition; Queen Susan of Chehalis, sister of Chief Yawnish; Yag^{w}ało, daughter of Samish Chief Petius at Bayview; Sally, widow of Tsenahmus, a Chinook chief; and Sneatlum noblewomen from Penn Cove. They were very organized ("bossy") and usually traveled with retainers sometimes described as bodyguards as a sign of their elite rank.

[6] Robert Walkinshaw, *On Puget Sound* 1929: 5.

[7] The late Cecilia Svinth Carpenter (1996, bibliography), daughter of a Nisqually mother and Lutheran pastor, lists these notebooks in her own bibliographies under Arthur Ballard, a near miss as described below.

[8] Glencove became the home of beloved YMCA Camp Seymour for over a century.

later (1880s), during a second wave of bona fide resettlers, does "official history" begin in this region. Overshadowed by the fate of Tacoma, which eventually lost its struggle with Seattle for supremacy on Puget Sound, the fortunes of the South Sound initially rose as Tacoma became the terminus for the northern railroad in 1873 (with service in 1885) and downtown Seattle itself burned down in 1886. But the Puyallup reservation, then as now, stood between Tacoma and all-important routes to the east.

The only obvious name appearing in the notebooks was that of Jerry Meeker, who was interviewed over several summer months according to a fee table in the back of Notebook A (¢/hour). Ironically, he was also a wealthy and famous real estate developer who helped dismantle his own Puyallup reservation to bring railroads and prosperity to Tacoma. After years of my own research, however, he earns sympathy as someone who had been burned out of two deeply-rooted home towns and then resiliently used the experience, as a Presbyterian capitalist, to prosper and nonetheless share. The Brown's Point salmon bakes that he started continue to this day between a square lighthouse and his timbered manse overlooking Commencement Bay, the expanse of Puget Sound north of the Narrows.

For four decades I have been researching, living with, and publishing on the Lushootseed Coast Salish of Puget Sound, especially speakers of northern dialects, but with a growing interest in southern dialect, sometimes distinguished as Whulshootseed (see appendix B). Located at the south end of the newly-named Salish Sea, Puget Sound includes passages, bays, islands, and inlets that provide place-based inspirations for aspects of native language and culture that attract scholarly and personal interest.

By luck, almost fifteen years into this project, I was asked to review story cycles submitted by a Lakota woman who had been gifted them and felt an obligation to make them available to readers, native and others. This was Smith's work, with a page of autobiography, and it lead me to a copy of his novel preserved by Robert Hitchman, which has been combined with the stories and awaits publication.

Alfred John Smith, with a rural education to the eighth grade and two years of Tacoma night school, earned his living as a carpenter and grocer, as well as writing within his own creative framework for general audience. Smith was raised in backwoods Wisconsin at Drywood, east of Minneapolis in Arthur Township, where he finished the eighth grade and early began writing for local newspapers. Married at 20 in 1906, he moved his family to Tacoma to work in the Todd Shipyards during WW I, then ran a grocery store (1919-29) near – what had been until 1903 and would be again in 1936 – the Puyallup Reservation, whose tribal leaders included Jerry Meeker.[9] His move toward more writing was precipitated by events of 1927 when

---

[9] Writing in 1935, just before Puyallup restoration, Smith summarized:

> There is no Indian reservation in Pierce County. The only remaining portion of the tribal lands which once comprised the Puyallup Indian Reservation consists of a parcel of land containing 43.75 acres belonging to the Indian school lands, community property of the Puyallup tribe of Indians.
>
> The Puyallup Indian Reservation was established in 1856 as a method of reconciling the Indians to the occupation of their lands by white settlers, and to protect the Indians from further encroachment by whites. In 1874 patents in trust were issued to the Indians for allotments of land given to them according to the terms

a speeding car crashed into his grocery, broke the plate glass window and pushed the building back two feet; his store was robbed; and months later his shots just missed the well-dress, talkative "Beau Brummel bandit" during a stick up.

In 1929 Smith served one term as elected Representative from the 28th District (western Pierce County) to the Washington State Legislature. He divorced in 1932, after 26 years of marriage and six children, and began concentrating on native lore and stories. In the 1930s he polished entries for guide books to Tacoma and to Washington State, local contributions to Works Progress Administration (WPA). By 1935, he finished his story cycles. During WW II, Smith moved as a federal contract carpenter to Kodiak Island, Alaska. Back in Tacoma on 5 October 1946, he remarried ten days later to Margaret Peterson, a woman born at Forks and raised among Quileutes of the coast. In 1948, when he was 62, he asked Arthur Ballard, Erna Gunther, and Jerry Meeker (then 86) for help with a novel, titled Old Lukh.[10] He fully retired in 1956, traveling by early motor home. Ill for three years, he died in 1971.

My obsession with the Minter notebooks, therefore, lasted beyond that first year, as my renewed research became, by turns, compelling, sad, quirky, bizarre, depressing, and again resolute. It brought together people who were simultaneously natives and homesteaders, real estate tycoons and displaced peoples, heroes and scoundrels. Indeed, my growing sense of angst about the ethnohistoric complexities of the native village at Minter, Washington, as well as a dynamic chronicle of its surroundings, kept me going in fits and starts. Here was a complex, adaptive, elite, and resourceful community to challenge prior static portrayals (including my own) of Lushootseeds.[11] Moreover, since Minter was in the south Sound, they were more properly Whulshootseed, speakers of the southern or so-called Nisqually dialect. This book makes amends for slighting them in the past, favoring the northern or Skagit dialect because it

---

of the treaty, and on Jan. 20, 1886, 167 of these patents were signed by the president. In 1887 Congress passed the Dawes Severalty Bill, which provided that any Indian who had a patent in trust became eligible to citizenship rights.

An Act of Congress in 1893 provided for the sale of Indian allotments to white buyers, by the Indians, particularly if near the cities of Tacoma or Puyallup. During the next ten years the greater portion of the Reservation lands was brought by white men. All that is now left of the Puyallup Indian Reservation is the site of the Cushman Indian School. This school was promised to the tribe as a part of the consideration for signing the Medicine Creek Treaty, and functioned as a trade school until 1920 when it was converted into a soldier's hospital. Upon completion of the American Lake Hospital, the Cushman Hospital became a tubercular sanitarium for invalid Indian children from Oregon, Idaho, Wyoming and Alaska. School work in the first eight grades is given. Chief Quo-School work in the first eight grades is given. Chief Quo-youp-kin, (Thos. Lane, 1852-1905) was the last tribal chief of the Puyallups, they becoming full fledged citizens in 1903.

[10] By tragic irony, Ballard's own life's work, *Listen My Nephew*, was withdrawn by his children while in publication and has been lost ~ misplaced for half a century. The Smith novel, therefore, provides a surviving if sideways look at what Ballard knew and had done.

[11] Jay Miller, *Shamanic Odyssey* 1988; *Lushootseed Culture and the Shamanic Odyssey* 1999; and many articles listed in the bibliography. Later ones, including this book, expand Wayne Suttles' insight that Salish feature an anchored radiance of nexus, rings, rays, and ramps.

had more speakers, more population, and the outstanding elder-scholar Vi Hilbert, a justly lauded national treasure.

By any count, therefore, my Minter "mysteries" have now gone on for over a decade. Most of the vital information was indeed gathered in that first year while I lived in Seattle. The torching of Minter was not worthwhile, except, however, for the price earned for logging off some trees. Instead it was another act in a tangled series of personal failures, painful deaths, and family tragedies that make the story iconic, ironic, and epic. As a place, Minter had a forgotten (~~erased~~ in academic jargon) early "history," which was largely native, privileged, and then brutal, before any official record.

Impressed by the ethnographic and linguistic data in these three notebooks, as well as by increasing awareness of the controversial fame of Jerry Meeker, I soon moved to substantiate the location, the resources, and the history of this terrain (now known as the Key Peninsula) that juts thumblike into southern Puget Sound. While the first two conditions were easy to meet, the third led to the appalling realization that "history" (in the sense of an Anglo-American coherent story written in English) began after the events chronicled in these notes and substantiated by archived documents. Many locals and a few scholars had written about this region, but none seemed aware of all that had happened decades before "official" history started in the 1880s, establishing "pioneer" family lines that are still obvious in this area and implicating their ancestors.[12] As is typical of the West, natives were rarely if ever consulted, except for outgoing elders like Jerry Meeker, about their own histories and homelands.[13]

Minter was long a home base: the nexus of place-based culture set in well-known space. "Place is security, space is freedom … place is an archive of fond memories and splendid achievements that inspire [and inform] the present; place is permanent … reassuring to … chance and flux everywhere."[14] Minter, however, was also a locus of trauma and pain, mentioned in these notes and confirmed in other widely-scattered documents.

After authoring several collaborations, books, and articles about Lushootseeds, I was well aware that native villages had been routinely burned out by settlers to claim these rich lands as their own, often "under color of homestead laws." Elders providing Land Claims testimony in the 1930s and 1950s, usually began, "They burned our homes at …." Every recent historical review adds to these generalities. For example, for Snoqualmies, "It was much easier to force the Indians off the land than it was to clear the virgin forest for farms. Protected by the presence of a small but powerful show of soldiers and gunboats on Puget Sound, settlers were able to frighten local Indians from their aboriginal villages [where] homes, tools, weapons, food

---

[12] Raymond (Father Thaddeus) Arledge, *Early Days of the Key Peninsula* 1998; Douglas Knapp, A History of Peninsula Lutheran Church, 1904-1979, 1985; Deanie Gallaghan, Minter - compiled from the Key Peninsula Civic Center Newsletter 1976.

[13] Lack of consulting has been devastating, especially the multi-million dollar failure to consult with their own elders by Lower Elwa Klallams and City of Port Angeles, exposing hundreds of graves at their ancestral village of Tse-whit-zen trying to dig a graving pond (dry dock) for new pontoons for Seattle's floating bridges. See Linda Mapes, *Breaking Ground* 2009.

[14] Yi-Fu Tuan, *Space and Place. The Perspective of Experience* 1977: 3, 154. Anne Black and Adam Liljeblad, *Guide to Methods Used for Developing, Analyzing, and Preparing Social Data Related to Attachment to Place* 2006.

supplies and ceremonial artifacts went up in smoke."[15] But these arsons, though still lamented by native families, were faceless – abstract legal matters of lost "improvements" and real estate costs.

Opening these notebooks gave names, Lushootseed ones at that, and, in a sense, faces, to those who had lived at Minter for eons. Via them, my previous ethnographic overviews of Puget Sound became more animated and nuanced by real people in specific daily conditions.[16] Notably, its headwoman (herein called Damasq for ease of reference) and a slave with doctoring power (Dr Simon) add greater complexity to standard accounts, as do the controversial deaths and disappearances of other community members at a time when Tacoma, intent on being the major city in the region, was frustrated by the Puyallup Reservation standing between its downtowns and railroad access to the inland US.[17]

Minter and nearby Glencove are deep in archaeological sites. A carefully screened visit to the records of the state archaeologist showed that Minter Pointe indeed had a long and intense prehistoric occupation that left a midden deposit that is (or was) eight-feet deep. In all, seven prehistoric sites, designated by Roman numerals, were marked on a sketch map of the bay. The relative sequencing by date and occupation for many of these, discussed in Chapter 2, are revealed in the first two notebooks.

My drive to Minter itself, however, confronted locked gates leading to prime waterfront property and beaches that, only in Washington State, are privately owned. (This issue of states rights and private ownership of beaches complicated the federal trial confirming federal-treaty-tribe rights to shellfish on local beaches. Everywhere else, including California and Hawaii, beaches are public property and officially designated as highways.) Fortunately, the state-owned Minter salmon hatchery happily provides public access to the creek and bay, where Puyallup tribal members erected their own fish trap during the contentious 1960s leading up to the famous trial when Judge George Boldt in 1974 confirmed native treaty rights to half the harvestable salmon.

---

15 Kenneth Tollefson, The Snoqualmie Indians as Hop Pickers, *Columbia* 1995: 41.

16 Recent abuse by university presses and supposedly-educated authors violating the technical (IPA) alphabet for accurately writing this complex Salish language has led me to several solutions. A few reviewers of my books have been overtly hostile to respecting the technicalities of Lushootseed, unwilling to respect the language on its own terms. Many complain that all these native names are too confusing to sort out. Based on years of effort to discuss those who lived at Minter, my range of naming strategies is based on the significant role of each person. If someone had an English name, such as Moses, that is used here. For others, when mention is occasional, I have used their native names without misappropriating or insulting the sanctity of their "real names," often passed on to descendants, who continue to "carry" them. A few names have anglicized versions, while key figures are given English equivalents, such as Gizmo, the town's craftman, and, to clearly identify her in her elite role, Damasq, the ranking woman.

17 Until a tunnel was blasted through the mountains at Stampede Pass, railroad passengers boated down the Columbia River to Kalama (named for a Hawaiian-Nisqually family), where they switched to track along Puget Sound to Tacoma. Reflecting their keen rivalry, Seattle was not listed on the train schedules in the hopes that it would likewise vanish, Murray Morgan, *Puget's Sound* 1979.

Filling in details from mainstay Eastern US archives (the other Washington = DC), moreover, delayed the finish of my research. But it also increased my suspicions about the timing of the two arsons, each occurring as another federal law loomed to secure native title to this homeland, or the village part of it. Instead, plank longhouses at both Minter and Glencove, where leading families continued to live for part of the year, were burned out a decade apart.[18]

The pivotal federal documents behind the torching of Minter, moreover, had their own nefarious purpose – namely, the abject alienation of natives from their ancestral communities and communal tribal lands. Providing legal title to their ownership "private" lands was intended to "pulverize" a tribe's communal integrity; asserting the primacy of private property (government endorsed "selfishness") deliberately intended to be at the "expense" of tribal cohesion.

This Act of 3 March 1875 (18 Stat 402, 420) permitted those who "abandoned their tribal relations" to homestead as individuals under federal laws on the public domain "to induce Indians to leave their tribal life on the reservations and to take up the habits and customs of civilized life in white communities." A Circular of Instructions issued by the General Land Office on 25 March 1875 specified that each "make affidavit that they have adopted the habits and pursuits of civilized life." Witnesses, hardly disinterested, to each "signed" (X marked) document were local white settlers and debtor merchants dependent on native labor and purchases.

A decade later, on 4 July 1884, about the time the refuge at Glencove was burned out, Congress passed a specific Indian Homestead Act to encourage natives to act like alienated whites while retaining an ethnic identity.[19] This act was especially beneficial to Sauks and Chehalis in Washington State, providing them with a land base in their homelands even as they survived by scattering thinly through the region.

Looking at the wider context shows more of the general pattern. This kind of cross-cultural, global perspective is properly that of anthropology, and it is to that field that I have allied myself, with reservations. Anthropologists – informed advocates – watch, witness, and synthesize from the sidelines in their writings, while historians actually wrap the story around themselves – but for very Euro-centric reasons. Their version of history is told for general readers in a national language, not in the idioms of imperiled communities. Native idioms are ignored, or, worse – distorted. Here I will seek to bend the English to suite the Lushootseed, rather than follow common (colonialist, settler, arrogant) practice. The American English-only hostility to other languages, unlike the multilingualism of neighboring Canada and Mexico, has and is doing harm to native communities. For example, in later years, the Minters became famous for public gorging at eat-all feasts that gained them a designation that best translates as "chompions," as used here, though "engorgers" will also be used.

---

[18] The 1874 homesteader at Minter was neighbor Calvin Burkett, who quickly transferred his claim to an employee, who then sold it to Calvin's ex-wife. Glencove was claimed in 1884 by William Rains and family. George Minter and family from Nebraska homesteaded the point during the second wave of settlement and so his name entered official regional history. Burkett and Isaac Hawk first filed on lots near Minter in 1866.

[19] Felix S Cohen's *Handbook of Federal Indian Law* 1942: 186, 222. The 1884 homesteads were held in trust by the Bureau of Indian Affairs for 25 years, and sometimes extended for another 25 years, unless, through a bizarre process, the native person applied for and was granted, on testimony of local merchants, bosses, and officials, a "certificate of competency."

I want to be unsettling, but in insightful ways. For example, Native American remains the politically correct term for those whose ancestry is rooted in the Americas. In Canada, the appropriate term is First Nations, encompassing Aboriginals, Inuit, and Metis. The name much more in use, especially among the people themselves, however, is Indians, though it came from a mistaken hope that early Spanish ships had reached India. It has persisted, though modified as American Indian, fueling the confusion and distortion that are basic features of colonialism – serving to keep everyone unsettled. Whenever I can, however, I will use *Indien* in this book (for the Indies, instead of India), adopting the solution of Europe and French Canada, apart from American US burdens and confusions. No single name serves all purposes or all times.

Three Notebooks

Opening three bound, grey-cloth-covered notebooks, still bearing their price stickers (.35¢) from the University of Washington bookstore, reveals strongly angular writing, rich in detail and full of native Salishan words rendered in remarkably good transcriptions. Most of the specific letters used to write them down in these notebooks derive from a technical system proposed by linguists in 1916, setting the oldest date for the writing of these notes. The most recent date is 1955, when Jerry Meeker, their source, died.

Though newspapers and other records usually list Jerry as a Puyallup, even as he worked to dismantle this reservation and its tribal membership, this claim derived from his Minter-born mother Sally. His father Jim had moved south during the 1850s Skykomish diaspora throughout the Sound.[20] The Skykomish fork to the north and Snoqualmie to the south are tributaries off the Snohomish stem and all three tribes were "officially" to be resettled by treaty on the Tulalip Reservation, though federal agents knew there was not enough room for all of them. Of further note, as Sally was a native speaker of the southern dialect and his father spoke the northern one, Jerry learned to be fully fluent in both major Lushootseed dialects.[21]

To identify Jerry's Minter scribe, I found and questioned all those once familiar with this type of Puget Sound research. Increased Internet proficiency helped me to locate (and "resurrect") several anthropologists then in their 80s, who had been involved with Sound natives in the 1930s, 40s, and 50s, but they could shed no light on these notebooks. Fearful that Minter could turn into an everlasting wild goose chase, I went on to other projects.

At first, it was the outer forms of the notebooks that led me on. Their purchase stickers, cloth covers, and pen ink in several colors assured me it was someone working locally, but none of the faculty or graduate students that I knew (or knew of) could be linked to them by comparing handwriting samples or research topics. My contacts with scholars in Indiana, Philadelphia, New York, and London raised various possibilities, only to have all of them

---

20 The fate of the Skykomish tribe, Jim's own, remains baffling, though a strong clue appears in Arthur Ballard's writing about one of its ruthless slaving families, marauding from their upriver refuge. Retaliation from downriver warriors probably dispersed this stronghold and, with it, most of the Skykomish. During the Treaty War, Patkanim ~ Patkadib forced almost 300 Skykomish downriver, a major disruption that further scattered them.

21 Thus, within Whulshootseed, some Puyallups spell their own version of the language as txʷəlšucid. Each river entering the Sound, of course, once also had its own dialect and heritage peculiarities.

dashed. A possible link to the 1950's Indian Land Claims sparked other possibilities that also soon led to dead-ends.

My later attempts focused on the notebook's inner contents such as the inscriptions themselves instead of their outward forms, which strongly suggested they were probably done in 1948, because the "recent" death of a centenarian who must be Reverend Matthew G Mann (1843-1945) is mentioned in notebook C. Later, the name of the scribe (Alfred John Smith) jumped out of an all-too-familiar source by Arthur Ballard, the renowned regional amateur who had early been ruled out as having been the scribe himself.[22] Like any search, the successful quest ended not far from where it began, but with better understanding of why.

Indeed, after being led widely astray by a quest for an academic, the carpenter, housepainter, and hack who was Alfred John Smith[23] devoted 1948 to concentrating his literary efforts toward understanding native home life in Puget Sound, aided by recognized local authorities, both native and scholar. Because he was not an academic, his record keeping and identifying signature was more relaxed, adding to the challenge of using Jerry Meeker's information.

Today as then, the Puyallup River flows into the bay now ringed by the City of Tacoma, whose founders worked with Jerry to abolish his reservation. The Puyallup Tribe has managed to survive, thankfully, clinging to a tiny but valuable land base at the shipping port. Ancestrally, they occupied this river along with nearby islands and the shores around the constriction known as the Tacoma Narrows, which serves as a geologic bellows for circulating the tidal flows of Puget Sound.

The rich soils of the Puyallup flood plain were developed into extensive berry and fruit farms, which relied heavily on Indien "stoop labor." Thus, at the same time as the Puyallups were being threatened and "extinguished," other natives from throughout the region were flocking there to earn cash by working the Fall harvests, leaving their own home villages vulnerable.[24] Puyallup lands became the most urban in the region, with the give and take of

---

22 This turning point came (after 18 months) at the end of Labor Day, 2001, when the word Minter jumped out at me from Arthur Ballard, Calendric Terms of the Southern Puget Sound Salish, 1950, based on Leona Cope, Calendars of the Indians North of Mexico, 1919. A reference to other notes by Smith from Lewis on Hood Canal adds to the mystery since these are now lost, and are not among the papers of WW Elmendorf at UC Berkeley.

23 Erroneously seeking a scholar named Smith resulted in false leads. A brief flicker involved Alfred (Fred) G Smith, a Micronesianist at the University of Oregon and University of Texas until learning that his middle initial was G. An Alfred John Smith was the only person of that name listed by the UW registrar, though he is unknown to the Alumni staff and so cannot be traced further. He attended UW from 1948 to 1950, transferring from Santa Monica City College. He graduated with a BA in English and Spanish on 10 June 1950, and became a Seattle school teacher. Efforts to trace membership in local anthropological societies drew a blank. Norman Lerman (*Legends of the River People* 1976: 5) describes, for 1950, that his own fieldwork collecting Chilliwack stories was "to qualify for admission to the anthropology department at the University of Washington" and provide the subject of his MA thesis. This was exceptional since most regional fieldwork was being done by enrolled graduate students.

24 Indeed, while they were away working at the Puyallup harvest, the Sauks were burned out of their North Cascades main village. The next year (1889), the Quileute village of La Push, on

increased suffering and compensatory cash settlements. Throughout this book, Puyallup tribal members remain in the background, as they have requested.

During the 1970s, rival tribal leaders exchanged gunfire. Puyallup activist, Bob Satiacum, confounding what happened at Minter, was convicted for arsoning rival native businesses as well as other crimes, but he fled the US and was given political asylum by the government of Canada. Only after his death was his body allowed back for burial at the Puyallup cemetery, near Jerry Meeker and his family. Today Puyallups earn millions of dollars from successful gambling operations that once included a moored paddlewheel riverboat, the *Emerald Queen*, for the same reason that their reservation was coveted initially – they are strategically located on the waterfront of the City of Tacoma, the hub of "old money" in Washington and the Northwest, as well as the vital I-5 corridor.

Minter in Place: Truth vs. History

Early America was supposedly a "wilderness," even though fire, sweat, and human hands over many millennia had actually groomed it into a park-like setting (a "tendedness").[25] All too soon, migrants made it over-harvested, polluted, and ~ or destroyed by commercial exploitation so that the scarring after-effects of Euro-American presence are now all too obvious. Natives pride themselves on living *with* nature not *from* it. When, ravaged by epidemics and land loss, they could no longer care for their native landscapes, these lands reverted to the so-called "wilderness" perceived by early deadbeat Europeans, giving credence to the lie. At Minter, natives were perceived as "wandering" by season and "drifting around in canoes" when they were actually on regular rounds, rings, or commutes to their ancestral "grounds and stations" (to use the terms of their treaties). Edwin Starling, the first local Indian Agent, based at Steilacoom, wrote erroneously in 1852 that "In their canoes they float through life, wandering in different seasons to the places abounding most in the different kinds of foods,"[26] as they well knew from eons of residency.

Because variously burning out, torching, or arson (a "crime" backed by guns, dynamite, and the Law) were crucial in "shifting" ownership from Indiens to settlers, some of the philosophical aspects and practical quirks of **fire** will be noted from time to time in this book, and pondered again in the finale.

Providing any kind of global "truth" about the past five hundred years in the Americas is a daunting task. Instead, we will look locally at Minter – one spot of shoreline along southern Puget Sound in the far US Northwest (of western Washington State) which is remote in time and

---

the verge of being designated the heart of an established federal reservation, was burned out by a would-be claimant with the loss of over thirty houses. The Bureau of Indian Affairs, fulfilling its mandate, protected the site and bought new lumber so people could rebuild. Sauks and Upper Skagits continued to suffer great hardships for a century until they received joint federal recognition in 1972.

25 "'Wilderness' is the thought product of a people who see themselves as separate from environment ... no longer in direct contact with nature," See Fikret Berkes, *Sacred Ecology* 1999: 154.

26 Arledge, *Early Days of the Key Peninsula* 1998: 14, #9.

close in space (once a short drive or boat ride ten miles northwest of Tacoma until urban sprawl bottlenecked traffic on the Narrows Bridge(s) to much extend the drive time).

Set at modern Minter Bay (sometimes called Minter Beach), these three notebooks, despite the best of intentions, were originally misfiled among Pioneer papers at the University of Washington Libraries because they were confused with those of Ezra Meeker – a famous early settler, writer, and Oregon Trail booster – who made and lost a fortune as the Hops King of Washington. Instead, the Meekers of Minter, through Jim the father, took the last name of Ezra because he was their employer, and thus patron of Jerry Meeker's family. Other early pioneers in these records, unfortunately, were grasping arsonists, torching one (Minter), then, a decade later, a second (Glencove) native settlement of these families. What may have been forced by the financial desperation of homesteaders, nonetheless ended in personal failure and tragedy for at least one of these families – the Burketts.

Instead, for natives, what these notes reveal is an "intense belonging" based in residency, regular seasonal commutes, and thorough familiarity with the life web of this locale passed on over many generations. These native inhabitants are linked through both ancient and on-going experiences with this very nurturing place, which also once served as a campus for the training of noble children. Indeed, a better recognition of these contents, corroborated in other widely-scattered documents, reveals multiple truths which are always lurking behind "official" or "booster" history.

The worst of this inquiry, for me, is that, a decade apart, these two Native American settlements were burned out, though no one seems to have been badly hurt or killed outright. Their "white" neighbors knew when natives would be away stocking up food. Since food, kin, and other refuges were locally available, exiled natives could flee in their canoes along the shoreline to avert dire starvation, exposure hazards, and intense suffering. They moved on to other seasonal camp sites, or homes of kin, and began again.[27]

To find out who some of these burners were in Washington Territory (a state after 1889) and why they acted as they did, as already noted, I had to visit the other Washington (DC, city not state), where the records of these homesteads still reside, a century and a half after application and "prove up" finalized the sales.

Thus, in thoroughly quirky, bureaucratic, "government work" fashion, to learn about the West, I had to go East, making sure to initial, date, and time by hour and minute every scrap of paper that was laboriously retrieved for me from the innards of the old US National Archives (AI) in downtown DC.[28] Concerned with an ethnography of research, I also tried to figure out

---

[27] In the uplands of the Cascade Mountains, however, such torchings had a more brutal impact because havens were fewer and more remote, as were kin refuges and vital resources. The Sauks, for example, could only live on unwanted terrain after their major town on Sauk Prairie was burned out and homesteaded by armed threat. These no-man's-lands were river sandbars, wedged between the forests claimed by loggers and the rivers claimed by licensed fishers. In time, violent settlers on the bountiful Sauk Prairie turned weapons on each other, giving rise to the legend of a native curse upon their lost homeland.

[28] During research on Minter I spent much time in archives across the US; where virtually all of them had staffing and cataloguing problems that only got worse as key people retired without adequate heirs and whole units imploded. In April 2004, the UW Anthropology Department

how certain documents ended up where they were least expected, and why certain collections became scattered.[29]

Sometimes, as with ever-elusive Minterite Isaac Hawk, there was no clear paper trail until a chance remark – by a lifelong Minter resident (though she properly calls her locale Elgin) about an old bachelor Fred Hawk who sometimes provided well water to her grade school – finally opened the way to a fuller biography of this wealthy landowner. Growing suspicion of a Masonic connection among the principals was confirmed when I visited their graves near Olympia, the state capitol, where they lie with other members of this fraternal order in one of the oldest settler cemeteries.

At Minter, moreover, a century into the history of the United States, a decade before known local history, and twenty years before the Frontier was officially declared closed in 1890, evidence scattered in federal and regional archives can now be understood against the contents of these three previously anonymous notebooks preserved in Seattle. Figuring out the mysteries in these notebooks and other documents is the subject of this book, as well as a goad for my occasional wry commentary in footnotes. As a novel ethnographic source, these notebooks are also an independent test on what has come before and after in the professional scholarly literature.

Errant Documents

After I had exhausted all the UW public archives, I knew that one other stash of materials remained on the UW campus in the Burke Museum but access was restricted (not to say closed entirely). Fortunately, a more sympathetic, if brief, director, through the help of a friendly curator, granted access to the clinching files.

Though I did not plan it that way, these notebooks were best tackled after I had thirty years experience in Puget Sound. At any earlier stage, too much of the record would have been baffling and impossible to ferret out. Even with that hindsight, however, many of my missteps came from making wrong or hasty assumptions. Chief among these was quickly ruling out that the scribe was specifically Arthur C Ballard of Auburn. Yet everything I know tells me that he was the lynchpin for all the Lushootseed research done during the first half of the 1900s, especially in the south Sound. Thus, instead of stopping with the assumption that he did not do them, I should have realized more quickly that he was the most likely person to know who had actually done these notebooks and probably had a hand in introducing that person to Jerry Meeker and local fieldwork.

"killed" the Roy Webb Library, scattering and trashing materials representing the full century of its faculty and scholarly history. All these archival tragedies added to other depressing aspects of Minter, though the few archival heroes appear in my acknowledgements. Nor has cost saving shifts to digital media been all that helpful since colors, textures, and tell-tale smears do not always appear with any clarity.

29 Eldridge Morse's history of the Treaty War, sent to Herbert Bancroft and now at UC Berkeley, notes of Wallatchett Bay "sometimes called Cut Throat Bay. The old Indian name is Solhoochett Bay. There were men stopping here many years ago, one had his throat cut by Indians, hence name of Cut Throat Bay, the rest all left, and for many years one person lived there. In 1868 GW Lathrop and David Daniels began logging there …" (1880 #17: 20).

The internal politics at the University of Washington among dean's office, anthropology department, and the Burke Museum also played a heavy-handed role. Here is where experience, patience, and timing paid off, again in hindsight. Ballard was the premier authority on southern Lushootseeds, an amateur in the fullest sense, who did it for abiding (if obsessive) love ("his only vice," he said). He helped ease all early academic fieldworkers into these native communities, beginning with John Peabody Harrington in 1910, and blossoming with Thomas Talbot Waterman in 1918, then later Erna Gunther, Marian Smith, and many others. Regrettably, his family suppressed all his research as he died, so his great contributions have remained largely unrecognized.

In 1951, when Seattle had its own Anthropological Society, Ballard was honored with a lifetime achievement award. He was presented with a check for $50, the title of "Field Research Assistant in Anthropology," and more importantly, published an article pulling together thirty years of work on the native calendar systems, inspired by Waterman, his first professional colleague.[30]

My own copy of Ballard's publication was a gift from either Erna Gunther or Viola Garfield; but I had never found in the various archives any of its typescript, supporting notes, or other evidence. With my growing (though false) realization that a Burke Museum car (based on car oil and mileage tallies inside the back cover of notebook A) was probably involved in getting the interviewer to Brown's Point, Jerry Meeker's home, I yearned to look in the forbidden Burke archives.[31] I knew that there were so-called Director's Files from the time of Erna Gunther and before. These had been kept off limits because they included unflattering letters about colleagues and salary stubs protected by privacy considerations.[32] A new director with a Northwest specialty, for the first time in forty years, gave me an opportunity to look at these files, ostensibly to seek the use of museum cars during the 1930s and 1940s. While such records did exist for the 30s, none seem to have been kept for the Second World War, and it now looks like Al Smith used his own car.

Nonetheless, among Erna Gunther's Burke papers there is a typed and corrected draft of the Ballard 1950 article. Had I not already known her SC ~ MSCUA files and the notebooks, I would not have recognized as readily the significance of this Ballard draft. Adding to the extra-legal complexities, the journal editor, Leslie Spier, Erna's ex-husband (by contract not marriage license), would have known Ballard from his time at UW, and clearly still admired his efforts. Indeed, a vast support network mobilized to get Ballard's lifework into print in time for his honoring. Checking the month terms, Ballard includes close, but not exact, quotes from the first notebook <A56-9>, thanking "Mr Alfred J Smith, a volunteer student of Indian life and lore" for his notes from (a) Skokomish Robert Lewis and (b) Puyallup Jerry Meeker. Indeed, in his burst of newfound interest, during 1948, Smith produced three notebooks and a novel, relying on his

---

30 Ballard, Calendric Terms 1950: 10-11.

31 The late Wes Wehr played a heroic role since he saved these files from a dumpster decades ago and convinced the Burke to keep them. It now appears that Smith used his own car and used these figures, like his meticulous word counts for each of his works, to keep track of accounting and pricing details.

32 Needless to say, obvious pay stubs could be easily set aside without a glance, though it goes without saying that a weekly salary from 1930 would not buy a snack today.

twin tale collections from 1935, when he worked with many native elders on place names, as well as a lost poetry volume.

Raised in backwoods Wisconsin, Smith started writing early for local newspapers. Married at 20 in 1906, he moved his family to Tacoma to work in the Todd Shipyards during WW I. He divorced in 1932, after 26 years of marriage and six children. During WW II, Smith moved as a federal contract carpenter to Kodiak Island, Alaska. Returning to Tacoma on 5 October 1946, he remarried ten days later to a woman, Margaret ??, born at Forks near the Washington Coast and raised among nearby Quileutes, sparking his return to writing about native home life.

His interviews with Jerry Meeker served as background for his novel, and the three notebooks were left with Erna at the Burke, used to augment Ballard's article, then were taken to the archives (probably by Erna herself) to become erroneously recatalogued under the much more famous Ezra Meeker name. Since Erna left the Burke, then called the Washington State Museum, under duress when the new museum was built, it now seems likely that her papers were not transferred in an orderly fashion. Many went to the archives, but her own fieldwork notebooks and some editing projects remained behind at the Burke. Some were included in the Director's instead of her own research files because she held that position for decades.

Another article in draft is a last (only?) joint effort by Erna and Mel Jacobs toward publishing Ballard's paper on the Green River salmon weir in the 1956 *Davidson Journal of Anthropology*, a departmental serial edited by graduate students and named in memory of a faculty member whose death seriously upset the course of the department. Daniel Sutherland Davidson, an Australianist, had been hand-picked by Erna to become chair but died of a heart attack before he could lead Anthropology into the future.

Since the three Smith-Meeker notebooks are in Special Collections (SC, former MSCUA), but the context for quoting from them is in the Burke Museum, the confusion over their attribution, dating, and motivation can be traced to the sad and abrupt departure of Dr Erna Gunther from this museum she had guided for decades. She took her seniority and fame to the University of Alaska, where she experienced the 1964 earthquake, then returned to Seattle, continuing research and writing projects until her death. There is no record that she ever talked about or used the Minter notebooks herself.[33] For a time after she returned to Seattle, Erna was my neighbor, but long before these notebooks and other manuscript materials became of interest.

Nexus of Pivots, Rays, Rings, Ramps

Like an anchored canoe rippling the water, Lushootseed culture has been described as an anchored radiance, with its vital energies flowing in rays and rings from a pivotal nexus at the center, which is its source and summary. Expressing human culture, this enmeshing web

---

[33] Other materials she was editing have already had happy outcome, by my own efforts. With Erna's death, more manuscript pages typed by Morning Dove ~ Christine Quintasket, a native Colville author, came to my attention and, retrieving them from an attic in Yakima, I edited her autobiography as *Mourning Dove* 1990.

consists of personal ~ sensory; interpersonal ~ social ~ institutional; and cosmic zones, discussed in greater detail elsewhere and abbreviated as SIC components.[34]

The Minter notebooks allow the restudy of this image because their data, once rearranged into topical chapters, comprise activities such as the annual harvesting that is ray-like and the ring-like social institutions of kinscape and landscape extending from a personal home hearth to ripple outward. Cosmic radiations through spirits, epic myths, rituals, and worldview are provided by Jerry's work with scholars, as well as existing ethnographies.

Missing from all prior discussions is recognition of ramps – a transposing of wholesale changes in the status, identity, and social community which serve to adapt a town over time and fate. At the personal sensory level are both Dr Simon, a freed slave, and Jerry Meeker, a tribal elder cum real estate tycoon who sold off much of the Puyallup Reservation. At the community level, Minter shifted its corporate identity in the aftermath of epidemics, slave raids, and hostile take-over of its town sites. Though I was initially surprised by this new insight, my recheck of the ethnography shows that there is an indigenous sense of such radical shifts in the concept of the "capsizing" of the world to start new eras.[35] This phrasing, as so much else, is best described for Twana, where it is called "the capsizing" (*sp̓əláč*).[36] The equivalent in Lushootseed is *g*^{w}*al*, though Jerry himself used the term *dsak*^{u} [*ʣak*^{w}, compare *ʣal* "turn over, upside down" or *ʣaq'* "topple, fell"].

Overall, expanding on Wayne Suttles's insight for the Katzie on the Fraser River "while local villages had far-ranging social ties through marriage and kinship, along with wider

---

34 See Jay Miller, A 'Struckon' Model of Delaware Culture and the Positioning of Mediators; *American Ethnologist* 6 (4): 791-802 1979.

35 Meeker to Marian Smith, Reel, Frame 0898, Cf *LD*: 87, 88. Of course, knowing to look for change led me to the early and important excavations on Pender Island, where "dating between 4500 and 3000 BP ... shows the nearly full development of Northwest Coast culture — the memorial or funeral potlatch based on direct evidence for feeding the dead, craft specialization, masks and ceremonialism, different labret types indicating social ranking, wood working, three-dimensional sculptural art, and a continuity of marine subsistence … overall evidence … indicates that head deformation gradually superseded labrets as a visible sign of high rank in the Coast Salish region. The logical inference is that the system of social rank remained while only its visible expression changed … The basic belief system … has considerable similarity with that of the ethnographic Coast Salish. First, there are the representations in the archaeological record of owl, eagle, salamander/lizard, serpent, wolf, fish, mountain goat, and humanoids which conform to the spirit powers recorded ethnographically. Second … the ritual of feeding the dead is clearly shown by the discovery of spoons at the mouth area of burials and of clam shell bowls in the hand or nearby. … Third, representations of ribs, joint marks, and backbones on some Pender artifacts indicate shamanic beliefs fully in keeping with the ethnographic belief system. See Roy Carlson and Philip Hobler, The Pender Canal Excavations and the Development of Coast Salish Culture, *BC Studies* 1993: 45, 49 (internal citations removed). In all, while these themes continue for thousands of years, their actual expressions vary over time, such as the present more-removed burning of food in open fires to feed the dead in contrast to this much earlier practice of putting spoon, bowl, and food in the hands and mouths of seated burials.

36 William Elmendorf, *Structure of Twana Culture* 1960: 536.

ceremonial relationships encompassing the entire region, the basic economic and spiritual bonds with a home territory were conversely both extremely narrow and intense, enabling an anchoring for radiance."[37]

In sum, the notebooks appealed for many scholarly reasons: assessing their reliability, discovering the name and dates of the scribe, exploring the complex (auto)biography of the Puyallup elder and real estate tycoon interviewed, preparing materials for future tribal use, solving the mystery of their misattribution by archives, restoring the erased history of earliest homesteaders as loggers and arsonists, fleshing out the local archaeological record with its ethnohistorical context, testing these data against previously published ethnographic models, and expanding our knowledge of traditional southern Lushootseeds in Puget Sound. Above all, the challenge of these notes is to set the record straight for one vibrant community at a specific place over several centuries during which it recreated itself after a series of traumas, setbacks, and triumphs. With a woman leader, shaman slave, and academy for elite families, it has much to contribute to our better understanding of local and global issues.

Lastly, in the following 15 chapters, the ancient web centered on the elite of Minter is discussed in terms of the source notebooks, allied documents, and key protagonists; the nexus at the native town itself, the rippling rings of landscape and kinscape, the directional rays of seasonal commutes, of food harvest, and of fishing; the jolting reversals of enslavement; the focal role of Jerry Meeker in many arenas, and the ramps that shifted community identities in the context of the later "official" if dubious history of south Puget Sound. Appendices detail aspects of native and trade languages, homesteading protocols, violence against property, and fuller biographies of Matthew Mann and Arthur Ballard.

---

[37] Jay Miller, Lushootseed Culture and the Shamanic Odyssey 1999: 63.

Within this overall context, Lushootseed has several ways of turning space into places. The world itself is *swatixʷtəd* = "land, country, world; place, region," with related words for *swətixʷtəd* = "all manner of plants, the entire plant kingdom" and *swatwatixʷtəd* = "trees, forest" (*LD*: 245). Broken apart, its morphemes indicate a meaning for the earth as an implement {*–əd*} for spreading around things {*-tixʷ-*}. It is mobile, not static, and dynamic in keeping with its active growth and changes.

In addition to this full word, other morphemes convey a fixed place, such as the suffix –*ali* = meaning a "usual place," such as *hudali* "fire place, hearth, stove"; *stubšali* = male plant; –*alič* = "bundle, pack"; *–alits'a'* = "clothes": *–alikʷ* = repetitive creative act, often done with finesse; *–aliqʷ* = "hat" (*LD*: 28). Of particular note, geographical terms often use the same lexical morphemes as body parts, such as the "face of a cliff" using the morpheme for "face" = –*us*, a point of land as a "nose" = *–aqs*, or a side appendage as an "ear" = *–adi*. More generally, *gʷəd* = "down, below, beneath" can be modified to mean land = *–ulgʷədxʷ* (*LD*: 99).

Society itself was organized into increasing inclusive special units: (a) hearth mates (*hudali LD*: 312) eating together, (b) within a cedar plank household (*al'al*, *–altxʷ LD*: 320), (c) among houses (*al'al'al LD*: 320) of all local residents, (d) of birthright (*gwədᶻ'ali LD*: 98) locals ~ those born there in contrast to inlaws, visitors, and foreigners, (e) including all seasonal settlements, towns, and resorts (*dxʷuq'əlb LD*: 183, 296), (f) inter-community networks of close kin (*q'ušəd LD*: 197 = "feet together") and people (*iišəd LD*: 345 = "feet apart"), (g) along creeks (*dᶻəlixʷ LD*: 90, 302) of tributary drainages, (h) within the entire drainage of a watershed basin (*stulək LD*: 346).

The expanding concentric rings of the landscape include the hearth, house, canoe, inlet and creeks, Sound, and the known world. The increasingly more inclusive rings of kinscape feature a person (Ego) enmeshed among peoples forming a family kindred, intergenerational *sept*, and diffuse *intersept*. The rays are grounded in local residence sites, projecting outward into the four directions according to economic resource by seasons. Of note, while the annual commute to gather in groceries for the coming year took people onto the land; the fisheries, in reserve, brought these resources toward the people.

Unique to this study is an examination of ramps, which several times totally changed the identity, focus, and meaning of the Minter community, and are unusually detailed in these remarkable notebooks done by Alfred Smith with Jerry Meeker on the advice of Arthur Ballard and Erna Gunter in 1948.

2 HOME BASE

Minter Bay, with an arced sandspit, is located on the upper east side of the Key Peninsula, facing Henderson Bay in upper Carr inlet. Case inlet flows along its west side, with Gig Harbor across on the far eastern shore, just above the Tacoma Narrows. These names were conferred by the American Wilkes Expedition to honor of its officers and equipment, erasing (except for a rare scholarly manuscript) their aboriginal place names. This chapter begins their recovery, beginning with resident humans.

Residents

Ten individuals figure prominently in these notebooks, identified, as noted, by accessible native names, available English translations, and evocative nicknames. These are 1) Damasq, my name for the headwoman (tšiałits'a); 2) her son Lashibya; 3) Broken Tooth (), the champion eater; 4) Simon, slave and shaman; 5) 18 George and his brother 6) Gizmo (kay'wey); 7) Moses (*wi'ayłpəx̣*), with suspicious Snake power; 8) Jim Hummelgood, a cousin; and 9) Jim and 10) Sally, Jerry Meeker's parents. To fill out a dozen, 11) Lucy Slugham Gurand, an elder twenty six years his senior, provides support for 12) Jerry Meeker's own information given to Alfred John Smith, the scribe.

In the 1850s, the first American Indian agent, Edmund Starling, gave the Minter population as 60, and George Gibbs numbered half that (27), but the better informed agent of the Hudson's Bay Company (HBC) in 1853 listed the resident Hotle-ma-mish with 43 men, 59 women, 29 boys, 36 girls, no slaves, no horses, 167 total population, 5 guns, 40 canoes, speaking the Nesqually [Nisqually, Whulshutseed, Southern Lushootseed] language.[38] Such a large number suggests that their "training academy," formerly called a "secret society" in academic writings, was in session when this census was taken.

Without these three UW-SC[39] notebooks and Jerry Meeker's own example, the wider affiliations of the Minters would have remained obscure at best. The closest approximation appears in court records, In her masterful summary of the ethnohistorical documents of the south Sound, introduced as evidence into the massive federal-court ~

---

[38] James Douglas, Private Papers (second series, 1853: 23), census inset after 424, in Herbert C. Taylor Anthropological Investigation of the Medicine Creek Tribes Relative to Tribal Identity and Aboriginal Possession of Lands Docket 234, Defendants Exhibit 129, 1974: 401-473 Coast Salish and Western Washington Indians II, 1974: 475-694. While Taylor lists his source as the British Columbia Provincial Archives, they have only a typescript (B/20/1853) and a microfilm (737A) of the original at the Bancroft Library at University of California at Berkeley -- one of the papers "borrowed and never returned by a noted California Historian" (Clarence Bagley, *In the Beginning* 1905a: 88). Taylor later devoted much time to assembling such census records to estimate the native population of Puget Sound.

[39] SC = Special Collections, formerly Manuscripts, Special Collections, and University Archives [MSCUA]. Coded letters and numbers refer to residential units in the main house [square brackets for Right, Left, Back + identifying #] or to the written notebooks <angle brackets for volumes A, B, C>.

treaty-right ~ fishing case of Judge George Boldt, Barbara Lane,[40] famous expert witness, expressed "reasonable doubt [about] the Hotlemamish of Carr Inlet [as] assigned to the Squaxin Island reservation" since, she noted, William Elmendorf[41] reported that Twana regarded the Shwotlmamish as a "branch" of the Puyallup, as these three notebooks indeed confirm.

The Town

Minter Bay of the mid-1800s included three big houses, each with several families of about 20 people per house, and some smaller "inferior" ones.[42] These were the winter "permanent" homes, where all the public foods and materiel assembled throughout the year were stockpiled, shared, and consumed. During this time, the leading house downsized a few times and relocated to the point. The other two, called "poor houses," were "above" [up bay] toward Minter Creek. These smaller "poor" houses included a few of the rich people,[43] who gave feasts with dancing and singing, but only the primary "rich" house had the prestige to invite in people from outside villages to be guests.

Done independently of the notebooks, a detailed survey map for Minter Bay by John and Marcia Winterhouse (on their honeymoon) identified separate archaeological sites by Roman numerals: Lyle (I) on the east side (off the map), the point (II), near the modern road end (III), and across on the west side along the upper inlet (IV, V), the Oyster plant at Cedar Point (VI), and on the bank (VII) with a view out though the opening of the sand spit. Matched up with the notebooks, the main house and academy were at VI, then, after the worst of slave raids, it was moved across the bay to II on the point. Sites IV and V are the two small "poor" houses incidentally mentioned in the notes.

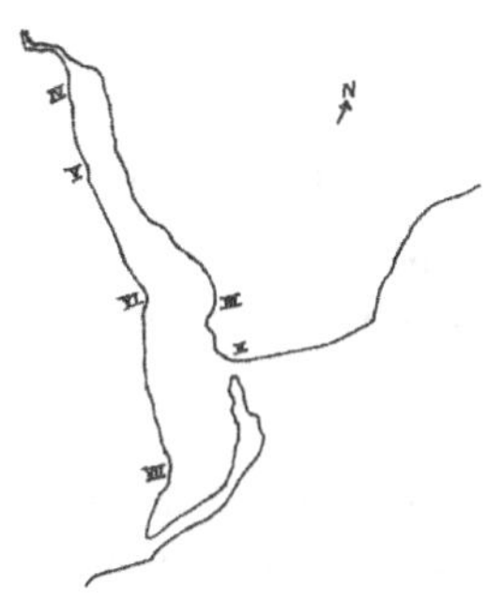

< §5 local sites >

Raised in Tacoma, John Winterhouse consulted with locally well-known Jerry Meeker, while his bride wrote notes on the envelope of their new marriage license, before launching a cabin cruiser on loan from the Burke Museum to make the shoreline survey. Other locals who helped identify these sites were listed as Thomas Myers of Tacoma, Mrs. T.T. Fuller of Seattle, a

[40] Barbara Lane, Anthropological Report on the Identity, Treaty Status, and Fisheries of the Squaxin Tribe of Indians 1972: 6-7, 13; her Puyallup Report 1970s: 3, merely notes that the Hotlemamish of Carr Inlet were close allies of the Puyallup, as were the Nisqually and Duwamish.

Relying on her summary and testimony on behalf of the Lushootseed tribes and reservations, the Boldt decision upheld the treaty right to fish half of the allowable salmon. Another long trial before Judge Edward Refeedee in the 1990s affirmed the same treaty right to shellfish.

[41] William Elmendorf, *The Structure of Twana Culture* 1960: 292.

[42] Twenty is an ideal average since these notebooks mention about 72 people variously spanning five generations affiliated with just the leading house.

[43] Again, after a struggle, what seemed to be written "sick" turned out to be "rich."

Minter descendent; Earl H Knapp[44] of Purdy, and J Meeker. Other families added details. The Smiths recalled natives still visiting Minter to fish. H. Secor of Gig Harbor, who started and sold the oyster farm, found bones while digging on his land at Minter IV, as did Meyers when he bulldozed (!) off a level area near Minter II.[45] Detailed maps of II and IV indicate where trenches were dug, while II also shows the Thomas Meyer home and boathouse around the point on Henderson Bay.

Alerted to the depth and complexity of Minter, in September 1952, the newly-formed Seattle Young Archaeologist's Society negotiated with Meyer to test this shell midden on the point(e) of Minter Bay, only to be immediately disappointed as a new concrete bulkhead "destroyed" the site. Dale McGinnis, a local who became an archaeologist, dug at Minter in 1973-74, noting "Lots of activity and disturbance" and recording three radiocarbon dates averaging 1200 +/- 270 years BP, suggesting a thousand years of occupation.

For this first ranked house at Minter, an early named leader was Broken Tooth, an old man with eating (gorging, chompion) power who lived during the generation before Sally Meeker. As an adult in his prime (early 1800s), he had led one of the other two houses at Minter. In the later 1800s, these two lesser houses were led by *siya'walxʷ* and by sʷ*a'dax̣əm* (sxʷ*adax̣əm*). Broken Tooth's spirit power enabled him to eat huge quantities but never get full, making him wealthy enough from winning bets to rise in local prominence. Jerry never saw him, nor did his mother, but he knew a story about him being invited to Hood Canal (Mission Creek) to gorge on salmon mulligan and to Gig Harbor, where he totally ate out his host (and saved Minters from enslavement if they had lost the competition, see below).

Broken Tooth preceded *walatšalq*, the first [?] husband of the headwoman Damasq, as leader. Though unstated for Minter itself, chiefly families with many sons often placed them in charge of other houses within their community, with birth order determining house ranking if all of them were fit, able bodied, skilled, and active. Because of the gendered division of labor, leadership was vested in the chiefly couple, with the husband supervising men and the wife coordinating women in their activities.

As public leader, *walatšalq* <B12>[46] attended the December 1854 Treaty of Medicine Creek. Their daughter *gʷoldowts* [*gʷoldoxʷts*] married a man named Hawk from Nisqually Flats (intriguingly the home of pioneer homesteader Isaac Hawk), and their son (headwoman's grandson) John Hawk settled at Skokomish, where he hosted many visiting scholars as well as Jerry Meeker.

By right as her husband, this nominal male leader of the whole community fronted for his high-born wife. He had become {"chief upon marriage to the chief of Minter's daughter. He was not a chief or chief's son among the Puyallup. His wife [Damasq] remained the *real* leader at Minter. He helps her in planning.... Her first husband came [from] right there at Minter. He

---

[44] The Knapps worked as brush pickers, a demanding outdoor job providing greenery to florists, as did Elmer and Helen Skahan, who keep a large sorting shed beside the road.

[45] John Winterhouse, A Report on an Archaeological Survey of Lower Puget Sound 1948. Warren Caldwell, UW grad long at the University of Nebraska before retiring in Idaho, mentioned two related surveys by women, Ethel Carlson in 1938 or Florence Howard (who traveled by canoe) in 1949.

[46] Again, for explanation of the content of these bracket styles, see Chapter 1, note 3.

must have been son of a chief. She was a woman chief because her father was a chief' <A52>}. The spiritual source of her authority, her spirit power song (for *yilbix* = women's riches) was accompanied by a pole pounded against the house roof, usually held by her son Lashibiya <A6>.[47]

Lashibya was famous for having been a "bum" until he married and transformed himself into a good provider {"became an expert because he began to study it and train to get to be good" <B24>}. He became the spiritual trainer at Minter through Jerry Meeker's early teenage years until Jerry entered reservation school in 1878, presumably when Lashibya died. He was the last member of the training academy that had made Minter famous through the early 1800s.

This chiefly couple had two slaves <A45>, a Lummi (*t*^{u}*lubi*) woman who ended up among the Nisqually and a fascinating Snohomish man called Simon (*dak*^{w}*iłał*, *dak*^{w}*ilał*, Chapter 8) in English. These slaves lived in separate huts, each of them eight feet square, with just enough room for a bed [bunk] and small fire where they cooked their own food. They worked hard, getting all the water, firewood, and most of the food, though the "chief's wife" cooked all of it to keep it morally untainted. The chief did virtually no physical "work," but instead managed everything via his~her wealth power.

Later, the main house was sometimes said to be led by the same man known in turn as Moye's (from Moses) and then as *wiyaypəx* (*wi'ayłpəx̣*). His mother was Puyallup and his father Klickitat from eastern Washington. Via a grandfather, he was first cousin to both Sally Meeker and the Minter headwoman, serving as her advisor along with Tyee George. While holding this leading house together after Minter was burned out, Damasq outlived all of her children but a daughter and a son (below). Strangely, she is not listed on the diagram of the leading household, though a blank square (see figure #6) is marked in the back opposite the doorway, the most likely sheltered abode for her chiefly family <A13, 52>.

During the 1855 Treaty War, natives of this region were confined to Fox Island, but, afterward, this household stayed on at Minter during winters, encouraged (and led) by Damasq until they were burned out by homesteaders in 1874. Their household then moved to Glencove, where a new house was built by a team comprised of Jimmy Hummelgood,[48] q̓əsiad, James Meeker, Jerry with his half-brother John, and Speym. Glencove had been Minter's prime fall fishery, and source, during all of October, for huckleberries and mushrooms. In time, the Glencove house, eventually used to dry salmon, was also burned out by settlers <A18>. The

---

47 yilbīx^{u} (as written in the notebooks) was a spirit that only came to those of high rank, with gender-specific gifts. It lived in a house full of fish and animals, and its servants looked like humans rather than other creatures. It gives ~ gave its male human partner the ability to have game and fish drop dead on command at specific convenient locations. This was the power given to the bloated boys at Minter (below). Where appropriate, it also provided whales. It is a wealth power, along with the more exclusive tiōłbax^{u} (tiyułəbax̌^{w}ad) and heyida (*dx*^{w}*hi'ide*) who provide abundance (Jay Miller, *Lushootseed Culture and the Shamanic Odyssey* 1999: 59-60. Herman Haeberlin and Erna Gunther, Indians of Puget Sound 1930:71, assume the tribe with this power northwest of Lummi is Nooksack instead of Musqueam). Possession of this power, in female mode, indeed qualified Damasq to be the real chief of Minter.

48 Puyallup Land Commission Report (page 129) calls him Jimmy Homalgood. In 1889, his family consisted of James, aged 36; Alice, 31; Jack, 13; Snyder, 10; and Rosa, 5 (Edwin Eells, Box 3, Folder 12A, #516-520 WSHS).

Meekers, more and more, had been summering away from Minter working on pioneer Ezra Meeker's farms, helping to increase his fortune. Many of the other Minter Bay residents can be traced after their diaspora (<C4>, Chapter 10).

In 1927 for Puyallup land claims, Lucy Slogham Gurand,[49] aged 85 {91} and living in Quartermaster Harbor, sat on the witness stand. She was born decades before Jerry, when Minter was fully occupied and memories of raids and enslavements would have been fresh. Her testimony is the clearest statement on its prominence as an elite training facility. In all, she recalled 12 houses at Minter, but one was especially huge, "sort of a theater house; [where] they trained the boys and girls ... Lots of dance[s], all night , all day … Lots of paint [worn]."[50] The other houses varied in size from 20 to 60 feet.

Presumably, Lucy tallied the three distinct archaeological sites on Minter Bay to reach her total of 12. At this time, the big house (150 feet long) was on the north side, having been moved across from the spot (where the oyster plant with huge shell mounds is now on the south side) after the massive Cowichan/Nanaimo slave raid. Homes up to 60 feet long stood in the other residential locations, and the smaller houses probably housed slaves, poor relations, and stored foods. A hollow tree stump hid special treasures, then, after Minters moved away, stored their dried salmon.

For these same land claims, on 25 March 1927, Jerry Meeker, identified as a 65-year-old farmer living at Brown's Point, was deposed on the Puyallup Reservation.[51] When citing property losses, Jerry noted, "I have seen about six buildings at Minter" constructed of great big pillars covered by stringers and crosspieces bound by twisted hazel boughs.[52] Side walls were ten to twelve feet high, with inside platforms occupied by families. Woven mats lined the inside walls, and the open interior of the house was where children played at night after the doors were closed up.

Of particular note, he said the early Minter big house was over 100 feet long and 50 feet wide. "This particular kind of a big house was a training house [academy] to train their young ones, and also there was a sort of secret fraternity [Growlers guild ~ sect] among the Indians, and they used to train their young people into this secret fraternity.… They lived in that house. That is what you would call, in English, professors, the ones that trained the children."[53] Trainers mentioned in the notebooks were the unnamed father of the brothers Tyee George and Gizmo, succeeded by Lashibiya, son of the headwoman. After a devastating slave raid, this huge house was abandoned in sorrow. In addition, there were dwellings whose size varied with their contents or the importance of their residents.

---

[49] The lone native on Vashon Island, her tombstone dates 1836-1929 were supplied by the Puyallup tribe when they marked her grave in 2008. See Appendix E.

[50] Lucy Gurand, RG 279, Docket 203, Box 1897, Folder 5: 34 – from RG 123, Box 3693, Volume IV, 1125/1276, 23 March 1927; Duwamish and others 1933: 650.

[51] Jerry also testified for the Indian Land Claims Commission on 13 June 1952 in Seattle (below). See other testimony on burned villages in the last chapter.

[52] Duwamish and Others 1933: 628.

[53] Duwamish and Others 1933: 629.

Home

Main Household

The bigger house had been where Jerry's mother Sally was born and lived. Nearly the whole band lived in that house (Appendix G). It had 6 or 7 fires spaced along the center of building. It had a flat [shed, one slope] roof set on beams across the width. Gummy pitch was used to seal up the seams. The inside was completely open, without partitions or dividers between the walls. The doors were at each end, not on the sides. Each door was made of two slabs set side by side. The door was always open during the day, but closed at night. In older times, the doorways were set low so a person had to stoop a little to get inside, making him vulnerable. Such short openings were a feature of grand and potlatch houses to keep off-balance any invited guests before their good intentions were clear.

About 1860, still fully occupied, the main house at Minter (that best known to Jerry) downsized, after losses to epidemics and fewer visitors, to a rectangle about 50 or 60 feet long, with about five upright posts down the middle of the building holding up the one-slope shed roof <A30>. Beams were fastened lengthwise between the notched uprights, and also across from side to side to fit into notched side poles set up along the walls. These cross beams were tied with ropes made of small hazel or cedar limbs (withes). The outside and roof were covered by cedar planks tied onto this framework of posts and beams. Inside, a bench about three and a half feet wide ran along the inner walls of the house, except for the doorway. Each family had a section along this platform, with rows of piled up baskets, boxes, and household goods instead of dividing walls separating off the family sections. The only door was at a short end of this building.

Outside in the path of sunshine, a cribwork or rack of poles, each one about three inches around and twelve feet long, was built for raised up storage and drying salmon during November when about 50 sticks rested between these poles, each one holding 4 or 5 split open dog salmon <A33>. The rest of the year, all kinds of things were stored on top of this lattice work, to keep them out of the way. A similar rack was also used at Glencove where, when he was older, Jerry helped to build a small replacement house.

In summarizing the house at Minter that survived the longest, Jerry said to Marian Smith that it had [with clarifications]

No mats [as inside insulation]

No center posts [mid-line supports]

Flat roof – horizontal [planks]

Grooved roof boards [interlocking for runoff]

Pitch – end to end [length]

Vertical wall [planks overlapped so there were no drafts]

Slanted wall boards [outward at top for drainage]

Door at ends [A door at each end, presumably for dramatic entrances and exits]

No pit [floor and fire set at ground level]

Marian Smith's sketch diagrams show the orientation to the shoreline of the house at Minter and the one at Gig Harbor. Jerry indicated that this main House at Minter was placed parallel to the south side stream on Cedar Point where the Minterbrook oyster plant is now, with the very accurate notation that the area was a "creek at low tide and bay at high tide." The east door therefore faced the Sound and the west one the hillside. Neither one faced the beach on which the house stood. By comparison, the big house at Gig Harbor ran side to side across a point, so its doors were at right angles to the beach in front ("faced the beach at each side"). Jerry said the biggest house he ever saw was at Gig Harbor and it was 400 feet long, enough to hold 10-12 families.

Houses were moved when the ground "got sour," or after a raid because "they felt so bad."[54] After the worst slaving raid, the main house at Minter (about 150 feet long) was moved from the south to the north side of the lagoon. The "old lady" [Damasq] who was leader kept her ceremonial objects in the abandoned house on the south side because it was "where her ancestors were." Presumably, she had used the hollow stump for her dancing poles before this. The tree stump then served to store the dried salmon that Minters continued to preserve there during Jerry's teenage years [1870s].

Land and sea foods were abundant nearby. Deer were mainly along the east side of Carr Inlet, and berries along the west side. Flounder and sole could be speared during low tide. A wild cranberry bog (stlɛ'hol)[55] stretched from Purdy behind Henderson Bay toward Minter. Overall, Minter's territory embraced ties by kinship, visiting, and use to nearby places such as Gig Harbor, Steilacoom, North Bay, Arletta, Wollachet, and other waterfront abodes.

Overland trails, providing safe passage away from waterways, led from Gig Harbor and Port Orchard to Purdy, then on to Minter, to North Bay, or to Rocky Point. Trails were used only for emergencies, such as escaping from attacks or conveying urgent messages and warnings <A107, 111>. All regular travel and harvesting relied on canoes with a variety of appropriate sizes and shapes.

In all, Minter came to rely not on tradition but on transformation. Once a premier training academy, after traumatic epidemics and slaving raids, Minter's identity shifted to that of engorging Chompions, who engaged in intercommunity rivalry by out-eating everyone to win wagers and fame. Today, Minter is directly involved with the Puyallup Nation through input into the Minter state hatchery due to the federal Boldt court decision, 70's fish-ins that made that claim, and the direct link of Elmer Skahan (1919-2004).

Elmer was an enrolled Yakima whose mother Lucy Guard, a direct Minter descendant, graduated in the first class at the Puyallup neighborhood school. When Daniel Varner, his great great grandfather, was burned out of Orting in the Treaty War, they moved to Minter Spit. His great grandmother married a "white man from Nebraska," and, on the spit in 1865, gave birth to Elmer's grandfather. His family tradition says there were then three communities at Minter, the

[54] Marian Wesley Smith, Microfilm Roll 3 (Reel A1738), British Columbia Archives, MSS 2689, Box 6, Folder 9 (Houses); Royal Anthropological Archives MSS 2794.

[55] This term is probably intended to be ƛ̓ałx̣ulč ~ ƛ̓ałx̣əlc "cranberry" from ƛ̓ałx̣ meaning "to pop, crackle" (*LD* 1994: 152).

native one on the exposed point, American loggers nearby, and a Metis one on the spit.[56] During one epidemic, probably smallpox (evidenced by a local native place name), his grandfather said that natives at Burley hoped for relief by undergoing treatment in sweat lodges, plunging into the bay and reentering the lodge, but most died before their third immersion. Elmer also recalled that George Minter, who homesteaded the point after the Burketts left, gave potatoes and other garden produce to visiting natives to keep their goodwill.

56 This now-bare sand spit, which shelters Minter Bay, would have blocked a view of the big house on the south side, especially if trees were growing on it. Lt Puget's survey with Vancouver crewmen missed seeing this community, but were confronted by locals, probably at Glencove, when they put a net into the bay to catch a fresh lunch.

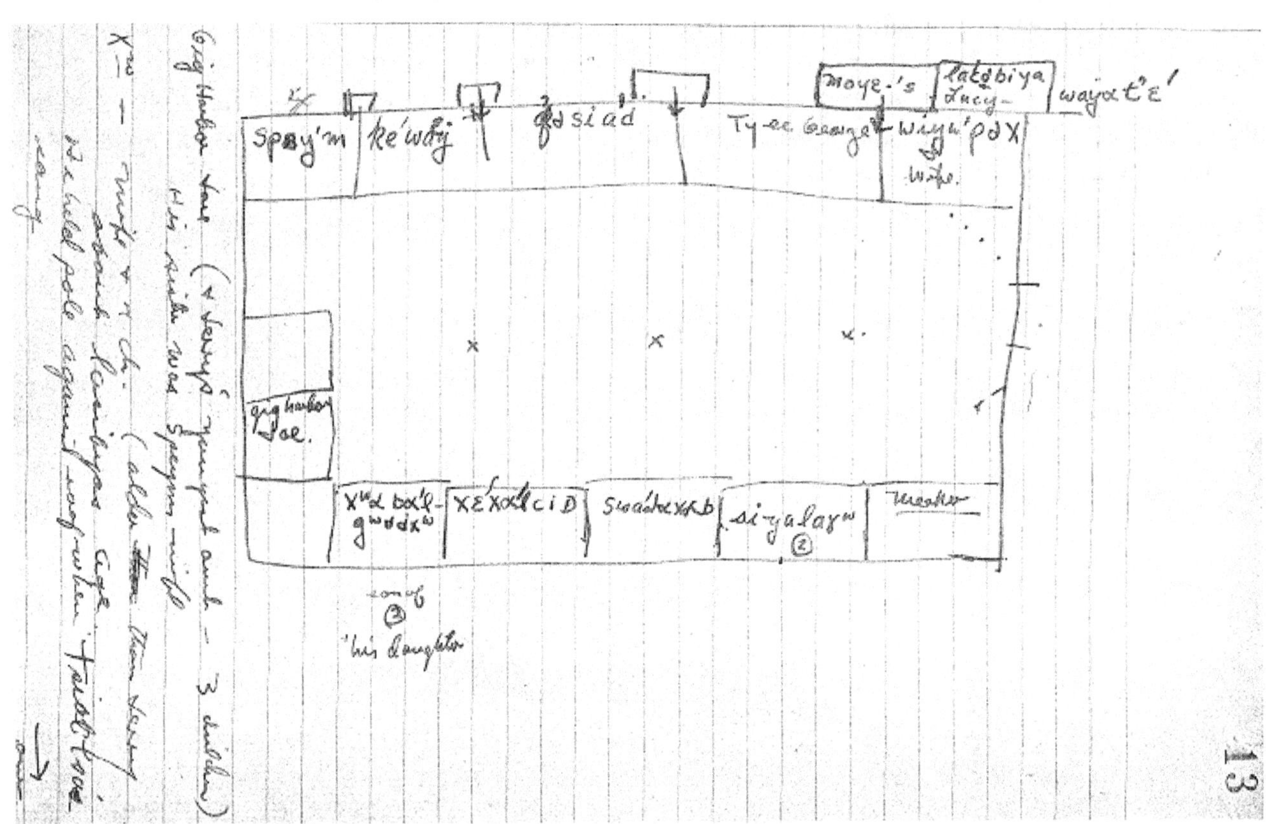

< §6 Sketch of Family Sections in Main Household >

< §7 Interior View about 1870 by Kenneth Greg Watson >

3 LANDSCAPE

Lushootseeds, including Minters, were bound by two overlapping systems of relationships, known familiarly in kinship studies as rays of "mud and blood." One involved fixtures of the land and waterways, along with various means of transport, as discussed in this chapter. The other, treated in the next one, involved family considerations of kinship, particularly the inheritance of shared corporate identity, hereditary names, abilities, and resources. Both radiated out from a pivot or nexus, such as a home hearth or a focal ~ key person, serving as the Ego (reference node) in a kinship diagram.

A glaring exception to this dichotomy, considered in terms of life shifts, was slavery. Totally alone, cut off from their kin, a slave was not a person, but instead only occupied a (s)place. Known by the name of her or his birth tribe (as a collective insult), a slave lacked any self-identity, according to the literature. Yet the life of Dr Simon, slave and shaman at Minter, corrects this record in terms of actual personalities, complexities, and potentials.

Minter's own variant of the traditional culture can be summarized in terms of general ethnography. Contrary to local white folk history, Minter was not merely occupied semi-seasonally (except in its final decades), but rather was the focal ~ base point from which natives dispersed with the seasons to commute for groceries taken from air, land, and sea. A former claim to local fame, also, was its resident academy for training the children of neighboring elite families.

Assembled from reordered pages of the notebooks and my own prior books, Lushootseed culture can be presented in terms of actual names at Minter.[57] Cedar and Salmon, mainstays of the entire Northwest, were also vital along Carr Inlet. Straight grained and long lasting, cedar trees were carved into canoes of various sizes, or split into planks for boxes, chests, cradles, and houses, particularly by Gizmo [k̓ə'wəy, R2], their skilled carpenter. Cedar bark was shredded to make into clothing, branches were twisted into rope, and roots were woven into baskets. Of five possible salmon species runs, varying by size and habitat, Minters relished three (coho, chum, pink) after the communal effort expended to catch, trap, dry, or smoke them nearby (See Chapter 7). For Minters, a varied diet was assured by east-bay deer and west-bay berries along Henderson Bay.

Place-Based Order

Culturally, the increasing building blocks of this society were the **house** (including hearth mates, locals, and distant kin); **canoe** (transport, access, and conduit across time and space); **inlet** (and feeder **creeks**); the **Sound** (distinguished by habitat as forest, prairie, river, or sea), and the known **world** (including the annual swirl of spirits around and through it). After they were

[57] Again, coded letters and numbers refer to residents in the diagram of the main house [square brackets for Right, Left, Back] or to the volumes of the written notebooks <angle brackets for A, B, C>, + page # number.

traded north, horses dominated land transport, rivaling canoes in some areas. Pasturage became a new concern, at the expense of unfenced camas prairies eaten into oblivion by livestock.

Tribal terrain was interlinked with others by waterways, portages, and ridge trails.[58] Most Lushootseeds were identified as "tribes" in terms of an entire river drainage, affiliated to resident immortals through spiritual bonds and rituals and to more remote peoples and places through visits, marriages, rituals, and trades.

In terms of the overall Puget Basin, Marian Smith[59], relying on Jerry Meeker and her fieldwork among the Puyallup and Nisqually, devised a spatial model for describing how native peoples related to their watersheds. She explicitly recognized that the greatest allegiance and loyalty coincided with the entire drainage system of Puget Sound.[60] Viewing her units as increasing in size better indicates the progression.

Therefore, within each watershed, group cohesion, loyalties, and affiliations expanded in terms of (a) hearth mates eating together at the fires in one household, (b) residents of all neighboring houses, (c) birthright locals - those born there as distinct from inlaws, visitors, and foreigners, (d) seasonal settlements, camps, and resorts, (e) wider community networks, (f) tributary waterways, and (g) the entire drainage of a river basin.

Each river constituted a "tribe," designated by the endings of *-bš* (*-bsh*), if more cohesive, or as *-bix^{w}* ~ 'bunch,' if more dispersed. (The familiar -mish ending seen on local maps is the English version of *-bsh* in Lushootseed, during the M to B shift among native speakers.)[61] Rivers and streams with bank-side trails linked all of these together, while trails along and across ridges gave access to separate tribes. Membership and acceptance within each drainage derived from the subtle, discerning, and valued regard for customs such that insiders, in contrast to outsiders, understood the complexities of "the feud, the snub, the verbal innuendo" and accordingly "were appropriate guests for a ceremonial feast."[62]

Traditionally, the crux of the entire system and the basic reason for gathering people together was the winter display of spiritual bonds with particular immortal powers and spirits. No one could be successful without such help. For centuries, leading families had bonded with the most powerful spirits in their locales. Lesser family members, some commoners, and even a few slaves (like Dr Simon) also had spirit partners, but these were less powerful than those of leaders.

Near Minter, Thomas Waterman,[63] the first full-time anthropologist in Washington State, identified places (by number #), in his classic survey, that were likely local abodes of species

---

58 Elsewhere along the major rivers of the Sound, this series is person, house, town, branch stream, and entire drainage of a watershed.

59 Marian Smith, *The Puyallup-Nisqually* 1940: 7; The Coast Salish of Puget Sound 1941: 197-211.

60 For reasons still unclear, barring his sometime New Yorker cussedness, linguist Melville Jacobs strongly objected to this model.

61 Though more appropriate for the next chapter on kinship, *-mix^{w}* [Lushootseed *-bix^{w}*] is a proto-Salish suffix with the complex meaning of "life force, people, breast, milk, world," Aert Kuipers, *Salish Etymological Dictionary* 2002: 205-6.

62 Natalie Roberts, A History of the Swinomish Tribal Community 1975: 79.

63 Vi Hilbert, Jay Miller, and Zalmai Zahir, *Puget Sound Geography* 2001.

powers rather than foodstuffs, particularly Dogfish's Water (#141) at Wauna, Bullheads (#159), and Black Bear (#169) under Gravelly Lake. Even more awesome was the recalcitrant earth at [Filucy] Ellice Bay (#145), who overpowered the Transformer, the merpeople off Fox Island (#154), the hand emerging from American Lake (#168), and McAllister Creek (#163), site of the Treaty of Medicine Creek, that was itself named in Whulshootseed for the doctoring power infused there. Dead Place (#142) probably held tree burials, before neighboring Lyle was homesteaded.

Great traumas are recorded in these place names (below), memorializing the Minter side of Carr Inlet in a way that serves to emphasize how epidemics took a toll there. Lt Peter Puget himself reported stout local men with faces "much pitted with the Small Pox."[64] Since Minter had been a protected and secluded locale where noble children were sent for training, these epidemics had the same emotional impact as that of a devastating disease scything through the students of an elite private school.

Minter was probably infected through its contacts with the Washington coast, perhaps through the Satsop trail and Hood Canal, if not an actual meeting with Spanish naval explorers, since the 1782 smallpox pandemic across the Americas probably originated in Colonial Mexico. Such direct encounters seem likely because of the casual way natives reacted without panic or flight to the sound of British gunfire from Lt Peter Puget's crew.

Since these place names (in original spellings) are the only direct evidence for the prior reputation of Minters as mighty defenders before their devastation by epidemics, each will be considered in turn.

> # 140 ^{Tu}sxo'tlEb from a stem meaning "to bite" on the sand spit which separates Burley lagoon from Carr's inlet where the Sxo'tlEba'bc or "people of a village here possessed the reputation of being great fighters." A myth recounts that once the people of this site were all killed except a pregnant woman who later gave birth to twins, a boy and a girl, by whom the group was perpetuated, and the village built up again. [Edward] Curtis gives the name S'hotlbabsh as the term for the people "at the southern end of Case Inlet." This is clearly an error, since his term exactly corresponds, barring the different system of orthography, with the one here given.

This place is probably "place of biting" [dəx̣ʷsx̣əƛ̓əb]. Of course, since Jerry Meeker gave this 'biter' [eater, gorger] name for Minter itself, it appears as the name for those of the upper, middle, and lower portions of Carr Inlet, including Henderson Bay. The identification of Minters as "fighters" instead of "eaters" points to an historic change ~ shift in their competitive strategy that is best explained by the depopulation from epidemics – as is highlighted in adjoining place names.

---

[64] Similar devastation is recorded in place names from the Fraser, where the epidemics were spread by face-to-face native contacts, long before Europeans arrived, and were blamed on indigenous causes that threatened the lives of misguided local shamans.

Landscape

142 Ska'ikaiyuale "corpse place" on a creek north of Huge [now Minter] creek with an aboriginal graveyard where the bodies were hoisted into the trees.

The meaning here is indeed 'dead, corpses, ghosts' (plural) + -ali = "corpses place."

143 ^{Tux}sxo'tEb "pestilence" Huge [now Minter] Creek.

The word for disease, 'pestilence' is now spelled sq^{w}utəb, and compares with x̣əɬ = 'sick, infirm'.[65] In this form dəx^{w}sx̣utəb implies smallpox pestilence. Such names in the vicinity of Minter indicate great tragedy because these natives had no immunities from European diseases, especially early on. Minter and its academy was ground zero for this devastation, with refugees probably moving later to the more isolated locale at Burley, whose own native settlement (indicated by a lone house post) had earlier been completely wiped out.

House

Key nodes in this overall system were cedar plank houses located along the shoreline at places like Minter that were strategically rich in local resources, such as a salmon stream, marsh, prairie, berry patch, and hunting territory. Even spirit beings lived in such houses, though only special people could see them as such. Beyond this house node of co-resident kin were at least three concentric rings occupied by allies, by competitors for regional status, and, third, by strangers.[66] During the late 1800s, US officials, citing public health, broke up and burned down these communal homes in favor of single family dwellings, built with milled lumber, though many kinspeople shared these rooms.

The basic arena where gender, rank, and sanctions were and are most fully expressed was this traditional communal house, now carried over as the public ceremonial longhouse used for winter Siyowin (Smokehouse) worship. This longhouse was also the setting for the shamanic Redeeming rite, the major public religious expression throughout the region, with each enactment customized to features of locale, personnel, and the resident immortal helpers, especially the "Little Earths."[67] Today, as in the past, during winter in such longhouses, families display both massive or mobile insignia conferred by spirits and confirming their claims to rank and pedigree. Massive examples are carved and painted support posts, while mobile ones include designs, insignia, and sacred animated shields.

---

65 *LD*: 194, 305, 263.

66 Natalie Roberts, A History of the Swinomish Tribal Community 1975: 82.

67 In the arena of international prestige, regions and tribes had distinctive ceremonies, with Puget Sound especially noted for this Redeeming Rite, as well as the use of paired objects whose name *sg^{w}ədilič* is analyzable Lushootseed (Bates, Hess, and Hilbert 1994: 100). In addition, communities were also adopting ritual guilds with distinct internal grades of membership, such as the Growlers, spreading from powerful nations along the central British Columbia coast.

The floor was hard-packed and clean-swept dirt, as noted, with family fires along its edges. Beside the walls were risers (bunks, platforms) of finely adzed planks set at less than a yard above the ground. A stack of storage boxes and baskets arranged between side posts separated off family compartments. During the day, the side bunks were cleared off, but at night they were layered with beds of cattail mats, animal skins, and woven blankets for sleeping. In ordinary houses, plain houseposts were draped with baskets, traplines, skins, fishing tackle, and other possessions to keep them in view, safe, and handy. Decorated houseposts were kept covered except when public events were being hosted there.

Each house was once owned by a group of siblings who succeeding in amassing the wealth, resources, and status needed to attract and reward the labor (of resident workers) needed to build such an imposing building. Its location was a hereditary site "belonging" (long assigned) to that family, usually at a sheltered and productive fishery. Large and famous families had several such house frames. Each was built at or near an important resource which they "owned" – in the sense of acting as the managing host for the sustainable harvesting and dispersal of that bounty rather than its exclusive, greedy extraction by themselves alone (as the English word "own" implies). Sharing was a valued privilege. When Minters visited or hosted, the goal was sometimes a challenge to eat someone out of house and home, in gratitude for their offered generosity. Eating contests were a measure of wealth and status.

Today, reservation community halls, sometimes inspired by styles of ancient housing, are used for ceremonies, feasts, and gatherings, particularly in winter. These buildings and events continue such binding traditions. Regional networks also continue, now named in terms of modern reservations instead of native rivers and watersheds, though there is considerable overlap between these past and present locations.

The aboriginal parklike old growth forests and the rugged terrain left few level spaces where people could live, so each house in every town had about fifty occupants, with family location within the house reflecting its rank in local and regional society. Thus, with a door at the front or side, the owner of the house and his family had the best protected spot in a back corner, away from the drafts and dangers at the doorway. They constituted a nobility, providing skilled leaders for shifting community tasks.[68] The hallmark of nobility was being hard working, steady, generous, and reliable, like Jerry Meeker and his parents. They successfully managed major communal projects, such as building a house, weir, or fort; leading a raid; or hosting an event such as a winter dance, return foods feast, reburial, or potlatch (invited give away).[69]

Along the sidewalls were families of ordinary common folks, who contributed food, labor, and upkeep to the household in return for the prestige and security of living with wealthy relatives. Poised at the least desirable and most exposed places in the front of the house were slaves, who had either been captured in raids, purchased, or born to their lot (Chapter 8). Each family had its own hearth fire along a side of the house floor, since eating together as a 'commensal unit' was what defined close relations and trust (see Kinscape, Chapter 4). Refusing offered food was tantamount to a suspicion of sorcery. Nobles usually had more than one wife, but each seems to have had a separate fireplace hearth to feed her own children and their

---

[68] Jay Miller, Back to Basics: Chiefdoms in Puget Sound 1997: 375-387.

[69] In the later money economy, Jim Meeker was straw boss for Ezra's hop yards, recruiting and deploying native laborers to build up an impressive family fund.

playmates. The elite, as elsewhere, also had more than one home, each strategically located near favored resources, terrains, or seasonal advantages.[70]

On important occasions, particularly during winter, the head of the house hosted public events on behalf of all the residents. Accordingly, most families moved out to stay in other accommodations, either nearby homes or mat tents, to make room for welcome guests. For these events, two or three large fires occupied the middle (along the long central axis) of the big house. Huge amounts of food – which had been gathered by slaves, housemates, and kin so it could be cooked by women under the direction of the senior wife of the host – were served throughout the festivities.

In Jerry's youth, as noted, families broke up into summer harvesting groups of about a dozen people each. Details of these food quests (Chapter 6) formed the seasonal commute. The Meekers joined with Lashibiya, siyaləxʷ, q̓əsiad, sxʷadax̣ub, and Hummelgood. Speym went with Lashibya to Long Branch, and with xəxal'cid to Lakebay. Tyee George rejoined the Suquamish, and Gig Harbor Joe paddled across the inlet to his namesake community. Gizmo and Moses stayed with Damasq at Minter <A110-112>. Sally Meeker liked to camp at Arletta to visit with her cousins, James yukots Coates and his brother General Marcellus Spot, Puyallup Catholic leaders. Women clammed during one over-night stay at Still Harbor of McNeil Island, apparently as a gender specific outing, though some children (daughters ?) must have also been along.

Everyone was back in Minter by December in time for the feasting and ceremonial season. Those with power from immortals became "sick to sing," to renew their spiritual partnerships. While native doctors ~ shamans had curing powers that were constantly available, career powers returned every winter but departed every spring, traveling in a global spiral from the east to the north, west, and south before heading back eastward. As the tight bundles of dried fish were stored inside the hollow stump after Minters wintered elsewhere, so other valuables, especially religious objects (sacra), were hidden out of sight. Since generosity was a virtue and competition was constant, secluding them precluded requests to give them away or, on occasion, having them used in sorcery against the owner.

Winter also involved rites of elite, high-born initiation into the Growlers (Chapter 11) whose members spat blood and terrorized the audience;[71] of shamanic Redeeming travel to the land of the dead, sometimes to return with a spirit that enabled a woman to become pregnant; or of gambling contests playing the wheel game as teams sang and gesticulated. Minter from earliest report was a training facility for Growlers, with initiations and dramatic events staged on its beach.

Changes in social status – such as naming, initiations, puberty, marriage, or death – marked the occasions for generous hosting – for inviting in guests. The more prominent a family, the more people would be invited from furthest away. Important families had far flung networks of friends and kin, forged by marriage, adoption, gifts, help, trade, and social obligations. Only the prime house at Minter invited in other communities, while the poorer

---

[70] Elmendorf, *The Structure of Twana Culture* 1960: 269.

[71] Jerry's uncle Charlie wilq̓ʷ provided a realistic if skeptical opinion ("bunk" <A 101>) on Growlers and Redeeming (Odyssey).

houses hosted only each other. Possession of powerful dicta ~ words, a privilege of elite families, provided self-confidence, poise, and spiritual protection in such intertribal situations.

Canoes

Formerly defended by a "death ray" canoe spiritually bestowed on a resident boy, the more recent fame of Minter relied on its gorging ~ out-eating abilities. The one stand-out individual to be named was Gizmo [R2], carpenter and maker of cordage and canoes. Because Minter was on saltwater, it used a full range of canoe sizes and styles.[72] More than mere transport and temporary abodes, such vessels were fellow beings enlivened by rituals, names, and kinship ties to the carver and his wife (its "parents"), since both cedar trees and canoes had male and female genders. His woodworking was empowered by spirits such as Woodpecker, Cedar, or Adze, whose attributes infused both the carver and each finished piece. The grain of the cedar, coarse or fine, determined whether the vessel was male or female, with gender specific dicta needed to get the most out of its shape and speed. Paddles differed for use by men or women, having different shapes. Children learned to use toy canoes and to study water current conditions by paddling smaller vessels, launching larger ones as proficiency increased with age.

Six standard canoe styles are known as shovelnose, hunting, cargo, racing, northern, and Nootkan ~ Chinookan. Shovelnose, also called river, was ideal for sheltered waterways, and usually was poled. Hunting or trolling canoes, typically used by men hunting ducks, had pointed and raised ends. Women and families used the cargo or freight canoe, particularly to transport household equipment. Both hunting and cargo had a notch in the prow that served as its mouth when "food" was offered in thanks to sustain the canoe and assure safe travel. Thin and sleek, the racing canoe still appears in summer "canoe races" (water sport competitions by men and women), but, traditionally, it was paddled by eleven warriors intent on lightning raids.

Introduced from faraway ocean tribes, the northern or Alaskan style was the largest vessel available, often traded into the Sound. The most distinctive canoe had a prow with an animal-like head and snout. Used between the Columbia River Chinooks and West Coast Nootkans (Nuchahnulth) of Vancouver Island,[73] these ocean-worthy trading vessels involved considerable ritual and dicta evoking Wolves and Orcas. Nootkans developed it for hunting grey and other whales, though it includes some uncanny parallels to Alaskan umiaks, open skin cargo boats also used to pursue whales and seals.[74]

---

[72] As the region's vital vehicle, canoes have a vast literature that includes Barry Carlson and Thom Hess, Canoe Names in the Northwest, An Areal Study 1971; Leslie Lincoln, Coast Salish Canoes 1991; Hilary Stewart, *Indian Fishing ~ Early Methods on the Northwest Coast* 1982; *Cedar ~ Tree of Life to the Northwest Coast Indians* 1984; Thomas Talbot Waterman and Geraldine Coffin, Types of Canoes on Puget Sound 1920. My own 1999 overview of Lushootseed culture had undergone final draft and lauding reviews before I blanched to realize that it included nothing on canoes themselves and quickly added such a necessary chapter. The Minter notebooks further enforce their vital importance. Of note, families lived, ate, and slept in their canoes while traveling and visiting.

[73] This shared canoe style should also figure in the discussion of the antiquity of Chinuk Wawa, fostering its spread long before the fur trade.

[74] *The World Is As Sharp As A Knife*, An Anthology in Honour of Wilson Duff 1981.

As canoes were a mainstay of life, used every day near home and cached at the ends of trails, so they held members of important families after death. The wrapped body was placed inside a canoe after it had been fixed in the branches of a high tree, sometimes, if the family were wealthy, with another canoe overturned on top. The 1854 logger Michael Luark stole such a burial canoe from Eagle Island near McNeil, indicating that it was fairly new.[75] Often, an old, battered, unseaworthy canoe was used for such burials because it had less appeal to the living.

Horses[76]

After the mid-1700s, horses increased the overland mobility of Northwest tribes, both coastal and interior, shifting some populations into coastal pastures, as among Cowlitz . Early settlers, like the reliable George Gibbs,[77] distinguished between "canoe" or "horse" Indians, though such watercraft was the much more ancient means of travel along all waterways since vegetation, except where tended by natives, was thick and dense. Elk trails in the mountains, however, were easily usable by horses. South Puget Sound was more open, with many prairies maintained by routine burning to fertilize abundant these grasslands. With horses and other livestock, however, once abundant root foods soon vanished in favor of weedy pasture.

Horses returned with the Spanish to the Americas, where their fossil record is most complete.[78] After the successful 1680 Pueblo Revolt, hacienda livestock were traded over native networks to reach the Northwest within fifty years. Shoshoni traded horses along the western Rockies into the Snake River, and from there they spread around the Northwest interior and, through the Columbia River emporium, to the coast by about 1730. Spanish ships learned of horses along the Fraser River in 1792, and fur traders in the early 1800s saw Spanish brands on horses in eastern Washington and reported, "For a bridle they use a cord of horse-hair, which they attach [by a clove hitch] round the animal's mouth ... The saddle is a cushion of stuffed deer-skin ... The stirrups are pieces of hard wood, ingeniously wrought, and of the same shape as those which are used in civilized countries ... covered with a piece of deer-skin, which is sewed on wet and in drying stiffens and becomes hard and firm. The saddles for women differ in form,

---

75 Hazel Heckman, *Island in the Sound* 1967.

76 Horses and their trappings are discussed in Dawn Bates, Thom Hess, and Vi Hilbert, *Lushootseed Dictionary* 1994; Daniel Boxberger, The Introduction of Horses to the Southern Puget Sound Salish 1984: 103-119; John Ewers, *The Horse in Blackfoot Indian Culture* 1955; George Gibbs, A Dictionary of the Niskwalli Indian Language 1877; Helen Norton, The Association between Anthropogenic Prairies and Important Food Plants in Western Washington 1979: 434-449; Marian Smith, *The Puyallup-Nisqually* 1940a, The Puyallup of Washington 1940b, The Coast Salish of Puget Sound, 1941; George Stuckley and George Gibbs, Zoology of the Route 1860. More visually, the National Museum of the American Indian featured a comprehensive exhibit through 2012 called A Song for the Horse Nation.

77 Gibbs came to the NW from the California gold rush. His distinguished New York family and early schooling gave him a keen interest in native languages. A graduate of Harvard law, he became secretary of the treaty commission of Isaac Stevens, who wrote "geo: Gibbs attached to the Superintenency, a gentleman of ability exceedingly well versed in Indian affairs, appointed July 9, 1853." NARA M234 Reel 907 frame 0252.

78 Though there are a few tribal reports from the southern Plains that a small horse survived the Ice Age and was known to tribal ancestors.

being burnished with antlers of a deer, so as to resemble the high pommelled saddle of the Mexican ladies."[79]

In western Washington, especially Puget Sound,[80] horses were once presumed to have been brought through mountain passes by Sahaptins, especially Taitnapams, who colonized upriver pastures, but this now seems to have been a later occurrence. In Lushootseed, the words for horse and wolf are closely related. Elsewhere in the Americas, native names for horse derive from that for dog.[81] In Chinuk Wawa, the regional trade language, the terms for horse trappings clearly derive from French since they retain the article, such as la-sel for "saddle." All horses had rope halters.

During a pleasant moment on his rush to the Dalles, Theodore Winthrop was aided by two new friends, one he called an "Adonis" who seemed a "graceful centaur" for whom "no saddle intervened between them and their horses. No stirrup compelled their legs. A hair rope twisted around the mustang's lower lip was their only horse furniture.... He rode like an Elgin marble."[82]

In his early Nisqually (southern Lushootseed) dictionary, Gibbs[83] provides words for horse, saddle, and piebald breed. His word for saddle (*Hut-se'-lup-id*, with corrected hyphenation (*Hu-tse'l-up-id*) for roots of *tsil* "bear up" and *ap* "end, butt") literally means "to bear up the buttocks from below," and is clearly indigenous and not a borrowing from another language. Marian Smith,[84] premier ethnographer, noted there were only the pack and women's saddles. Men rode bareback or upon a folded blanket. A woman's stirrup (*gatscadeb ?*) was made from solid wood (alder, maple) with a wide half-circle cut out for the foot and a top hole for holding the leather strip fastening it to the saddle.

The wooden stirrup is noteworthy because it is "similar in design to other Salish objects and quite unlike the leather ones adopted later from Sahaptin horsemen." Indeed, "The horse or equine culture of the Sound occurred along the path of the prairie; at no time was it synonymous with groups dominated by Sahaptin influence." Instead, it was "more probably that the [coexisting] presence of the horse on both sides of the Cascades later stimulated contacts," including intermarriage.[85] Horses made possible extended bison hunts onto the Montana plains, encouraging distinct confederacies of Yakama and of Columbian Salish during the early 1800s.

Extensive, interlinked prairies were once characteristic of the Sound, maintained by routine burning to clear and fertilize huge beds of camas and other root crops tended by generations of native women inheriting family plots.

---

79 Gabriel Franchere, *A Voyage [1810-14] to the Norwest Coast of America* 1968: 204; John Alan Ross, *The Spokan Indians* 2011: 461.

80 Missing from all prior considerations are important aspects of gambling and heavy wagers placed on horse races, including established race tracks, such as that at the present Georgetown neighborhood of south Seattle.

81 *LD*: 226, wolf = *stiqayu* and horse = *stiqiw* follow each other on the same page. Gibbs (1877: 329) listed the word for "wolf" as the source for "horse."

82 Theodore Winthrop, *Canoe and Saddle* 1862: 142.

83 George Gibbs, A Dictionary of the Niskwalli Indian Language 1877: 321, 329-30.

84 Marian Smith, *The Puyallup-Nisqually* 1940a: 292-294; Puyallup of Washington 1940b: 22.

85 Smith, The Puyallup of Washington 1940b: 22.

Greater Puget Sound

Lushootseed natives had an extremely complicated social life based on rank, age, gender, and career specialties (Chapter 4). Their society was comparable to the complexity of farmers elsewhere in the world, yet they largely lived by harvesting the bounty that nature, with some bio-management, readily provided for them, though it varied considerably by place and season. Families did enhance plots and fields of plants with edible roots, such as wild carrots, onions, camas, and other bulbs; but this wise cultivation of nature was not the same as intensive farming. Nils Bruseth, an amateur folklorist in the north Sound, called it "reverse farming" since it involved weeding out some plants to encourage others to grow naturally.[86] Certain wild plant plots were enhanced by generations of women leaving seeds and roots in these moist locales. After traders from the Hudson's Bay Company introduced natives to potatoes, these prior talents at tending wild root foods allowed them to easily raise such tubers as a cash crop.[87] Traditionally, people commuted with the seasons to camps and stations near available natural foods. The climate was mild, due to the offshore Japanese and California Currents, and rainy, so the region abounded with plants and animals.

Chief among these foods were five species of salmon which (more properly, who, Chapter 5) spawned and died in the rivers, although in some years the runs were more abundant than others. In the notebooks, Jerry provided the most sustained discussion of a riverine fishery in existence. By working hard for a few weeks, a household could catch and dry enough fish to meet winter needs of the family and its guests.

Yet people did not live by fish alone. After the summer fish runs, families camped in the uplands and mountains to collect dozens of kinds of berries, which were also stored for winter use. Men hunted a variety of mammals, both sea and land, during the fall and winter, depending on where they lived. A whale straying into Puget Sound might also be taken. In the spring, fresh greens and early fish runs enriched the diet of stored winter supplies. By prudently and generously using resources which were locally "anchored," a household could add to their "radiance" throughout a greater Sound.[88]

Puget Sound, south end of the Salish Sea, has a surface that is 40 miles wide and 170 miles long, encompassing a thousand miles of shoreline, includes such ecologically diverse habitats as islands, deltas, tide flats, marshes, estuaries, shallow bays, and beaches. The Puget Lowlands region was successively formed by volcanism, plate tectonics "docking" huge islands eastward into the mainland, glaciation under the mile-thick Puget Lobe, and, most recently, sedimentation, including huge mudflows (lahars). During the Fraser glacial era (after 25,000 years ago), local rivers drained to the north into that major Canadian waterway. This inland sea, comprised of four adjoining basins complicated by islands and inlets, rarely has any wide open channels.

---

[86] Jay Miller, Dibble Cultivating Prairies to Beaches: The Real All Terrain Vehicle 2005; Vi Hilbert and Jay Miller, "That Salish Feeling…" *Studies in Salish Linguistics in Honor of M. Dale Kinkade* 2004.

[87] Wayne Suttles, *Coast Salish Essays* 1987: 137-151.

[88] Jay Miller, *Lushootseed Culture and the Shamanic Odyssey* 1999.

In the north Sound, Whidbey Island forms the outer edge of the largest basin, with Camano Island curving along its inside. It has 45% of the total area and receives 60% of the freshwater running off the Cascade Mountains. This main basin includes the entrance from the Pacific along the Straits of Juan de Fuca through Admiralty Inlet between the mainland on the east, including Seattle and Tacoma, and the Kitsap Peninsula, abutting Bainbridge Island, on the west. Vashon and Maury Islands, barely attached to each other at Quartermaster Harbor, block its southern end, just before the all-important Narrows. It receives 20% of the freshwater runoff. What is now called the Kitsap Peninsula, after a native leader, was once several islands which fused. Its twin peaks (Green and Gold Mountains) stood above the thickest glacier.

The south basin, receiving 10% of the freshwater runoff, is shaped like an irregular starburst or a deformed hand with seven fingers, each a longish inlet. The largest are Carr and Case Inlets, on the north side. Between them, projecting due south from the Kitsap landmass, is the Key Peninsula, the home of the natives at Minter. Islands (Fox, Anderson, McNeil, Hartstene, and Squaxin) direct the flow of main currents and tides. During the Ice Age, the Black Hills spillway took glacial waters south into the Chehalis River, which remains a widened route to the coast known as the "Salish Funnel" because ancestral Tillamook and Tsamosan speakers trekked along it to occupy the coast, where Chimakuans already lived.

The fourth basin, Hood Canal, to the west, has a separate, straight, open passage, albeit with a sharp bend (elbow) near the lower end. In ancient times, an easy portage took people and canoes from the south Sound through this channel to travel across the Straits of Juan de Fuca to Vancouver Island and present-day Canada.

The salt waters for Puget Sound rush through the south side of the Juan de Fuca Straits twice a day, with a quarter of this volume entering the Sound and three-fourths going north into the Straits of Georgia within the Salish Sea. With the Tacoma Narrows acting as bellows, either sucking or expelling at 6 knots (6080 feet ~ 1832 meters/ hour), the tides (spring-high, neap-low) move clockwise around Vashon Island to the north and eddy around Fox Island to the south, near the mouth of Carr Inlet. Since only a third of the total volume exits into the Straits at each tide, two dozen tides (two weeks) are needed to flush out all of the southern Sound.

Away from the shore, terrain is hilly, interspersed with lakes, and dense with tangled undergrowth, as historically reported, beneath a mixed forest of Douglas fir, red alder, grand fir, big leaf maple, and cottonwood. Scattered parklands, included oak and Douglas fir, were formerly kept grassy by an annual burn-over ritually set by young men.[89] Edible plants ranged from abundant berries to clover, cow parsnip, fern, wapato (wild potato), and camas. Plentiful game animals, living in diverse microenvironments, comprised waterfowl, deer, elk, bear, otter, raccoon, beaver, mountain goat, shellfish, ocean fish, porpoise, seal, sea lion, and the seasonal runs of salmon, smelt, and herring.[90]

---

[89] The boys engaged in mock combat before setting these prairie fires, presumably to transfer energies into the fresh growth as during other seasonal sports.

[90] Charles Nelson, Prehistory of the Puget Sound Region 1990: 481; Florence Howard, An Archaeological Site Survey of Southwestern Puget Sound 1949; John (and Marcia) Winterhouse, A Report of an Archaeological Survey of Lower Puget Sound 1948; Robert Burns, The Shape and Form of Puget Sound 1985.

Landscape

Cascading from its rim of mountain ranges, each river was once dotted with the winter towns, villages, hamlets, and seasonal camps (resorts) of a distinct tribal community.[91] Each fully interacted with all the others near and far to give order and meaning to Lushootseed life and culture. The larger basin is occupied by speakers of the northern dialect of this language, while the middle and southern basins are the home of southern dialects (Whulshootseed).

Today, all of the religions and sects of the modern world can be found among the native peoples of Puget Sound, but they co-exist with much more ancient beliefs and practices based in the landscape. Modern churches, however, have distinctly native features because families and communities continue to worship together. In the northern sound, assigned by US officials to Catholics for the past 150 years, cedar boughs freshly cut from the forest and flutes carved from cedar limbs augment the Mass. Similarly, Protestant churches on south reservations feature native designs and concepts such as the "Great Spirit" in their services. Some hymns are still sung in Lushootseed.

Two modern religious expressions, moreover, continue ancient beliefs associated with spirits of the land. One is called Smokehouse ~ Siyowin Religion because it uses public buildings built like ancestral, communal, cedar-plank houses, continuing traditions of personal spirit helpers and special regard to certain places, often remote and sacred, on the land and in the water. The other is the Indian Shaker Church, founded near Olympia in 1882 and incorporated under Washington state law in 1910. It blends ancient beliefs with those of Christianity into a distinctive pattern of worship now spread from California to Canada and Montana.

Relying on Cedar and Salmon, Minters made the local into the global, taking along outer house planks on their annual commute as well as canoes filled with gear to ease their hosts' obligations during visits. Moving through and across the landscape strengthened these extensive kin ties as relatives met and parted at different places, in the life style of Sally Meeker.

World

The Lushootseed world is believed to have passed through several epochs. Efforts by semi-divine (if sometimes bumbling) Transformers, originally in teams, led up to a last universal change, likened to a "capsizing." At that moment, everything came into its present form to begin the modern world. Across land- and sea-scapes, beings became immortal, some cast in stone. Each occupied a known or revealed place, where, over generations, its resources were shared with members of the leading local family. Often in epics, an ancestral spirit couple was placed upon or within each river, with their resulting children founding various towns and villages along its length to be nurtured by its staple bounty from water, uplands, meadows, and forests. The Puyallup drainage serves as one example, providing the greater affiliation of Minters on the basis of shared language, kinship, ceremonies, and foods.

---

[91] Though the seasonal distinction between towns and camps is fixed in the literature, elders speak of traditional summer camps as more like resorts. Of course, this may be more a reflection of their young age, while hard work was being done by adults, but the image is telling. Similarly, native settlements themselves require more varied and suitable English terms such as hamlet, haven, or town. Their seasonal movements, as noted, were not nomadic roaming but rather commuting among regular stations.

Leading, reliable families traced their own pedigrees from the epic of twin Starchild and Diaper Boy, who left the earth to become the Moon and Sun after marrying diligent wives and leaving many resourceful children (and powerful dicta) behind to lead seasonal activities and intermarry among crucial towns.[92]

While shamans, both men and women, still practice among the Salish, many of their curing functions are now shared with members of modern religious sects such as the Indian Shaker Church and Pentecostal Christianity. Indeed, one appeal of Pentecostalism for Lushootseeds has been the prominence of women in its history.[93] Today, members of these faiths are more friendly than in the past, recognizing that all emphasize possession by "Spirit" as evidence of a direct link with God, exuberantly expressed while healing the sick and afflicted by such members of the wider Indien community.[94]

Lastly, by notable comparison, as the tidal sea swirls around Puget Sound over a long cycle, squirted through the Narrows, so immortal spirits also circuit through the Lushootseed universe, arriving back in the Sound during the winter to reconnect with their mortal partner and empower his or her song and dance in smokehouses. They come from the east, like the Sun, and travel around to the north, west, and south before again heading east for the summer. The waters of the Sound, of course, move in reverse, coming eastward from the Pacific Ocean on the west. Furthermore, all of these systems are, in turn, reversed again in the land of the dead, interweaving cycles of life, time, and space.

---

[92] Fully discussed in Jay Miller, *Lushootseed Culture and the Shamanic Odyssey* 1999: 50-56, though the specific version told by Jerry to Thelma Adamson was Minter's own.

[93] Inspired by teachers at Bethel Bible College in Topeka, Agnes Ozman received "Spirit baptism" on 1 January 1901, leading to the 1906 Azuza Street (Los Angeles), to revival by William Seymour, a one-eyed black preacher, founding Pentecostalism, and to Aimee Semple McPherson's 1921 founding of the Foursquare Gospel Church and the Angelus Temple. Before 1920, Sarah Ober actively worked to recruit Washington Shakers into the Pentecostal fold without avail, even among those using the Bible, Cf David Buerge and Junius Rochester, *Roots and Branches* 1988: 95.

[94] Homer Barnett, *Indian Shakers*, A Messianic Cult of the Pacific Northwest,1957; Pamela Amoss, *Coast Salish Spirit Dancing* 1978: 81; Robert Ruby and John Brown, *John Slocum and the Indian Shaker Church* 1996: 154.

4 KINSCAPE: PERSON

At Minter, the web and puzzle of kinship intersected geographical places ("mud") and genealogical spaces ("blood") with four increasingly more inclusive aspects forming rays. Individuals, of whatever life form; constituted a **person** (composed of a gendered aging body, a mind, and souls – along with spirit allies). Radiating out from the focal person (Ego) are increasingly more inclusive networks; such as a **kindred**, either nodal for lower or stem for high social class; a **sept**, covering at least four generations; and, largest, an **intersept**. These are considered in the next chapter, after we discuss the nexus at the person.

Person

Personhood was engendered as male or female, aged as older or younger, and ranked as elite, freeborn, or slave. The leaders of households and communities constituted the elite title holders, "owning" (in the sense of holding and hosting) famous names, houses, and resource locations. Like the wealthy everywhere, they had several homes (massive fixed house frames positioned among varied localized resources), though the primary one was occupied during the rainy winter. Other members of the freeborn rank were commoners, valuable for their labor and support but otherwise undistinguished.

Lushootseeds along the shoreline emphasized rank and class, while those inland, upriver, and in the southern Sound held more Plateau ideals of a kin-based society. "Southern Puget Sound culture emphasized spirit quests and had a lesser emphasis on inherited privileges than the Northerners,"[95] and hence provided the birthplace for the more democratic beliefs known as the Indian Shaker Church, recognizing a universal, omnipotent God. Overall, native identities involved practical consideration to gender, age, rank, descent, residence, and waterway.

Gender

At Minter, gender equality was strong, like the Salish ideal. The highest ranking person, child of a prior chief and presumably an elite marriage, was Damasq, a woman serving as head or "chieftess," most obviously whenever she was between marriages or widowed. Otherwise her husband "fronted" for her by default as leader of the community, though he does not seem to have been known in public as a "real" chief – except by courtesy in lieu of claims to an inherited and instructed ("trained up") right. By being demure and indirect, Damasq displayed the breeding of a highborn woman.

Men tended to do some things and women to do others, a matter more of frequency rather than of rigid duties. Genders were and are defined by their actions, not by their overt body differences alone. Since the immortal spirits also had gender, a woman performing usual man's roles was presumed to have a male spirit helper.

[95] Natalie Roberts, A History of the Swinomish Tribal Community 1975: 32, 35, 77.

The entire community functioned like a salmon. Among the Fraser River Sto:lo to the north in British Columbia, the vital image of Salmon conveys a sense of mutual cooperation such that "women" are said to be like the backbone, and "men" like the nose, with the ready understanding of all fishing folk that "the nose is, of course, first, the forward tip of the head which is not followed but propelled by the backbone."[96]

Since these gender careers were mutually interdependent, they functioned best in terms of a married couple, who shared information when they were in bed together. Men killed and women cooked. A hunter gutted his prey and left it for his wife to pack home, as did a fisherman <A19>. At a salmon weir, the leader scheduled the unloadings by men before his wife apportioned the catch among all the women to process the fish for their family's use. Today, a person cannot properly display spirit power at "its" annual winter return without emotional and musical support by a spouse. Stable couples cooperated in endeavors, even as they observed sexual abstinence (ritual chastity), which was required for hunters before a hunt, women before harvesting, shamans before a cure, and warriors before a battle.[97] While a husband was in pursuit of food, wives and sisters prayed and sang to assist him, often lying very still to model the desired stand-still of game animals.

Noted hunters at Minter were spəym, lašibiya, and sxʷadax̣ub <B34>. The outstanding fisher was tsialaxa ~ tsiyaləxʷ, though his son Jim Hummelgood (xʷəbalgdəxʷ, xʷəmalgʷnəxʷ) did not follow in this career and instead hunted with lašibiya.

Children

From the time they were toddlers, boys were given toy tools such as paddles, bows, arrows, slings, and carving knives to practice for adult careers. As they got older, these toys got larger. Children spent much time paddling a variety of canoes. Girls were given dolls, toy needles, awls, and cooking utensils to play at sewing, weaving, and keeping house. Her first basket was "finished" during her puberty seclusion and given away to a worthy matron, who prayed for the girl's long life and increased skill.

Ordinary children were usually known by kin terms and nicknames until they were about twelve and received an ancestral family name.[98] Of course, in elite families, with skillful managers and reliable planners, children were named at a very early age, then went on to personally earn and acquire subsequent names over their lifetime. Salishan names could come through the father or the mother, but the father usually suggested the first one. Many names specified gender, but could be held by males or by females of proper families with the addition of an appropriate ending. Leader names, regardless of the actual gender of their current holder, were usually male and often ended in *-qən/-qəd* meaning "head," or *-qs* for "nose," as illustrated by the ending of the native name of Sally's Steilacoom first husband (Ce-col-quin). Female names often end in *–ul* "having" + *–itsa* "dress," such as that of Damasq's.[99] Transgenders ~

---

96 Crisca Bierwert, Tracery in the Mistlines: Semeiotic Readings of Sto:lo Culture, 1986: 340.

97 Pamela Amoss, *Coast Salish Spirit Dancing* 1978: 57.

98 June Collins, Naming, Continuity, and Social Inheritance among the Coast Salish of Western Washington 1966.

99 As noted, because of the taboo of silence imposed between the death of an elite name holder and the transfer to the next heir, Damasq's seems more of a female nickname, appropriate to

transvestites are not known for Minter or Steilacoom, though a few did occur elsewhere around the Sound.[100] Men and women expressed a skill in all of its ramifications. For example, as a canoe maker, Gizmo [R2] also produced paddles and made meshed netting.

Men

Men made the open-work clamming baskets, traps, nets, weapons, canoes, and houses. They did all the hunting, fishing, and woodworking – constructing fire-proof hearths; making cradle boards, adzing handles, carvings, and multipurpose planks; and building smokehouses for curing meat and fish. They gathered firewood (if no children or slaves were available), whittled long wooden needles for sewing cattail mats, and split the ironwood stakes (jokingly called "fish sticks") for cooking salmon and clams.

Carpenters had to combine spiritual techniques with manual skills to be successful. While every man could work wood, the building of houses and canoes called for experts. All specializations served to enhance family and personal prestige, granted by guardian spirits to provide a religious sanction for public success. As the sons (half-brothers only for Anglo Americans) of the trainer from the prior generation, both Tyee George [R4] and Gizmo [R2] shared in the successes of each other, their families, and ancestors.

For men, special careers included those of chief, warrior, doctor, and ritualist. In southern Puget Sound, a man could excel as canoe maker, hunter, storyteller, gambler, wrestler, gorger ~ chompion, or harpooner. While all men hunted, such career hunters honed the talents and powers needed to harpoon sea mammals or pursue mountain goats, wearing clothing and equipment, such as quivers, made of cougar skins. While sea mammal hunting was a south Sound specialty, as likely at Minter as elsewhere, hunting in the Olympic Mountains, while also likely, is not reported, though elk are briefly mentioned in the notes.

Women

Women took care of the house and family – drying foods; cooking meals; and weaving cattail mats, baskets, and, if noble, dog or goat wool blankets. Long in advance, they worked to gather, prepare, and dye necessary cedar boughs, bark, grasses, and roots. They made clothing and rain gear from softened, shredded cedarbark, which invigorated by lightly chafing the wearer's skin. In upriver and mountainous regions, leather clothes were preferred. Both men and women wore leggings when walking overland as protection from brush, and both donned snowshoes for winter treks.

---

her career. Her hereditary name as chief, therefore, was never inherited and so remains in limbo.

[100] Buried in the fieldnotes of Sally Snyder (Box 109) for the northern Sound are references to four transgenders, and words for them such as *sali'ib* "acting double," with the ending *–ib* "acting like." Located on the Skagit River, two male bodies dressed and acted female. On the Snohomish River, an overprotective mother encouraged her son in female pursuits. At Darrington, a woman became an avid hunter, which was highly unusual because typically females gave life and men took it. Actual hermaphrodites were thought to be the result of the mother eating wrong, especially female, foods.

In historic times, mobility improved. Because of their kinship with Klickitats across the mountains, Minters would have had access to horses and specially tanned leather through inlaws; though it remains unknown, except possibly by archaeology, how and if these were acquired. The James Douglas 1853 census reported that there were no horses at Minter. They could have been brought over when horse herds from arid eastern Washington were pastured on moist western slopes, or when some Minter men went across to trade, or, most likely of all, as gifts from their Sahaptin inlaws. In his brief memoir, Willy Frank explained how such horses could have swum across the Sound and been ridden up the peninsula to Minter.[101]

By season, women gathered roots, berries, and shoots; dried and smoked fish, venison, and shellfish; prepared skins; shredded cedarbark; spun goat and dog wool; made baskets and weavings; tended children; prepared meals, and carried wood and water – if there were no slaves to do these tasks. Healthy, fertile, moral women acted as midwives or nurses, to assure the wellbeing of the newborn and mother.

Rank, family pedigree, diligence, resourcefulness, and resilience were highly valued among Minters, as by other Lushootseeds, yet each person must rely on a personal link with an immortal, who shared some portion of the all-pervading power (vitality-energy-force) from the Creator. Such access was made manifest in the success of community efforts under the guidance of elite leaders. Though men were the acknowledged holders of these positions, their primary support came from close kin and affines, both women and men, aged and young.

Rankings

Minters were distinguished by social class. Families were ranked as high born, noble born, ordinary, or slave, with public authority qualified by age (old to young) and by gender (man to woman). Elite status was validated by the continuous personal and public successes of family members across many generations, assuring their reputation for self-confidence, generosity, competence, and authority. Nobles took the lead by arranging successful group hunts, winter ceremonials, giveaways, elaborate cures, and the building of houses, canoes, huge nets, and fish weirs. Of note, these nets were as equally effectively in the water as in the air (at Quartermaster Harbor, Day Island) or in the forest, snaring either fish, flocks, or herds.[102] Minter specifically was noted as the recent home of Chompions famous throughout the Sound. Earlier, as noted, they had been trainers and warriors, before epidemics and slave raids took a huge toll.

In his classic discussion of human social classes and ranks among the Coast Salishans,[103] Wayne Suttles[104] argued for a societal model that was like an inverted pear because the majority of people considered themselves to be noble, worthy, respectable, and moral. The narrow bottom of the pear was occupied by the low class, and the very base by a small number of slaves. Usually, these memberships are called the upper class, the lower class, and slavery, but these terms obscure degrees of rank within the upper class. Indeed, while most people had only a class identity, members of elite families always held names which had long been famous intertribally.

---

[101] Willy Frank, Voices of Washington State 1980.

[102] Cf Thomas Waterman, place # 171.

[103] This section improves on the section on Classes in Jay Miller, *Lushootseed Culture and the Shamanic Odyssey* 1999: 89-93.

[104] Wayne Suttles, *Coast Salish Essays* 1987: 3-14.

Thus, while houses and towns might be attributed to a social class on a local basis, rank was a matter of regional recognition. At Minter, that recognition came to be identified – at the end – with their gorging fame, while earlier it was extolled by their prestigious academy.

Based on present-day patterns, every region had and has certain families, those with honored names, that clearly stand out from the other nobles. These families were the obvious elite and they passed on names which were well known in the international network. They were the equivalent of a Roosevelt, Vanderbilt, Kennedy, or Astor, rather than a Jones, Smith, or Miller.[105]

June Collins[106] has distinguished these titles as "renowned names" because holders of such names owned several big houses at locations variously endowed. Indeed, in Lushootseed, such a person or family is called *hikʷ si'ab*, in the sense of a grandee, "big" in terms of authority, respect, sharing, and ability.[107] In a few instances, such an owner had several large houses (actually, architectural frames), each near an important resource.[108] The wall planks or mats moved with the family to enclose their current residence. That he (or they) could coordinate the building of more than one large home further spoke to his (their) leadership abilities. While any leader was usually too busy to hunt and fish regularly, his wives did harvest roots, berries and clams. In return for skillful management, a leader received gifts of meat and fish from followers.

Based on observations at modern day reservations, where some families are still called "low class" behind their backs, the distinguishing characteristic of such people is that they are inconsistent, given to binges, and so can not be relied upon to always behave well at public gatherings or to help out readily in times of need.[109] Leaders would indicate places where the bloodlines of other families were "weak" because of bad or shameful behavior by an ancestor.[110] A great but subtle insult occurred at a public gathering when a noble spit on his left little finger

---

105 Homer Barnett, *The Coast Salish* of British Columbia 1955: 247, note 3, cites Comox "superlative term[s] of address for an aristocratic" woman and man using *ti-*.

106 June Collins, Naming, Continuity, and Social Inheritance among the Coast Salish of Western Washington 1966.

107 In this context *hikʷ* means "big, high, most, very" and *siʔab* is the term for "honor, respect, nobility," derived from *ʔiʔab* "wealth, rich, abundant" and the *s-* nominalizer.

108 William Elmendorf, *The Structure of Twana Culture* 1960: 271, 317 called this "plurality of site residences."

109 Susan Kenyon (The Kyuquot Way: A Study of a West Coast (Nootkan) Community 1980: 86), a British subject from Wales, gained her understanding of Nuuchahnulth social organization when a Toquaht chief reminded her that the system was much like her own: The elite carefully trace their *descent* from illustrious, famous ancestors, while everyone else relied on *kinship* networks. Thus, nobles relied on both descent and kinship, but commoners traced only kinship.

110 By implication, Lushootseed thought that the common substance shared by family members was "blood," as in popular European notions of kinship. The continuing importance of "bone" in rituals indicates that it too was important. In many cultures, "blood" comes to a child from the mother, "bone" from the father, and this arrangement may have once been Lushootseed belief. Along with factors of residence, kinship, as noted, combined "blood" and "mud," especially in the wet Northwest.

and held it up because this meant that the person he was referring to was of slight consequence.[111]

Some families are simply lazy, but others frustrate because they vacillate across the spectrum of good and bad behaviors. Their position is so unsure ~ unreliable that they binge – sometimes they devote much time and effort to putting on a good front, but other times they will appear drunk or unruly at gatherings, where they are quietly but grudgingly tolerated. High class Lushootseeds realize that the undistinguished have a "tough" life, but good people and families are expected to show "pluck" and rise above uncertainties and momentary hardships.

Now as in the past, there are families who are famous and elite, others who are respected, others who were stolid, and others who are looked down upon. Similarly, in certain contexts today, reservations are distinguished from separate native communities. Because of their legal and federal advantages, those placed on reservations with a full compliment of rights from the treaties of 1855 sometimes maneuver to slight in public those leaders whose reservations were established by presidential order or recent recognition since these people have a more contentious relationship with the federal government. Lastly, those few tribes who are described as landless – variously lacking treaty rights, federal recognition, or trust land – sometimes meet with open hostility from the leaders of treaty tribes, both at native gatherings and in the US district courts. These attitudes seem to be carry-overs from relationships between the classes and among ranking families.

Houses and towns that appeared prosperous and generous have always received more respect and attention. The basis for this prosperity, according to the Salish, was continuous relations between the leading family and local immortals. In the most successful of families, these relations were intentionally so diverse that their households were filled with a range of specialists – in crafts, culinary efforts, medicine, command, management, and religion – who were vital to the intertribal network of protocols, trade, kinship, ceremonies, and hospitality.

> “people felt free to travel only in areas where they had relatives. If a person visited a village where he was related but was not known personally, he identified himself by calling out the name of a distinguished ancestor from the village and the nature of his own descent from this man or woman. He was then entitled to a friendly reception, food, and shelter. Failure to behave in this way meant that the visitor was unrelated and therefore an enemy who should be dispatched at once.”[112]

Other expressions of rank were the private ownership of desired resources, such as fisheries and trade items; strict rules of inheritance, particularly from father to the oldest son and from mother to the oldest daughter; the ownership of houses and slaves, and the possession of family wisdom (*x*^{w}*dik*^{w}), sometimes called “advice ~ lore.” Many of the details of this wisdom – in addition to own family history, complex genealogies, gossip about other families, and full accounts of spirit quests by ancestors – include moral aspects of the Golden Rule and Ten

---

[111] Homer Barnett, *The Coast Salish of British Columbia* 1955: 191, confirmed for Gulf of Georgia Salish that holding up a little finger was a way to belittle other families. Any ceremonial use of a left hand, however fleeting, was also insulting.

[112] June Collins, Multilineal Descent: A Coast Salish Strategy, *Currents in Anthropology* 1979: 251.

Commandments.[113] These practicalities were complemented by a range of esoteric knowledge, ranging from prayers used during life cycle events of family members to a special set of powerful words (dicta) to control the minds of all intelligent life forms, from humans to animals to weather spirits.

Often these enchantments, sometimes called hexes, magic spells, or formulae, were associated with the houses of particular leaders and were passed on to descendants of families who had been resident there. Bits of these formulae might also be sold to a person outside the family for a high price. Though often regarded by scholars as a separate religious system, these dicta were given to the family ancestor by the Creator either directly or through the efforts of the Changers who did "His" bidding and prepared the world before human arrival.

For the neighboring Twana, hallmarks of nobility included birth, wealth, personality, and spirit powers.[114] Birth pedigree referred to descent from families of good "blood" and reputation who worked diligently to maintain this status by industrious productivity and ambition. Wealth took the tangible form of slaves, canoes, dog or goat wool blankets, fur robes, sea otter pelts, bone war clubs, and dentalium shells – all of which served as currency in the overlapping intertribal network of gifts and trade. Personality referred to an even temperament, dignity, regard for others (compassion), generosity, industry, self control, and pride. The greatest of spirit powers bonded to the most elite families, conferring wealth, wisdom, property, progeny, and good fortune.

While a child started with the advantages of a good birth, subsequent training instilled the self discipline needed to undergo the rigorous ordeal that achieved spiritual purity. Such training was a determining factor in the molding of a personality suitable for the acquisition of powers that allowed an adult to enter the ranks of the elite. The entire family contributed to this training, although older family specialists were usually "paid" (compensated) by the parents for taking the time to teach particular lessons, as was the case when three elderly "uncles" taught Old Pierre the epic of Katzie genesis.[115]

A special training academy at Minter established its early prestige, and other "schoolhouses" are reported for other regions where the children of noble families were educated and initiated together, establishing another set of fictive kinship ties among classmates. These sometimes blossomed into actual ties of marriage and descent, much as in modern prep schools.

---

[113] Wayne Suttles saw the crucial role of this concept, known as *snəp* in Straits Salish, emphasizing its improbable moral tone such that "it is hard for an outsider to believe that it was not generally known that one should not lie, steal, or throw rocks at his grandmother, but this was the Coast Salish fiction." Today, such aphorisms continue as "truisms" used by native politicians and others to say something appropriate yet neutral at gatherings, such as reminding tribal members to stay out of cemeteries after 3PM, when ghost become active, unless one has special spiritual protections.

[114] William Elmendorf, *The Structure of Twana Culture* 1960: 322, 327-336.

[115] Diamond Jenness, The Faith of a Coast Salish Indian 1955: 65. Old Pierre was unusually precocious and his mother very determined so this training started when he was as young as three, with intensive lessons after he was eight years old.

Chief

Known as "first nose, to nose before," ($sd^{z}ix^{w}qs$, "one" + "nose")[116], a leader's specialty was a grasp of the human condition – its emotions, needs, foibles, and concerns. He or she epitomized dignity, open-handedness, restraint, wealth, and knowledge of traditions within the community, diplomacy and generosity with outsiders, and haughty disdain before enemies. Years of careful marriages among other prominent tribal families and ceaseless training of children in their lifelong responsibilities were intended to produce members of this high rank. The major Minter house traced inlaws from Muckleshoot, Suquamish, Klallam, Chehalis, and Klickitat.

Sometimes a chief would deliberately stigmatize him/herself to have an excuse for a potlatch. For example, in the early 1800s, at Suquamish, *šalqəb*, the second chief, after Kitsap and ahead of a young Seattle, deliberately went too close to his hearth so his blanket caught on fire, giving him an excuse to host a potlatch to cover his embarrassment and to show people he was generous. Such staged dramatics as a cause for generosity were an aspect of the chiefly role that has been generally overlooked in available publications.[117] Since respect and position relied on such ongoing hosting, such "all too human" occasions provided reasons that seemed less self-serving.

Shadow Politics

The leadership of Damasq at Minter provides insight into Lushootseed polities, which is generally said to be minimal. Puget Sound politics, instead, is a mask, cloak, or shadow for aspects of kinship, rank, training, and economy. Leaders were senior kin of prestigious families with proven success. They coordinated care, labor, food, and ecology for their local community, as well as integrating it into the greater waterway and watershed. While most tasks were led by those most skillful, the political leaders specialized in "the human drama," able to sympathize and direct community members. Within the larger region, those living downriver, who could block salmon runs, had more influence than those upriver, where salmon spawned. Chiefs did virtually no physical or muscle "work," but instead managed everything via their wealth-power, oversight, and persuasion. At the core of their reliable labor force were slaves, who did their bidding and supplied daily needs. Healthy children and their spouses also strengthened this position. As noted, chiefly families with many sons often placed them in charge of other houses in their community, with birth order determining house ranking if all of them were fit, level-headed, able-bodied, skilled, and active.

Leaders relied on pedigree and training to withstand the constant criticism that was their lot. Their success was judged by their abilities as hosts, sustaining loyalty and labor to accomplish needed communal tasks, especially construction projects for houses, weirs, canoes, and containers. They controlled special knowledge, especially dicta, to apply spiritual pressures on workers. Keeping everyone healthy, active, well-fed, and cooperative thus assured the

---

[116] *LD*: 91,179.

[117] See Jay Miller, Suquamish Traditions, *Northwest Anthropological Research Notes* 1999a. Reprinted in Evergreen Ethnographies 2015.

continuity of their community and family. Spirit powers concerned with wealth, bounty, and success bolstered their status.

Both men and women of elite families were leaders, but Euro-Americans, during the very reign of Queen Victoria, nevertheless denied official roles to native women. At treaties and public meetings, men kept the advantage. Broken Tooth, who instituted the engorging power that saved Minter, was of the same generation as walatšalq, who attended the December 1854 Treaty of Medicine Creek while married to Damasq. Americans did not recognize women as leaders, and certainly not as treaty signers, especially when the military was in charge. In his notebook autobiography, Jerry repeated this prejudice, denying that women could be chiefs despite his family's own experience at Minter.

Jerry was careful to specify in these more private notebooks that pedigree was crucial. Damasq's husband became {"chief upon marriage to the chief of Minter's daughter. He was not a chief or chief's son among the Puyallup. His wife remained the real leader at Minter. He helps her in planning…. Her first husband came [from] right there at Minter. He must have been son of a chief. She was a woman chief because her father was a chief" <A52>}. Her power was *yilbix* (women's riches), with a song accompanied by a pole pounded against the house roof and usually held by her son Lashibiya <A6>. [??] She held the leading house together after Minter was burned out, and relocated it to Glencove <A13, 52>.

In sum, Damasq carried the chiefly pedigree at Minter, aided by a powerful Wealth spirit, and presumably dicta from Star Child. As a woman, especially when foreigners were involved, her husbands fronted for her in public settings, though she clearly managed behind the scenes. Her family included walatšalq <B12>, daughter g^{w}oldox^{w}ts and son Lashibiya. Lashibiya was last trainer at the reduced academy that had made Minter famous through the early 1800s. He died about 1878, about the time that Jerry Meeker entered the schoolroom (of Rev Mann?) at the Puyallup Reservation. Damasq had the support of her two slaves <A45>, a Lummi woman and the Snohomish man called Simon, who became a shaman (Chapter 8).

Later, when Damasq was old, the main house was sometimes said to be led by Moye's (Moses), who, via a grandfather, was first cousin to both Sally Meeker and the Minter headwoman. During the 1855 Treaty War, Damasq was muted by these circumstances, but, afterward, she led households at Minter and then at Glencove, built by teams of men. At the end, the Glencove house was used to dry salmon until it too was destroyed by a settler family <A18>.

Family pedigree, training, and ability provided community and tribal leaders, who worked through kinship, sharing, and hosting to maintain their leadership positions. They planned well and supplied local needs, even as they oversaw the burning off, planting, and harvesting of wild foods. With help from spirit powers, they were integrated within the cosmos for the benefit of themselves, their kindred, their community, and the overall interspecies ecology.

Because the Minter headwoman cooked the meals, so the food would not be morally tainted by her slaves, these continued domestic duties may have lessened her chiefly rank. More likely, though, such cooking aided Damasq's reputation for generosity when visitors were there, or was a function of her age in a household where the children were grown and gone.

Warrior

Warrior powers only occurred along the coastline, where open access made necessary such community protection and defense. As a singular exception to expected behavior, a warrior should be forceful and aggressive, dominant, imperious, quick-tempered, implacable, and despotic.[118] He alone could flaunt a hot temper, stamina, indifference to physical risk, and a willingness to be mean in inflicting pain. His dagger and club were so closely associated with the killing of men that displaying an unsheathed weapon at a public event was tantamount to a declaration of war. A famous warrior had a palisade built around his house or established a nearby fort for added security.[119]

While men were defenders, women were sometimes seen as instigators. As an apt example, much farther north in Alaska, Tlingit women are expressly said to have worn weighted labrets in their lower lip as a reminder that their unguarded words ("loose lips sink ships") caused wars.[120] The added tug of the labret served to remind them to be reserved and "watch their lips" when they had something to say.

Among Lushootseed neighbors, the war between Lummi and Stockaders for the present mainland near the mouth of the Nooksak River started when an insulted wife tangled her fingers in her Lummi husband's hair to hold on to him until her Stockader brothers could behead him.[121] Though the Lummi took over this mainland, they could not successfully use its resources until they first hired, then intermarried to inherit, proper Stockader rituals and prayers (dicta) to assure river weir fishing success.

Both Kitsap and Talibot,[122] famous and fierce, served this warrior role at Suquamish when Minter was in its prime. Twanas[123] reported that Minters "had never seen any war; they did not know what it was like," indicating they had no warriors then, overlooking the past slaughter at Burley indicated by place names noted by Waterman.

The most famous Minter warrior was a boy who lived through his terrifying encounter with a great power and carved its horned snake image onto the prow of a canoe that he kept secluded. When Taitnapam slavers attacked Minter, he uncovered the canoe and all those who saw it were instantly struck dead, zapped by a bolt shot through this image.

Doctors

Shamans had both career and curing spirits. He or she often had a separate house, for the privacy needed during cures and because most people were rightly suspicious ~ scared of such power. Yet their presence in a settlement brought security from attack by spirits or hostile shamans. Their duties were to explain the cause of hardships, treat the sick, and counteract

[118] Pamela Amoss, *Coast Salish Spirit Dancing* 1978: 10.

[119] Jay Miller, First Nations Forts, Refuges, and War Lord Champions around the Salish Sea, *Journal of Northwest Anthropology (JONA)* 45 (1): 71-87 2011, Spring.

[120] Frederica de Laguna, *The Story of a Tlingit Community* 1960: 120.

[121] Jay Miller, *Lushootseed Culture and the Shamanic Odyssey* 1999: 17.

[122] The name *talibot* means "war club."

[123] Elmendorf, *Twana Narratives* 1993: 18.

malevolent sorcery. While shamans were generally treated with deference (tinged by fear), a doctor who was a member of the family was the best of allies.

No doctors are reported in the Minter notebooks except for Dr Simon, the eventually-freed slave, a highly unusual instance. Instead, those at Chambers Creek receive repeated if passing mention in the Joseph Heath diary, and Dr Cataammouth was a close ally of the pioneer Chambers family. Unless they were creating an occasion for generosity, the cure by a Twana with Lizard power of a Minter woman whose own spirit had gone to Mt Rainier also strongly suggests a lack of local shamans – killed off by diseases, angry patients, or competition. It may well have been that, in the aftermath of combined epidemics, slaving, and warrior attacks, their fame as Chompions became their distinctive community career specialty. Moreover, the role of Minter in training and initiation into the Growlers academy may have precluded other more common shamanic activity, especially individualized expressions in favor of this highly elite collective one.

Slavery

Two tiny houses at Minter were the homes of slaves, a female and a male, belonging to Damasq. We know nothing of the woman after she joined Nisqually, but the life of the Dr Simon[124] has been pieced together (Chapter 8). Born noble, he was never a typical slave; his work involved little drudgery and much excitement.[125]

[124] Jay Miller, Dr Simon: A Snohomish Slave at Fort Nisqually and Puyallup 2002.

[125] A more typical case is John Kettle, freed at Suquamish, who sold shellfish to Seattle markets, prospering from his life-long drudgery, See Jay Miller, Suquamish Traditions 1999a: 130.

5 KINSCAPE: PEOPLES

Kin groups (often called corporate ~ bilateral ~ cognatic) among Coast Salish have long interested scholars. The study of kinship in Southeast Asia as well as the central Northwest Coast has revealed increasingly more inclusive (and diffuse) units such as family-based groupings, traced through both father and mother, known as **kindreds**, either **nodal** for lower ranks or **stem** for the high social class. These diffuse into a **sept**, traced bilaterally over a wide region for at least four generations, regardless of where members were living. These kinspeople interacted with members of nearby comparable units – in rituals, games, feasts, and marriages – to form "overlapping intervillage social units, which Suttles,[126] with some misgivings, called **kithreds**, referring to kith of country or neighborhood. Herein they are called **intersepts**.

Geographical, linguistic, and residential considerations made up what has been called the "tribe," though this label has become a discredited term among academics, even as it have become enshrined in federal Indian Law.[127] Instead, each watershed, basin, or drainage embraced cultural overlaps that were tribally and linguistically distinct. Elite intermarriages and social interactions further confounded notions of tribal boundaries and consistency.

Hereditary names, especially renowned ones, serve as the labels for these groupings, though some moderating consideration is always given to the moral qualities of inherited traits, such as "good or bad" blood (*stulig^{w}əd*)[128] and family resemblances traced as body peculiarities, abilities, and personalities. Jerry's own name lehaldx^{w} is a good example, because its preceding holders had lived on both sides of the Cascade Mountains and spoke languages of very different stocks, but, as Jerry noted, hearing that name immediately identified its original locale and sept as anchored at a Nisqually town {"These were famous names, and one knows … the exact village the name comes from … to differentiate them from the other [commoner] people" } <A43>.

Kinship links traced through both father and mother aligned Lushootseeds into discrete kindreds – bilateral (both sides of a family) descent groupings associated with households. In most cases, each formed a "nodal kindred," where the node was a bond of parent and children or, after those antecedent's death, that of siblings, often brothers who jointly owned a winter house. For most families, a kindred had cohesion only as long as it had a dominant node, sometimes expressed as attenuated family prestige derived from previously hosted events.

Of particular note, however, was the permanent node based in an elite name, the basis for a "stem kindred" which continued over time because succeeding holders of that name stemmed across generations. Since the system was and is bilateral, the actual inheritance of that name was

---

[126] Wayne Suttles, *Coast Salish Essays* 1987: 221, note 5.

[127] A tribe is now regarded by many academics as an unstable transitional stage, caused by colonialism, after the breakdown of a chiefdom, between a band and a chiefdom, but it remains the preferred native term based on common homeland, language, and social patterns. Lawyers and judges continue to insist on its use in courts because its political meanings are embedded in federal law

[128] Its derivation seems to be *tul-* = flow *-ig^{w}əd* = inside body, *LD*: 115, 230.

optional, to some extent – passed to the kinsperson with the best success in upholding overall kindred honor, prestige, reputation, and generosity. All those publicly aligned with the "stem name" comprised the diffuse sept.

Tracing kinship bilaterally, through both father and mother, makes for large numbers of relatives. Siblingship, however, counted foremost, so that the birth order of ancestors continued to apply down the generations. The child of an older brother was always senior to the child of a younger one. Kin were regarded as close or near, literally as q̓ʷu'šəd 'feet together' and iišəd 'feet near'.[129]

Important families asked their leader's opinion before sending out messages of intent for a betrothal or marriage. For example, Gig Harbor Joe's sister was married to Speym, and, through that link, he asked to marry *tsəltsi*, Sally's sister <A114-116>. Joe came ostensibly to visit his own sister, providing the opportunity to propose first to the girl. With her assent, he then asked permission from her parents and of Sally and Jim Meeker. They consulted with the rest of the family, and all agreed. By receiving approval from the leaders, this marriage was protected from the bickering that often damaged hasty arrangements, and could escalate into violence.[130] The couple was married at Minter after everyone came back together about November 1st. Joe gave gifts to her parents, and they gave something in turn to the married couple, probably a canoe. He also gave prestigious Indian blankets, woven of goat wool (*gʷasdolitsa*). At Minter, Damasq [Tsi'alitsa] used to weave them, along with Tsialaxʷ's wife.[131] Wool from a special breed of woolly dog also produced valuable robes, but these are not mentioned for Minter. George Gibbs, while living nearby at Fort Steilacoom and assembling his Nisqually dictionary, had a pet woolly dog named Mutton, whose hide has been at the Smithsonian for over a century. A medium-size dog, this pelt serves to correct the prior misunderstanding that woolly dogs were small.

Twin Kindreds

To rephrase, in addition to these considerations of personal identity, free or slave, Lushootseeds traced kinship through the "bloodlines" of both parents.[132] The immediate family

---

129 *LD*: 197.

130 Brothers were obligated to protect their sisters and avenge reports, or even rumors, of wife abuse. Rank, honor, industry, and respect were important considerations. Two contrasting examples are the attack at Fort Nisqually by Patkanim, Snoqualmie leader, and his many brothers in response to the rumored domestic distress of their sister. A local white, Wallace, was killed by accident, leading to the imposition of US justice and the hanging of two brothers. By contrast, during her brief first marriage to an Upper Skagit, Angeline, Chief Seattle's famous daughter, raised pampered, was publicly denounced as lazy by her husband and immediately returned home.

131 Again elite are alike and the European equivalent would be embroidery by ladies in waiting to the Queen.

132 June Collins, Multilineal Descent: A Coast Salish Strategy 1979: 243-254. Twana, more compact along Hood Canal, had terms for these kinship units, such as the kindred (*sčəla'*), blood relations, and inlaws (affines), See William Elmendorf, *The Structure of Twana Culture* 1960: 327, 348.

grouping (derived from four grandparents) is technically called a *kindred*, while the huge extended family, which was and is transnational or intertribal (through eight great grandparents), is a called an *intersept*.

Salish kinship has been recognized as the prototype for all the Native Americas because its "distinctive … bilateral organization" and "variability in regard to rules of residence," made it "more widely distributed in North America than any other type of social organization," and suggest it was "the original type from which most other North American systems have arisen."[133] Its defining characteristics are gender, age, and decedence (whether a linking relative was dead or alive).

Among ordinary kinspeople, a *nodal kindred* formed around its senior member(s), often the grandparents as a long-married couple. After the death of the last surviving spouse, the kindred regrouped around their children, the siblings led by the eldest, if fit and able, and so on through a generation or two. Leading families, however, formed a *stem kindred*, which continued across generations because the stem consisted of the line of holders of its famous name, conferring control of locations and resources that made up the "estate" of these nobles. Influence from Wakashans of Vancouver Island may have fostered occasional *ramages*, descent based on birth order, especially a seriated line of eldest sons or eldest daughters who were expected to intermarry with first-borns to maintain the ramage rank.

Traced through all of the bloodlines of great grandparents, a sept had its own network that even now extends beyond space and time, as a "nondiscrete, nonlocalized, property-holding group."[134] It existed wherever and whenever its members lived, and included ancestors from the past and children yet unborn. It had no fixed size nor place, except in family lore explaining the origin of its famous names. It was managed by the oldest able elder (male or female), who provided guidance about the proper use and conservation of resources, as well as the transmission of names, positions, dicta, and artifacts within the kindred.

If it contained a famous name, stories about past holders of that name and their fea(s)ts served to specify places where the kindred indeed had a birthright through past actions, particularly on-going partnerships between the spirits of these places and family members. The most powerful spirits dwell in remote locations, either high up in the mountains or deep in the water, either ocean or river. Its most prized possession has been called 'wisdom' (*x^{w}dik^w*, also advice, teachings, know-how, lore), which included special formulae (*dicta*) to control activities for good or ill, genealogical details, and epics from the beginning of time.[135]

Household

Spaces along the four walls of a house were usually assigned by rank. The high born were in the sheltered back, nobles in the corners, ordinary along the sides, and slaves exposed in the doorway, though they could never really claim any place as their own. At Minter, as noted, ranks were also associated with separate houses. The major house, where the Meeker family

133 George Peter Murdock, Algonkian Social Organization, *Context and Meaning in Cultural Anthropology* 1965: 31.

134 Wayne Suttles, *Coast Salish Essays* 1987: 210.

135 That Salish Feeling … , Vi taq^{w}šəblu Hilbert and Jay Miller 2004.

lived, was of highest rank, with lesser ranks in two other "poor quality" houses. The "poor" houses included a few nobles as leaders, but were tainted by this mixing of classes. The two known slaves each had a separate 8-foot outbuilding, away from these multi-families.

Senior siblings, as nominal owners of a house, lauded themselves by carving and painting evocations of their spirits on the houseposts located in the center or corners of the house. Painted houseposts were the rule; carved ones were the exception. None are mentioned for Minter, so the dancing pole of the headwoman provided a movable substitute. Since she seems to have been a sole survivor,[136] the actual owners of the major house were probably the cousins (by American reckoning only, since they are all siblings for natives). These close kin of Damasq (the headwoman [B2]) would have included Sally [L1], Moses [R5], and Henry [L4], who all shared grandparents from Minter and Klickitat.

In addition, a strong leader might arrange for the building of an especially large house, called a "potlatch house" in English, where he hosted public events and out-of-town guests were billeted. It was just this ability to accommodate large influxes of invited people that defined a central native town (a hub) and great leader. As noted, only the prime house invited in outsiders, while the "poor" houses invited only other Minters <A94>. Though not mentioned in the notebooks, which mostly concern the time after the mid-1800s, Jerry's 1927 land claims testimony noted the Minter "schoolhouse" was over 100 feet long, where training, eating contests and winter dances were held, attended by large crowds. In the aftermath of their devastation by epidemics and slaving, Minters downsized into the 50- by 20-foot houses that Jerry knew as a child.

Successful efforts had to be sanctioned by an immortal's blessing, for either career or curing abilities. While any of these "spirits" could provide a career, only the most powerful, for good or bad, gave doctors the ability to cure or to kill. Any large community was sustained by many career specialists, organized by its leaders, and both healed and protected by its doctors. Moses [R5] had Snake power, but used it selfishly; he "disappeared" in consequence. Among the Twana eat-all visitors (Chapter 11) was a man with Lizard power that enabled him to return the wandering spirit of a Minter woman. In thanks, Damasq, herself town leader and wife of the acting headman, passed out valued dentalia shells to these visitors.

Overall, therefore, while Lushootseed people have adopted the goods, clothes, boats, and housing of mainstream society, their most creative response to Euro-American society has been in terms of religion, beliefs about their place in the universe, epitomized by the co-efforts of John and Mary Slocum near modern Olympia in founding the Shaker Church after 1882.

Indeed, Sound natives coped well with the pivotal economic presence during the first half of the 1800s of the British-ruled Hudson Bay Company, trading for furs and labor at Fort Nisqually in the heart of Whulshootseed territory. Problems increased, however, when American squatters, settlers, and would-be homesteaders, encouraged and bankrolled by commercial lumber and mining operations shipping to California (especially San Francisco), took over their lands by fair means and foul under the color~cover of title and "protection" of

---

[136] A family of 9 is suggested for her, probably parents and 7 siblings <A 52>. Since this was the chiefly family of Minter, there was probably more than one wife and mother for all these children, who nonetheless regarded each other and their cousins as close siblings. For the English to better represent the Lushootseed, the term should be "sibcuz."

Anglo law. Co-resident in an area, these settlers knew only too well when villagers would move away to garner foods elsewhere, leaving their homes unprotected and ready for arson by neighbors intent on homesteading an already developed location.

Intersept (~ Kithred)

Living along waterways facilitated frequent interactions, except where hostile intent or enforced tariffs set up native obstructions ("tollgates"). Throughout the entire Northwest Coast, its commonalities were never homogeneous, but rather the result of a complex series of overlappings with neighboring communities, regardless of their ancestral languages. Suttles,[137] with misgivings, called them "kithreds," derived from Old English "couth" for familiar country and neighbors, though "intersept" (punning on "intersect, intercept") is more apt. Renowned hereditary names come to the fore in these networks since prestige relies heavily on standing in allied communities, in turn, reinforcing status and rank at home. As Jerry noted, {"These were famous names [from an] exact village" <A43>}. Underpinning such prestige was a valued currency of wealth that included slaves, canoes, goat ~ dog wool blankets, fur robes, pelts (especially of sea otter), clubs, dentalia, and, after European traders, guns, factory blankets, and silver dollars.[138]

Elmendorf insightfully highlighted five overlapping population networks, from Chinook to Klallam, for Twana, living in their more discrete territory, and his findings apply equally well throughout the coastline. These kithreds, moving outward throughout the southern Salish Sea, were concerned with local eating contests, disk gambling games, elite intermarriages, secret society [guild] initiations, or warfare at more remote locales. In corroboration, Suttles plotted genealogies centered from Musqueam to show overlapping intersepts among neighboring Coast Salish, as Dorothy Kennedy[139] has done moving out from a Squamish standpoint further to the north.

Maps and charts in the *Sto:lō Atlas* also add a totemic dimension since certain families in various communities trace their ancestry to a sky being or a transformed primordial Animal, as either progenitor or patron.[140] Leading families across intersepts, sharing the same totem, regardless of language or locale, use its image as their identifier, often bolstered by an epic account of their common origins. At Gig Harbor, near Minter, residents traced descent from transformed Killerwhales, emblemized by two rocks representing the mother Orca and a platter where food offerings were daily left for her and her family.

Families forged links by seasons. During summer economic efforts, families moved widely, camping with chosen kin, as Sally Meeker often did, for companionship in the work of harvesting from nature. During winter, families hosted key members of their networks at public events, where they were housed, fed, and gifted. Leading families with renowned names, as

---

137 Wayne Suttles, *Coast Salish Essays* 1987: 221, note 5.

138 William Elmendorf, *The Structure of Twana Culture* 1960: 331.

139 Dorothy Kennedy, Looking For The Tribe In The Wrong Places: An Examination Of The Central Coast Salish Social Network, 1993; Threads To The Past: The Construction and Transformation of Kinship in the Coast Salish Social Network 2000.

140 Keith Thor Carlson, *A Sto:lō and Coast Salish Historical Atlas* 2001: 25.

noted, like the wealthy everywhere, had several cedar plank homes[141] strategically located to take advantage of local natural resources as well as travel routes. Their hospitable favors to guests and visitors added to their reputations.

Inlaws were particularly important both for extending far-flung, radiating connections and for their role in transforming food into wealth. Blood relatives had to be fed and supported without reserve or question, while inlaws stood at a remove such that a return gift was expected when they were given food. In consequence, inlaws served to turn perishable foods into permanent wealth items to nourish family prestige and rank.

The extent of the Minter network is shown by its range of marriage ties as well as the final dispersal of the community members among neighbors <C4>. The Meekers settled at Puyallup, where Jerry advanced church, school, carpentry, and sales into his own prosperity. Tyee George, though Suquamish, also moved to the Puyallup Valley, and his granddaughter married among the Klallam. Speym went to North Bay on the other side of the Key Peninsula at the head of Case Inlet, then later took land on the Squaxin Island Reservation. Hawk, Damasq's grandson, settled at Skokomish on Hood Canal.[142] Hummelgood married into Duwamish and had kin at Muckleshoot, though he stayed at Joe's Bay (~ Lake Bay) and joined Mary Sloane and family when they dried fish at Glencove, and sometimes back at Minter, which continued to feed its residents even after they did not live there all winter. Jimmy Cross's family mostly died out. He had married Betsy, a Nisqually woman, and moved to the Puyallup Valley. His one grandchild at Muckleshoot, George Cross, had children there, while his brother Silas Cross and family lived in the Puyallup valley.

From Minter, descendants moved over the globe during the past century. Jerry's grandsons fought in Asia and Italy during WW II, and one brought back a Catholic bride.

Comparisons

Canadian Coast Salish recognized both owned property and "commons," which applied to "hunting territories, clam beaches, fishing grounds, camas and wapato areas, berry patches, and weir sites."[143] Corporate-owned properties include "sturgeon and salmon fishing sites, clam beds, cranberry bogs, wapato ponds, Indian carrot plots, camas grounds, egg-gathering sites, waterfowl refuges, bear-hunting areas, sea mammal hunting sites, and mountainous areas where mountain goats were hunted."[144] On Vancouver Island and the mainland, "the types of descent group-owned marine, intertidal and riverine resource areas include clam gathering areas, raised duck-net sites, bird-nesting areas, islets for sea-mammal hunting, reef-net fishing sites, fishing rocks in the Fraser Canyon, fish weir sites on the Cowichan River, sturgeon trap sites, and some

---

[141] William Elmendorf, *The Structure of Twana Culture* 1960: 271.

[142] Hawk's wedding to Emily Hines and move to Skokomish is mentioned by Edwin Chalcraft. *Assimilation's Agent* 2004: 110.

[143] Kennedy, Threads To The Past: The Construction and Transformation of Kinship in the Coast Salish Social Network 2000: 323.

[144] Kennedy, Threads To The Past: The Construction and Transformation of Kinship in the Coast Salish Social Network 2000: 204.

of the small fishing streams and bays."[145] Pentlatch at Comox Harbor owned a burial grove, where coffins were set by height to accord with rank.[146] Claims to clam gardens were asserted by rock walls built along the shore.[147] Within prairies, burnt-over regularly, women of a matriline, regardless of where they were married or living, inherited rights to tended plant gardens.[148] Overlap was expected; elders and lawyers have recently argued that firm boundaries are a colonialist tactic to disadvantage First Nations.[149]

The role of the House is much debated by academics, with Kennedy[150] denying it any validity. Physically, this building served as "food processing and storage, workshop, recreation center, temple, theatre, and fortress."[151] Among the matrilineal northern tribes, the house is the pervasive unit, and its influence was felt in the south, where some communities strove to assert claims to a similar but unique house as an aspiration rather than a routine feature. Thus, standout examples include the Whale House (*sałułtx^w*) comprised of five high ranking Comox communities near Cape Mudge,[152] and the famous Painted House of the Snoqualmies east of Seattle.[153]

Salish houses, repeatedly, have been called "similar in many ways to a 'House' in the sense of European nobility [holding] property, tangible and intangible, names of heaven-born First Ancestors, confidential knowledge (*sniw'*), ritual property (*ts'uxwten*), legends, songs, dances, secret words, medicinal remedies, and ceremonial prerogatives.[154] All of these are place-based, as inalienable patrimony, such that "senses of place focus attention on the connections and interrelations between myth, legend, ancestor, spirit, song, identity, language, property, territory, boundary and title."[155]

In his unpublished notes, Diamond Jenness, closely attending to his own elder interviews, carefully distinguishes between corporate ownership and the commons.

> The real political unit was therefore not the village, but the big house occupied by a number of kinsfolk – an enlarged or genealogical 'family' to which the Saanich applied the term *hunit's'lakum*, and we in speaking of the similar European nobility use the term House. Each Saanich House, as we many call it then, possessed its own long shed-roofed dwelling,[1] its own camas beds on Galiano and neighboring islands,

---

145 Brian Thom, Coast Salish Senses of Place: Dwelling, Meaning, Power, Property and Territory in the Coast Salish World 2005: 308. These data are used despite potential native displeasure because of his tainted near-slave status among Sto:los.

146 Kennedy, Threads To The Past: The Construction and Transformation of Kinship in the Coast Salish Social Network 2000: 60.

147 Judith Williams, Clam Gardens, Aboriginal Mariculture on Canada's West Coast 2006.

148 Kennedy, Threads To The Past 2000: 215.

149 Thom, Coast Salish Senses of Place 2005: 390.

150 Kennedy, Threads To The Past 2000: 329.

151 Wayne Suttles, The Shed-Roof House, *A Time of Gathering*, 212-222, 1991: 214; Kennedy, Threads To The Past 2000: 76.

152 Kennedy, Threads To The Past 2000: 52, based on Barnett 1955: 25.

153 Vi Hilbert, Jay Miller, and Zalmai Zahir, *Puget Sound Geography* 2001: 178 #9.

154 Homer Barnett, *The Coast Salish of British Columbia* 1955: 141, 191; Jenness, Saanich fieldnotes, 1935: 52; Thom, Coast Salish Senses of Place 2005: 85.

155 Thom, Coast Salish Senses of Place 2005: 409.

> its own set of ancestral names or titles, and its own stock of legends, songs, and medicinal remedies.[156]

The accompanying footnote expands on such privileged property:

> #1. Almost any departure from established custom might become the privilege of a House, heritable by later generations, and by them alone, provided the public had ratified it; and the public ratified it when during some potlatch it heard the statement of claim without demur and accepted the gift that followed the statement. All such privileges or rights, however, hinged upon proof of lineal descent, and the most obvious indication of such descent was the possession of an ancestral title.[157]

At Duncan, Cowichan Houses owned nearby weir sites along the river, but

> "On the other hand, the sea near the villages, the hunting grounds and berry patches round about, were common property; any villager, whatever his station in life, might fish and hunt wherever he wished within the village territory."[158]

Elite families owned property that included several houses, as noted, occupied throughout a year at seasonal resource sites, famous art works, and claims to epics, songs, displays, and rituals. Senior members, both men and women, of elite families doubled as religious and political leaders, depending on the season. Summer was devoted to economy, and winter to religion.[159] The lowest class was largely immobile, confined to a small area from birth to death, and marked by a strict provincialism.[160]

An apt comparison to Nuchahnulth ~ Nootkan kinship and noble descent indicates "The situation among the people of the West Coast is not unlike that of medieval Europe (a comparison suggested to me [a Welsh national] by a Toquaht chief) where the descent principle was fully utilized only by the elite of society and where the common people neglected to trace their genealogies the further they were removed from aristocratic rank.... In addition, both principles need not be of equal importance for all members of the group."[161]

Salish kinship interwove several factors, with age and birth order highly significant. "Relatedness to members of the society can include companionship, affinity, friendship and adoption, as well as biological ties."[162] Marriage and coordinate rank networks rely on propinquity and residency. "Effective affiliation with the elite owners of such sites required not just kin ties, but also residence, the investment of labour [sic], and, in former times, the acquisition of an ancestral name belonging to the group represented by the elite residents … an individual could, at any time, withdraw his allegiance by moving to another village. Similarly,

---

[156] Diamond Jenness, Saanich fieldnotes 1935: 29.

[157] Jenness, Saanich fieldnotes 1935: 29.

[158] Jenness, Saanich fieldnotes 1935: 29.

[159] Cf Kennedy, Threads To The Past: The Construction and Transformation of Kinship in the Coast Salish Social Network 2000: 7, 160, 326.

[160] Kennedy, Threads To The Past: The Construction and Transformation of Kinship in the Coast Salish Social Network 2000: 125, based on Smith, *The Puyallup-Nisqually* 1940a: 410.

[161] Susan Kenyon, The Kyuquot Way: A Study of a West Coast (Nootkan) Community 1980: 85-86.

[162] Kennedy, Threads To The Past 2000: 73.

an in-marrying woman attained a form of membership for the duration of her marriage. Her offspring's membership to the natal village began at birth, although a child's status required formal socialization through the bestowal of an ancestral name, usually occurring around puberty, which marked the individual as a fully-socialized adult, now capable of receiving and distributing goods."[163]

Among Central Coast Salish, the kindred is generally known as "one family."[164] The overall unit has been called a sept, but this generally means an endogamous group like a parish, though, over time, with the incest taboo, a sept tends to become exogamous, like the Salish intersept (extended kindred). In practical terms, the functional category, aptly noted for its flow, is the "bloodline."

Tribal names, illustrated by a standard Lushootseed area map of the Sound,[165] show that downriver ones usually end in *–bsh*, while those for upriver end in *–bix^w*. Of particular note, the origins of the latter suffix, which implies something basic, link it to bloodlines since "**-mix^w* = life force, "mana," person(s), animals, world, land, river; woman's breast, milk."[166] Kennedy[167] misconstrued this as an argument for place instead of geo-political namings, and cited two counter examples that instead, on close inspection, support the more general argument. The upriver Puyallup site[168] ending in –bsh was located in a huge prairie that "had strong contacts with the Nisqually villages to the south of them" on saltwater. The Suquamish shoreline site[169] ending in -bix^w is associated with a place name making reference to "diarrhea," and thus with both blood and less cohesive connotations.

In all, the pursuit of ancestral land claims in British Columbia has refined our understanding of Salish kinship, property, and ecology. Kindreds, especially stem kindreds, retain their important role in these societies, as do larger intertribal events for confirming the prestige and pedigree of names and possessions of the septs and tribes.

Constituents

Salish kinship has long been remarkably flexible and versatile. Its kin ties flow from blood and sharing, while intersept ~ kithship follows from marriage and includes inlaws. Traced through both mother and father (bilaterally), kinship follows "bloodlines" that are free flowing from past to present. Its full compliment of components have yet to be fully examined, so an attempt is made here to delineate them. They include at least six features involving both nurture and nature, as well an organizational gradations from core to fringe.

---

163 Kennedy, Threads To The Past 2000: 321-22.

164 This term is x^{W}ənc'aləwəm in Halkomelem, x^{W}ənc'ɛləwəng in Saanich, nch'ay'u'am in Squamish, Kennedy, Threads To The Past 2000: 163.

165 Jay Miller, *Lushootseed Culture and the Shamanic Odyssey: An Anchored Radiance* 1999: 16.

166 Aert Kuipers, *Salish Etymological Dictionary* 2002: 205-6, with a whole page of examples for this Proto-Salish suffix.

167 Kennedy, Threads To The Past 2000: 50.

168 Marian Smith, The Puyallup of Washington 1940b: 20 #9.

169 Warren Snyder, *Southern Puget Sound Salish: Texts, Place Names, and Dictionary* 1968: 133 # 44.

DESCENT carefully traced from both parents, especially in terms of pedigree, with recognition of close kinship bonds that embrace the eight great grandparents; more distant generations might be traced through the inheritance of ancestral names within a stem kindred.

RESIDENCE at familiar resource locales associated with family members, foods, and materials. Wealthy families had more than one house, shifting with seasons, harvests, and events among their dwellings, as well as making prolonged visits to distant kin and friends. Patrilocality was preferred, with other options fully acceptable depending on various contingencies of the couple.

INCORPORATION ~ INGESTION of foods grown at particular locales and events, provided commensal (co-eating) groupings made up of the same nutrients fortifying all their bodies. Adoptees gained full membership via this process of eating locally.

LABOR contributed to the food supply by hunting and harvesting, to the construction of houses and weirs, and to the hosting ceremonial events sponsored by the household, family, kindred, or sept.

CLASS ~ RANK defined by "good blood" and "unblemished" pedigree distinguished noble ranks from generic commoners, with slaves a stigmatized group not fully human. Leaders of unquestioned rank sometimes flaunted the rules with impunity, proving their special status. By the same token, chiefly families provided social welfare, feeding the needy and taking in orphans or forsaken children to offer safety and security.

TOTEM as emblem, logo, and ancestor (progenitor or patron) linked a kindred to a venerable species and habitat, as well as providing vague behavioral characteristics, such a bird-like swiftness or bear-like grumbling.

INITIATION into the Growlers, Siyowin, or certain churches confer family ties upon members, who celebrate the date of their induction as another birthday and regard their age mates as siblings (sibcuz) and treat their inductors as parents. Today, a dozen song types serve to group Siyowin initiates according to the sharing of the same spirit with its own distinctive drumming rhythms. Formerly, all Growlers collectively shared the same patron spirit.

CORE / FRINGE gradations further define these memberships such that pivotal kin units, especially siblings, provide the nexus at the core of these groupings, with a blurring fringe along the outer limits of kin.

In all, Salish kinship interwove several factors of land and quasi-lineage, with age and birth order highly significant. Kin drew on biological ties and benefited from companionship, affinity, friendship and adoption. Intermarriage and ranked networks grew from propinquity, residence, labor, and family treasures, especially honored and ancestral names held up by the elite. One's natal village became a life-long focal point, aided by training and travel. Property and food circulated throughout the system of overlapping networks, including those of species and spirits specified in stories.

6 GATHERING GROCERIES ~ MAKING ROUNDS

Today, on the Key Peninsula, local landowners and amateur historians falsely report that natives only used this locale as transients (or, worse, vagrant nomads) passing through to gather foods for use in their cedar plank homes across the Sound near Tacoma.[170] From the notebooks and archaeology, however, we know Minter was indeed a stable winter village, and therefore "permanent" in terms of tribal identity and ownership. This periodic, "homeless", or seasonal visiting and harvesting pattern only began after epidemics, attacks, and burnings forced Minters to relocate to the relative safety of nearby reservations. The wealth of detail that Jerry provides in these notebooks about the timing of foods, places, and people met by Minters while on their annual commute[171] clearly indicates that they extensively used and managed these lands and resources. Again, by combining fleshed-out phrases and quotes taken from the notes, edited for readability, we get a keen sense of their in-depth knowledge of the resources within the regional landscape to harvest and prepare winter surpluses for use at their Minter residence.

While the wording has stayed close to Jerry's text, foods have been rearranged by season, topic, and technology, with some overlap, to make details about this commuting more informative. The notebooks themselves, however, remain the primary source for particular foods and practices.

A great value of these notes is their obvious link to prehistoric times when all of native technology used the products of nature. The only more recent exceptions that are mentioned, provided by 1856 treaty stipulations, were some metal hooks and gaffs bought from traders, or made by local blacksmiths.[172] It is vital to remember that much of this food getting, particularly salmon fishing, remains the economic and dietary mainstay of Lushootseeds and other native peoples. Today, motor boats instead of canoes, nylon nets instead of those using Gizmo's hand-twist cords, and factory-made fish smokers engage people in their ancient marine way of life, using improved technologies that have been sanctioned in several federal court decisions.

The seasons will be summarized first, followed by economic activities or specialties. In the next chapter, the management of the entire fishery of the Puyallup River and its five strategic weirs is especially noteworthy since nothing else like it is known for the Northwest Coast region.

---

[170] The ironically named E. A. Starling, first US Indien agent, charged in 1852, "In their canoes they float through life, wandering in different seasons to the places abounding most in the different kinds of foods," cited by Arledge, *Early Days of the Key Peninsula* 1998: 14, #9.

[171] "Commute" is a term now favored by natives to highlight their regular business-like visits to resource areas – the better to set in sharp contrast the misguided views of most Americans that Indiens "wandered ~ roamed" over the land without serious purpose. Consistent with their self-identification with salmon as co-residents, these "bright swimmers" are the final native commuters to return to Minter, managed by that state hatchery. During the US Colonial era, settlers were outraged that native hunting presumed on the lifestyle of European nobles.

[172] Some men, subversively, made fish gaffs from the farm tools handed out by the Indien agent to accord with the BIA program of making farmers out of natives, an agenda particularly absurd in the forested Northwest.

Winter

Fishing in Minter Creek diminished during all of November, while children picked nearby huckleberries and cranberries. In their increasingly free time, women began making baskets and mats. After a summer putting up foods to "feed the people," Minter families returned home for their religious season during December, known as "winter moon" (*heqᵘskas sluqalaD*), January, "little younger brother of winter moon" (əɬ *soqa stas*), February, "frog singing" (*waq̓ʷwaq̓ʷos*), when frogs croak and snow is only light enough to moisten the ground, and March, "strong wind" (*č̓pospuhɛgʷad*), when the Southwind tears up trees while "throwing out" winter.[173] Canoes and paddles were put away, and most people stayed off the saltwater <A56>. Only small fishing canoes ventured out timorously to get fresh food.

< §8 Winter Dance by Helmi Juvonen 1947 >

In December, Minter hosted ceremonies <B49>, such as those of the Black Tahmanawis, a secret guild also called Growlers. Lashibya was training Jerry for its initiation, but he died [c1878] before Jerry could graduate <A99>. This guild already had about 15 local members, including two of Jerry's uncles, and was (in)famous for its guttural song and blood spitting. Though a member, his uncle wilq̓ʷ denounced it as "bunk," revealing that the blood came from a

[173] Situated in South Seattle, this epic – explaining the blustery conditions of March in the Duwamish and Puyallup Basins of the mid Sound, as recorded in multiple versions by Arthur Ballard – is what led me to Smith as the notebook's scribe. Suspiciously, Calvin Burkett filed on his Minter homestead in March, when natives would have been most housebound, unless the headwoman and her close kin had retreated elsewhere. As stay-at-homes, though, they were less likely to appear near the land office to contest his filing.

cut under the tongue, not caused by supernatural powers <A101>. Like others in the south Sound, Minters confused the Growlers with the Redeeming Rite.[174]

< §9 Redeeming Rite >

Other winter ceremonies were specialized affairs that included activities such as gambling contests, war dances, and efforts by "singers", who helped those who were "sick to sing" (in the usual native phrase), in order to be able to release their pent-up spirit power songs. Only the prime house at Minter could invite outsiders to come to its events. The other houses merely invited each other <A94>. But prosperity also had liabilities. After everyone had put up their winter stores, these were likely to attract intertribal attacks, assured of gaining slaves and booty. Of note, Minter suffered one major slave raid among many <A95>; its leaders also planned counter attacks <A102> (Chapter 10).[175]

[174] Throughout the south Sound, memberships in the Redeeming (Shamanic Odyssey) Rite and in the Growlers were merged if not confounded in later memories, See Jay Miller, *Lushootseed Culture and the Shamanic Odyssey* 1999: 101. Retrieving lost vitalities was the goal of the Redeeming Odyssey, while the Growler elite assured privilege and intimidated the lowly. Because some have pointedly remarked that calling this the Recovery Rite made it sound "alcoholic AA," while Odyssey was too Greek, the rite is better described as "redeeming," acknowledging both its spiritual~religious and medical intentions.

[175] Jerry here refers to Minter in its warrior phase, before smallpox and slave raids took a heavy toll, and Minters became eaters. Twana references to Minters not knowing war may have been a taunt.

Spring

After wintering at Minter, everyone prepared for spring fishing. People began to stir in April, "relax" (qaq^{w}əlaB, 'rest haunches')[176] when good weather allowed for refurbishing gear and tackle <A57>. Minter households broke up in the spring as families scattered among their usual resource camps. During calm days in early March, **fires** were kindled to burn over berry patches, grasslands, and root fields to feed new growth with ash fertilizer and direct sunlight. Shellfish harvesting occupied April through July, starting with butter clams. Geoducks,[177] dug at the four lowest yearly tides, were best in June, less so in July <A55>.[178] They dug lots of clams from beaches between Raft Island and the mainland, and sometimes met Wollochet Indiens around Rosedale. Travel was by water, though trails were maintained to provide safe routes to be used during storms or attack when the waters were dangerous. Trails crossed from Gig Harbor to Purdy to Minter, or from Gig Harbor to Purdy to the end of North Bay at Rocky Point and on to Hood Canal. At Allyn, travelers had to yell across for someone to come with a canoe <A107> to get them across. As further corroboration of these notes, nearby Sherwood Creek had a big village, with the first sockeye run to be killed off by a sawmill dam.[179]

Households broke up into family kin groups to camp at favorite locales, harvesting and processing natural foods. At night, with a fire burning on a sand layer in their canoe, men speared lingcod, sole, flounder, and skate <A55>. After trolling for king [tyee, chinook] salmon on open water in May and June, they switched to various traps when fish started upstream in July. During June and July, herring, candlefish, and salmon squeezed through the Tacoma Narrows. Digging up and drying butter clams in May, June, and July; they dug horse clams in July and August <B33>. Puyallup women, camping overnight on McNeil Island <B39>, paddled their own canoes to take butter clams at Still Harbor. A drying stick would hold 20 butter clams or 10 horse clams, and two full sticks would be threaded onto one string <B8> for storage. Salmon, clams, and berries were dried at Lakebay camps, sometimes until October.

Big camps were set up in June and July at the Narrows for catching candlefish, herring, and salmon. People gathered from Quartermaster, Wollochet, Steilacoom, Minter, Gig Harbor, Puyallup, Nisqually, and Squaxin <A108>. For these two months, most families stayed for 3-4 days at a time, but Gig Harbors stayed there all summer since it was their own territory. Visitors would stay until they heard that the salmon had arrived in their own rivers <A109>. Minters

---

176 Again overly polite, the term literally means 'wide across buttocks'.

177 Geoducks are huge clams not waterfowl, whose name entered English from Twana, according to William Elmendorf, *The Structure of Twana Culture* 1960: 123.

178 The highest and lowest tides occur near the solstices, during the middle of the night in winter, ideal for fowling, and during the day in summer, ideal for claming, See Wayne Suttles, *Coast Salish Essays* 1987: 71.

179 Henry Allen, a Twana elder, reported with disgust this extinction of a cherished sockeye run; "Finally a pioneer named Sherwood built a little dam on the creek [to Mason Lake] and stopped [killed] the fish, and they named the creek after him [!!]," William Elmendorf, *The Structure of Twana Culture* 1960: 62. Two huge Sherwood brothers dammed the stream in 1852 to run a sawmill, Ezra Meeker, *Seventy Years Progress in Washington* 1921: 257.

camped north of the Wollochets near Arletta, where a large graveyard stretched along the shore to the steep bluff at Cromwell.[180] Purdy and Rosedale provided good flounder fishing <A107>.

Minters did not use the south side of Fox Island[181], but dug for butter clams in the bay at Sylvan. Sally Meeker, Speym, and Jim Hummelgood took their families to Still Harbor[182] on McNeil Island to dig butter clams in June <A110>. They stayed only one night, coming from either the Arletta or Lakebay camp. Jerry was too young to go along [probably mid-1860s]. Sometimes 6-12 women took their own canoes to this harbor for clamming in late summer.

The fission and fusing of kindred members throughout the summer is well illustrated in these notebooks. Families harvested along Fox Island, Longbranch, Lakebay, and Rosedale at Arletta, staying for about two months. Jerry's mother's family later went with siyalawhax, swadaxub, q'siad, and Jim Hummelgood. Speym, Lashibya, and xexulcid went to Longbranch and Lakebay <A111>. Gizmo and Moyes stayed with the chief's wife (in her old age) and did some local fishing at Minter and Glencove. Sally Meeker liked going to Wollochet country and Arletta because she was related there through Yukots' (James Coates) and his brother, General Spot (sxodubqud).

At these camps, the oldest active men were the leaders. People brought their troubles to them to resolve, and what they said was "law." Two prominent brothers related to the Minter headwoman were Tsialax^{w}, the elder sibling, and Swadaxub <A114>. Strangers would stay overnight at Arletta if it got too dark before they could move on. Usually they talked to these brothers to identify themselves and get permission to stay <A119>. Such consensus and public regard meant that suspicion or jealousy was avoided, except during marriage proposals, when competition between families was subtle but intense.

At Arletta, no food was put up for the winter. It was just eaten fresh day by day when the tide came in and out, exposing the beaches <A117>. Old people did a lot of gambling with visiting Wollochets, playing the stick game (*slahal*), or alternating between *sxax̣ts* in the evening

---

180 #142 Ska'ikaiyuale "corpse place" on a creek north of Minter [then Huge] creek with an aboriginal graveyard where the bodies were hoisted into the trees. North of Minter, TT Waterman recorded by number this place name, and the others in the next few footnotes, Cf Vi Hilbert, Jay Miller, and Zalmai Zahir, *Puget Sound Geography* 2001. Some have already been cited as evidence of identity shifts by Minters.

181 #154 Beti'l "sea person" in the cliff or declivity on the southern shore. A girl who once lived here was stolen by the sea people and married a husband down there. During storms, her kin on shore could hear her singing lullabies to her baby. Long afterward she came back with her sea children to visit. Ever since then curiously shaped pebbles wash up on the beach, representing toys made by the sea people to amuse these offspring. [This word is not in common usage but may derive from *bə-* 'again, anew' + ƛiɬib 'sing' to refer to the lullabies rather than the merfolk themselves, *LD*: 34, 239.]

182 #156 Suwo'xtld "steaming place" at Still Harbor on the north side of McNeill Island, named for the many clams cooked there by steaming in pits. [The more likely meaning is sweathouse ~ *swux̣təd*, suggesting that women had their very own sauna there.]

and *slehaləb* during the day <A103>.[183] Children played games of all kinds, while women wove clothes and baskets.

Once, when camping at Arletta, some Quartermaster Harbor men defeated Haida raiders, a few of whom escaped overland, where one was stoned to death. These local defenders were John Swan - Sally's uncle from Gig Harbor; Jim sqʷaqʷuyub - a Steilacoom; James Coates; Tsidat'alq - a Steilacoom; and "Jack" - from Gig Harbor, who was the lead warrior <A118>.

Tyee George (sʷətcabxłt') usually went to Suquamish where his wife was related, sometimes staying the entire summer. A trail from Suquamish went to Port Orchard and on to Purdy, but Tyee George always went by canoe <A111>. Gig Harbor Joe (kʷolyadxʷ) always went home to Gig Harbor, though the Meekers would meet up with him later at Longbeach drying clams and picking berries after salmon fishing was done <A112>.

About May, king salmon were eaten fresh as they pooled to go upstream in June. Night spearing (luring fish with fires placed on sand piled in the bottom of canoes) went on all year long for lingcod, sole, flounder, skate, bullhead, and, when they were best in the autumn, for porpoises and seals. Only the bullhead with smooth skin and smaller head was edible; the other kinds were not. A fisherman never packed or cleaned his fish. His wife proudly carried it from the boat and cleaned it <A19>.

Summer

As most foods became available, families moved out of Minter for the summer (*pədhedəb* < time of "hot"), a term lumping together May, June, and July because storms were few and it was always warm, pleasant weather. This was prime time for gathering food, beginning with butter clams, then digging horse clams in July and August <A55>.

Along their Key peninsula, Minters hunted, fished, and berried down to Van Geldern Cove <A105>. Deer lived mainly on the east side of Carr Inlet; the west side had a cranberry bog and many huckleberries. A high bank south of Glencove blocked access, but a dip between Glencove and Van Geldern allowed people to climb onto the plateau to pick berries. Minters camped at Lakebay to dry horse clams and huckleberries. At Longbranch, they met many Steilacoom people also picking berries and drying clams. Other Minters went instead to Purdy for clams and berries. Night fishing relied on torches <A55>.

People fished all summer, eating their catch fresh <A34>. Herring were gathered into canoes by paddling with a "toothed rake". This long pole was lined with pegged-in wooden barbs, later nails, serving as "teeth" to impale these fish, then rendered for oil. Porpoise oil was stored in deer bladders, to be served at meals for dipping from a clamshell dish <B48>.

---

[183] The late Bruce Miller of Skokomish, whose family home was next door to John Hawk, the Minter headwoman's grandson, learned that sxa'əts was played as a one-on-one power contest with each side's supporters betting on the outcome. Bruce recalled that John came to Skokomish as a baby, probably from Nisqually Flats where his mother had married, adopted by the headman from Hoodsport and his wife, the sister of Mowitch Man, whose ancestry was at least part Puyallup and Squaxin. John married a Duwamish woman, and their children are now at Puyallup, Swinomish, and Skokomish. Chalcraft (*Assimilation's Agent* 2004: 110) mentions the marriage of John Hawk to orphan Emily Hines on 18 September 1894.

Fall

Autumn (*pədtulos* > time of *talus* = salmon jaw used for soup) lumped August, September, and October, while November marked the time to finish drying dog salmon and return home <A34>. Each month was counted, particularly by women like Jerry's mother who, as noted, tied a new string around her finger at each full moon <A57>. Silver salmon were eaten fresh in August, when salal berries were being dried, before huckleberries ripened in September <A33>. Both grew for two miles along the top of a bluff for a quarter mile inland. Otherwise the forest was too thickly overgrown with trees and brush to get through easily.[184] In October, many Minters camped at Lakebay, picking late berries. Later, a small group went to Glencove to harvest nearby berries and mushrooms[185] that were dried at that camp <A19>.

In October, fattened dog salmon were dried in quantity for winter use, mostly at Lackey Creek on Glencove Bay. Men and women worked together for long, hard hours. Teams also went off in canoes, gathering mushrooms and huckleberries to dry on racks at Glencove. Women picked berries, such as ripe salal {"Indian sugar"} along bluffs in August, huckleberries in September, and many others in October. These grew abundantly in the hills between Glencove and Van Geldern Bay. Some berries were made into dried cakes, one inch thick by six inches around. Half of a cake mashed in water could serve six people <A59>. Dried wild lily bulbs, likened to horseradish roots, were sometimes sliced into disks and worn as aromatic beads on necklaces.

Men hunted in both spring and fall. They waited at stands along deer runways, or imitated the call of a fawn by blowing over a taut grass blade (see Hunting below). Waterfowl – such as geese, widgeons, and ducks – were mostly taken by night hunting (see Birding). In November, families went for two weeks to swampland near Glenwood, where men hunted and women jerked the meat <B37-38>. Nothing was wasted, even the blood was cooked as food.[186] No salmon were put away for the winter at Lakebay <B8>. They were either eaten fresh or partly dried for a later meal.

---

[184] Such underbrush was not found in old growth forests and so reflects the environmental collapse caused by Europeans.

[185] Mushrooms were not common fare. Repeated questioning, however, indicates that they were eaten, but only when gathered by specialists who knew the safe species from the poisonous ones. Jerry's report is one of the few clues to such botanical usages. The native use of mushrooms and toad skins as poisons is only hinted, See William Wihr, You Toad Sucking Fool 1995.

[186] While this is generally true, those with warrior power deliberately had to consume blood every so often to "feed" their spirit.

Groceries

Shellfishing

The big Fall job at Lakebay was drying butter and horse clams dug up with an ironwood stick (q̓aalid) – a dibble (*sqaləx̣*) sharpened at either end.[187] They knew where to dig by watching the clam necks [siphons] sticking above water. Usually Jerry's mother put away 15 baskets, sometimes 20 baskets, in one season.

Women did all the digging and smoking, though the men got wood for the long drying fires <B9>. A drift log was used as a heat rebounding reflector (5 feet high by 30-40 feet long), which Jerry called a "dutch oven," with the shucked clam bodies skewed onto two-foot sticks tilted toward the fire. One stick held either twenty butter clams or ten horse clams. After being smoke-dried, they were strung on doubled-over strips of inner cedar bark, which acted as a food preserver. One such string held two sticks of clams, and each string was further dried over a slow fire, hanging from the cross sticks set atop a cribwork, for a week or 10 days. These strings of clams were finally layered between bracken fern fronds, then trampled to compact them. A woman wanted 2-3 full baskets, loosely woven of cedar boughs (*cʷaxʷad* ?) about 1½ feet wide by 2 feet high. Each woman took care of her own section of fire within the shelter or house where shellfish were prepared for cooking, stringing, smoking, and final layering <B10>.

Hunting

Spring hunts began in April after fawns are born, with hunters luring does (females) by mimicking the calls of young deer by blowing on a blade of grass that was stretched across cupped hands, held tightly between the thumbs and index fingers <B36>. A lone hunter would circle inward, using his scent to repel the deer, driving it toward the center to be killed easily. If hunters had time, they carried a portion of meat back home, but usually they got an eager young man to pack it so he would look like a good provider. If they killed several deer, slaves and others helped to pack home the quartered meat. Because of their small size, hunters ate birds as they killed them. Ducks were taken in the fall and winter before they flew north in the spring. People did not eat hell divers [pied-billed grebe], except as a last resort, because they were tough, with too many sinews and tissues.

While the women and children picked, the men fished and hunted, training attentive 14 to 16 year-old boys to assume these tasks. These teenaged males would steer and paddle the canoe (or later, rowboat) <A21>, while a man speared fish or devilfish [octopus]. Boys and girls had to be 14-16 years old to leave the camp alone to pick berries, though the youngest children helped by picking close by. At 16-18, boys could hunt alone. Minter hunters were Lashibya, Speym, and swadax̣ub. The prime fisher was t̓siyalaxʷ, father of Jim Hummelgood, who instead hunted with Lashibya <B34-35>, indicating that personal considerations of abilities and spirit sanctions trumped direct succession from parent to child for economic careers.

---

[187] A dibble (from "dip" + "for," as in 'ladle', 'beetle') was multi-purpose, as effective for digging up roots as clams, though a brace might be added for more traction or leverage. See Jay Miller, Dibble Cultivating Prairies to Beaches: The Real All Terrain Vehicle 2005.

Groceries

Fall was prime hunting time.[188] Minters tried to store as much dried venison as fish for the winter. Traps and snares were set along deer trails. Sometimes a hunter waited at a strategic point [a stand] while two or three others "scared up" animals to run toward his poised bow and arrow. Lashibya led such drives. When all Minters were camped at Lakebay, hunters stayed out at a forest camp, sometimes sending back a deer each day. One man could pack out a whole deer after the entrails were taken out <B38>. The blood was carefully saved for food. Men continued hunting from Glencove, following a creek inland from the inlet between Glencove and Lakebay, making base camp near a stream in order to have running water for drinking and for cleaning (washing off) butchered game. After everyone was settled back at Minter in November,[189] hunters went off to a camp in the swampland near Glenwood (4 miles north), intent on filling out winter supplies.[190]

Most deer meat was eaten fresh, but some was thin-sliced and dried in the autumn. Elk was not common fare, living far in the Olympics and being too big to pack easily <B61>. A few that wandered into traps were enjoyed.[191] Elk and deer hides were tanned for use as moccasins, clothing, and bed covers.

Snares set along a runway consisted of loops of hazel branches placed where deer ducked their heads down, or behind a log where they jumped over. For small animals, a snare was attached to a bent sapling that sprang back up when released. Snares were also used to catch birds. Traps (pits covered over with brush), sometimes four or five that were spaced far apart, might be dug along the same deer runway. Trapped bears had to be killed since their fall into the pit was not fatal <B62>.

Small land animals were killed with bow and arrows, clubs, traps, and snares. Raccoon snares were baited with fish. Both raccoon and land otter meat was eaten, though the fur pelts were more desired. Squirrel, beaver, and mink were also hunted both for meat and furs <B64>. Otter (land, river), cougar, wolf, and coyote provided their pelts for clothing and bags.[192]

Gizmo harpooned porpoise, blackfish [orca], and seals <A24>. Such sea mammal hunting from canoes was distinctive of the South Sound.

Birding

Ducks were taken in aerial nets set along flyways beside marshes. Such a net was 14 feet long and 5 feet wide, with a narrow mesh. In tidal zones, attached floats lifted and lowered these

---

[188] For the Straits, bucks are best in the spring, while does and bear are best in the fall, See Wayne Suttles, *Coast Salish Essays* 1987: 34.

[189] November sometimes is pədƛ̓xʷay? meaning "time of dog salmon," *LD*: 157.

[190] Cf Moons <A56>, Year Cycle <B33> in the notebooks. Low hills here now surround the Horseshoe Lake Golf Course.

[191] Again, this reflects changed conditions since elk bones are abundant archaeologically.

[192] Mountain beaver pelts were preferred for baby bedding and clothing, See June Collins, Stillaguamish Docket 207: 58. This intriguing and wildly misnamed mammal appears as a love interest in epics, as well as the actual architect of trimmed trees and elaborate dens, whose construction debris includes gnawed lumps that can look like a baseball, See Jay Miller, Regaining Dr Herman Haeberlin 2004: Appendix G, 37-39.

nets along supporting posts. During a tidal change, feeding ducks leisurely floated and dove with the lowering current, but they always took the same route at liftoff and so hit the net <B64-66>. At Quartermaster Harbor, Puyallups caught ducks by hoisting a net above the water, stretched low and tight between two tall poles, to stun and snare them at dawn or dusk along their regular flyway.

Ducks were also speared at night on salt water, attracted by a **fire** blazing in the bottom of a canoe. As they swam up, the flames blinded them. The spear[193] was a 6-foot shaft with an ironwood head – lashed on with hemp and covered over with fir pitch, which had been boiled to smoothly coat and seal the point. People living on the rivers used bone from deer or elk for their spear heads, never bear. Sometimes, hunters could club waterfowl with a paddle. Duck (sqʷaləc)[194] varieties were known as black or rubber back,[195] orange nose, mallard, butterballs, widgeon, and brown head <B67>.

Other birds were also taken. Some were lured close with scattered seeds and then shot. Geese – whether snow, Canada, or brants – were trapped. Ruffed [Dusky ?] grouse [locally called pheasants] were lured with a scatter of crabapples and cottonwood seeds, then shot with arrows. In winter they "housed up" in trees and became virtually invisible.[196] When one was actually seen, the others seemed to be suddenly obvious. Helldivers were only eaten as a last resort because they were so tough <A69>.

Berrying

Berries were harvested and dried by women (and children) who joined together for company and mutual protection. In late June or July, blackcaps were eaten fresh. Both blackberries picked in July and salal berries picked in August were sun-dried. The few red huckleberries found in August were eaten fresh since they did not dry well (and supposedly tasted dull). In October and November, huckleberries were much prized. If it rained while these favorites <A58> were dehydrating, mat roofs and a low, smoky fire helped to spare them from mildewing. When partly dried, they were mashed together to fill the inside of a large basket.

The pulp was dried as cakes about 6 inches across. Some were ovals about 8" long by ¾ to 1" thick. Dried and smoked inside on a rack, such cakes were stored in medium-size, openwork baskets. To serve six people, half a blackberry cake was mashed in water. Sometimes

---

[193] As AL Kroeber insightfully noted, this duck spear with a 3-notched butt is the lone historic weapon with echoes of the atlatl that was used for thousands of years before the bow was adopted about a thousand years ago, leading to the strategic proliferation of forts and protective barricades along the coast, See William Elmendorf, *The Structure of Twana Culture* 1960: 109, note 80; Jay Miller, First Nations Forts, Refuges, and War Lord Champions around the Salish Sea, *Journal of Northwest Anthropology (JONA)* 45 (1): 71-87, 2011.

[194] The Southern Lushootseed (*LD*: 41) word for waterfowl that swim well is sq̓ʷalaš, while NL uses buʔqʷ.

[195] Though their Lushootseed name means "white wings."

[196] This seeming disappearance of grouse is explained in legend as a winter visit to the land of the dead where Grouse's daughter is married.

it was mixed half and half with dried salal berries, which only had to be soaked a little to be reconstituted <A59>.

Woven of cedar roots and bark, a storage basket held about 20 gallons. These soft baskets were 3 feet across and 2½ feet high. Water-tight covers were fastened down by lacing a cord through loops woven in along the top edge. A family wanted at least 2 or 3 basketfuls of blackberries, but most tried to put up as many as they could. To mash the berries to remove the juice, stone hammers – shaped like a small dumbbell with a thinned middle grip – were used <A58>. Hazelnuts were stored loose in big baskets <A60>.

Lastly, other important foods consumed at eat-alls but not mentioned in any of these notes were camas, dug as a bulb, silverweed roots, and acorns, which had to be cooked and leached of their toxins. Only in his last court testimony did Jerry add that these plant foods were found at American River, Connell, Steilacoom, Puyallup, and Olympia Prairies. Such expanses, carefully tended by generations of daughters, exemplified a native gardening that has not been well reported by scholars.[197] A key factor in their care was the routine use of **fire** to burn out last year's withered growth to provide fertilizing ashes.

Aptly termed commuting, Minters well knew the timing and locale of all foods and resources in their own territory, while also visiting other locations as guest kin to extend their web of kinship regionally among rich, poor, mortals, immortals, and those yet unborn.[198]

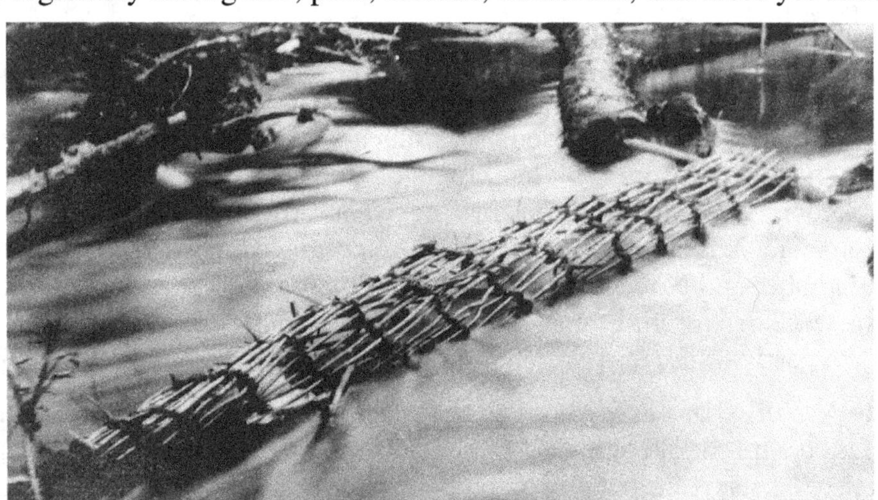

< §10 Basket trap set in a stream >

---

[197] His family's suppression of Arthur Ballard's material widened this gap since he collected a story where the Changer turned four quarrelsome women into maidenhair fern, skunk cabbage, wild artichoke, and sand rush, clearly linking plants to women.

[198] Though William Elmendorf, *The Structure of Twana Culture* 1960: 332 reported "All informants denied family claims on productive tracts such as clam beaches, root-digging areas, hunting or fishing localities, although equipment used or set up at the latter might be personally owned," the best locations were managed by the most renowned names, assuring bounty to leaders. In addition to these commons, however, there were private plots, such as clam gardens, which had been laboriously enhanced by family members over a long time (Chapter 5).

7 FISHING ROUNDS

Fish, particularly *Salmon* <A33>, was ~ is a mainstay food and symbol of Northwest Coast natives, joining with *Cedar* as the basis of the regional culture. At their every annual return, salmon, as fellow beings "who" lived as humans beyond the horizon, were welcomed as honored guests by special ceremonies and feasts. Fishing was a time of plenty, with much visiting and sharing among kin and the needy.

Minter fishers relied on canoe trolling gear in their bay and long basketry traps set into steams. Siyawalax^{w} [L2] and other leaders took care of the gear that was used every year by the community – first deployed by the elite, then passed on to others in turn by rank <B1>. Gill nets were used only at Gig Harbor and on the Puyallup River, never at Minter. Smelt, herring, and other small fish running in schools were swept into canoes using spiked rakes like paddles. When they spawned near a beach, a kind of drag or dipper seine was loosely woven of cedar or hazel branches <B1, B48>. These branches were split in two, flattened, and loosely bound up with twine to be 1½ feet wide and 3½ feet long. Poor people had their own meager fishing gear <B4>, especially if it was easily and quickly made like this seine, but only the wealthy had a complicated array of equipment to provide for any contingency.

Watercraft were essential for fishing. A large canoe of the wealthy held two or three families, transporting many passengers and goods. While everyone had small canoes, these big ones were few, prized, and welcomed. Families could never move around among camps unless they were related to those of the higher classes. All summer long, the rich visited with their "cousins." Those in the Minter big house *could* marry into the "poor" houses, but they would not have "good children." In fact, Jerry did not remember any "mixed" marriages into those poorer houses <B3>.

Mat houses, made of cattail panels formed into tents, were placed closer together when occupied by relatives. Often, separate mats were joined into a single dwelling for rich families, while poor outsiders camped apart. These poor also joined in the gambling, but a loser could claim back his last bet without any fuss if he declared it was all he had left <B4>.

"Uncles" such as Swan and tsidat'alq would visit with the Meeker family, but not bring along any of their fishing gear. They only came to gamble, staying for a night or two, then going back to their own family's summer fishery. They made it a point to keep coming back to gamble, indicating their continued good will. Food was shared communally, especially among kin, who were widely dispersed when they were members of leading families <B4-5>. Swan and others were fed {"as if they were at their own home"}. Jerry's mother knew how these distant relatives, though "poor," were related to her, but she never told Jerry specifically. Kin terms were used instead of names when speaking to them to indicate such closeness.

In one clear instance, she called Charlie Nichols and Jimmy Cross her "cousins" because her kinswoman Sxo'baya was their grandmother, though she lived in a "poor" Minter house, despite the understood high rank of her family. She died long ago <B6>. Jimmy Cross's family mostly died out. He married Betsy, a Nisqually woman, and they moved to the Puyallup Valley. He had one grandchild at Muckleshoot, George Cross, who had children there; his brother Silas Cross and family lived in the Puyallup valley.

Families left the camp at Lakebay in late Fall (November) to come back to Minter one by one <B40>. As creeks filled with increasing rainfall, the dog salmon run began. People used gaff hooks to capture these fish when they first entered the creek because, after 2 or 3 days of fighting upstream, their flesh got "too old" [mushy] to be good for eating. After a week in fresh water, dog salmon were too thin, especially the females. Males were best to dry because they did not get so "spawned out" as females did after laying eggs <B47>.

Minters relied on gaff hooks or a woven conical trap (sx^{w}i'əp)[199] facing upstream against the current to pen-up any fish that slipped backwards. When the Meeker boys did not have hooks, however, they built a small trap and one of them would splash above it to drive the fish inside while the other tossed them onto land. During a big run, no trap was needed since Jerry would sit down in a stream with his legs spread apart, while John drove fish downstream for his brother to pen up and fling out onto land. As is often recalled of those days long ago, "They were so thick you could walk across the creek on their backs" <B42>.[200]

Hooks were scarce and valuable, so only the wealthy had them. The old folks (when Jerry was young) had gaff hooks, but it was easier to leave basket traps submerged overnight, extracting fish in the morning. Traps would be placed above high tide, and each man owned his own since they were easily made. "But if you were not using yours during a run, you were expected to lend it to someone in need" <B43>. When Jerry was young, there were only individual traps. Poor people had no hooks, but instead used traps.

The average trap was 8-12 feet long, holding up to 10-12 fish with their heads wedged together at the closed end. Men cut the sticks that the women then tied and wove together. A single family needed a 6-foot basket trap. About half those in the Minter main house shared an extra large 14-foot long trap with a mouth 2 feet wide <B46>. These householders would dry their catch as a joint operation because the trap caught so many fish that they had to be processed quickly and efficiently to be preserved. Women prepared all the salmon they were given, without waste. One quick slash gutted the fish, scrubbing with a handful of moss and ferns removed guts and loose scales, and then precise strokes formed side fillets to be hung up to dry.

Individual families, while they wintered at Minter, hung their dried salmon inside from the rafters above their dwelling section. Afterward, when Minters wintered elsewhere, tight bundles of dried fish were left behind, stored on a platform inside a huge hollow tree <A35, C3>. For feasts, everybody contributed foods to serve. Winter supplies relied on dog salmon. Since summer salmon had much more fat, these did not preserve well. During cooking, summer salmon and porpoise dripped oil into clam shells that was saved, sometimes in deer bladders hung above the fire, until ready for use.

During Mythic time, every being had a human form that eventually changed into someone or something of the modern world while also retaining infrahuman (inner human) qualities. Here is a more understandable close paraphrase of the notes.[201]

---

[199] This name specifically means 'no end' in the sense of 'no exit,' replete with Sartrean echoes matched by native beliefs about very human salmon in their homes beyond the horizon.

[200] A sad but true statement since only streams on the west coast of Vancouver Island still bear witness to this remarkable denseness of a run, like a well attended marathon today.

[201] Jerry briefs this epic in Ella Clark, *Indian Legends of the Pacific Northwest* 1953: 26.

> There were five sisters living at tuh^{w}a'lq'^{u} (the weir [on the Puyallup River] above Orting running up to the Mt [Rainier, Takoma, Taxoba]). One of these women married a chief named ta'bu of the Twana on Hood Canal and they had a son. When the boy was 4-5 years old, he could visit back and forth between Orting and the Canal. When he was 6-8 years old, his parents began to quarrel violently. Finally, in a rage, they fought and this wife tore her husband to pieces.[202] As she and the boy packed up, she told him "do not forget the water" (taqo'ba) and that became the generic [snow-capped] mountain name "Tacoma" that whites have now limited to Mt Rainier. When they got back home, the Changer arrived and announced to the five sisters they would become mountains – Hood, Adams, Saint Helens, Baker, and Rainier~Tahoma. He said, "Now you will be useful, supplying rivers with water for fish to go up and feed the people" <B16-18>.

To underscore the importance of these immortal beings [with names capitalized] for the elite members of native society, the notes emphasize, with some reparaphrasing for clarification,

> {Those were first people and all the people in the Sound country were changed to Rocks, animals, birds (Blue Jay, Raven, Crow), deer, bear, mink, etc. Jerry did not know if any certain animals or things were the most ancient ancestors of Minter people. Such knowledge was highly specialized and only about half a dozen men of each band could count back in generations to the Changer and beyond <B18-19>}.[203]

Weirs

A major contribution of these notebooks is Jerry's detailed treatment of a river fishery <A73-89>, particularly the overall management of the Puyallup River from upriver at what became known as Stuck.[204] Along the Puyallup and other major rivers, people built huge weirs that looked like a slanted palisade wall made of ten-foot-tall poles. Women and children located the poles, men cut them down, and women, about mid-August, wove fiber between them to make

---

[202] Too polite, Jerry avoided mention of the intense jealousy among co-wives for their husband's attention that led to this dismembering, with the various body parts specifically flung to named locations, graphically and visually appropriate, throughout this region. The boy probably survives as the side peak of Mt Tahoma on Rainier.

[203] Certain rivers, tribes, or communities had special relationships as heirs, kin, or wards of specific immortal beings. Thus Thunderbird once lived where Lake Tapps is now and gave special protection to Puyallups, Snohomish came from Killerwhale (as now portrayed by a huge orca in front of their casino), and Skykomish from Grizzly, Cf Herman Haeberlin and Erna Gunther, Indians of Puget Sound 1930: 73.

[204] This Stuck River was just south of Auburn. Another Stuck was a high class Duwamish village near O'Brien. During massive 1906 floods, the White River moved into the channel of the Stuck and now empties into the Puyallup instead of the Duwamish, kept there by dynamite and dams. As such, the fishery described here has not existed for a century.

a fence. Gifted specialists then dove to place these panels against tripods {"derricks"} set into the river. The weir lasted through late October or November, when winter rains washed away the tripods, traps, and fence. Spring floods removed any remaining features. Fish traps were used for the salmon species known as silvers and humpies. Minters preferred to take dog salmon with gaff hooks in the creeks and smaller streams. Other Sound people also caught dog salmon with hooks, not traps, as two or three shifts of fishers rotated through each good location during the nights of a full run.

Puyallup weirs were located at Fife (kʷad) on Hylebos Creek, and along the river at 3-4 villages that included Alderton (sk̓ʷəspł = trout) and Orting (tsuwa'), as well as 2-3 villages at Stuck. Only 15-16 men along each river were specialists at building a weir <A74>. The overall fishery manager was a man named Walisxʷai at Stuck, [205] who was fluent in many languages, including Yakama (from east of the mountains) and any others spoken by regular visitors. He was "a real man," skilled and learned in languages, technologies, and diplomacy.

The Fife weir was managed by "old man" Kits'ap, who was a half-Suquamish local leader and related to Walisxʷai, the acknowledged chief. Kits'ap was mean, and once at a funeral killed the Indian doctor assumed to have slain the man being buried.[206] Walisxʷai was the _real_ boss of the "tribe" at getting and erecting the poles. He did not, however, boss the women; they knew how to work without male interference <A75> (though his wife probably oversaw their efforts).

The Stuck villagers would get the "first fish" and hold the proper ceremony, usually a big feast. When someone from a group had died during the year, a few of the live fish would be thrown back into the river as an offering. At every meal after any close kin (wife, husband,

---

205 Independent support for this man appears in the Waterman manuscript on place names, listing (p.25) A 302 StEx "pushing through," located on Stuck River north of the present town of Sumner, where some mythic inland whales pushed through to the Puyallup and saltwater. "Two 'headmen' here were Wa'losxoi and Kwiya'lx." Another man had many (reported as either a thousand or twenty) valuable dogs, probably shorn for wool since they were well treated and fed on salmon until slaughtered by soldiers during the Treaty War.

206 Arthur Ballard (1951 Deposition) distinguished at least three distinct Kitsaps – this "old" one at Puyallup, the famous one at Suquamish, and another from Ellensburg in eastern Washington who also lived in an immense house at the mouth of Newaukum Creek among Muckleshoots. Charlie Ashue, in the notes Ballard gave to Marian Smith, provided details on the execution, in a graveyard between Sumner and Puyallup, of a "bad" doctor by Old Kitsap "when he could hardly see." Old McKai (nakco'ya), a Tulalip married to a young Puyallup wife, was suspected of having killed two of Kitsap's daughters and the young man then being buried. Kitsap's wife guided his hand so he could shoot to kill. Afterwards, Old Kitsap went into hiding, but he was so old that the authorities decided to treat him leniently. There was no jail, so his son-in-law (Joe Taylor) settled him in the schoolhouse where Ashue was a pupil (about 1873). Kitsap sat by the stove and smoked his pipe. The teacher Rev Mann [note bene] said nothing. If he was thirsty, he would call out. The teacher would ask, "What does he want?" "Water." "All right, get him a drink." (Cf Marian Wesley Smith, Microfilm Roll 4 (Reel A1739), British Columbia Archives, MSS 268, Box 8, Folder 4; Royal Anthropological Archives, MSS 2794).

parent) had died, a portion of the food was similarly offered.[207] Some spouses threw it into the **fire** instead of the water. In native belief, if they didn't do that they would have a short life, while {"if they remember the dead, they will probably have a long life" <A78>}.[208]

After the Stucks were done, Kitsap's Fifes would be second on that weir, followed by the Orting men <A78>. Always, the people who built the trap were the first ones to use it, before they invited in neighbors. KoyopqeD and others were from Orting, and they could always get more fish later at their own small streams. Still, they would come to help all the others at Stuck. Walasx^{w}ai determined the alternate nights that these other groups could fish. Poor people would be told the nights they could use the trap without any charge. Young men volunteered to fish for people who were too old or too afraid to fish from the weir.

Every night, everyone gambled, sometimes betting slaves. Each family and village group would pool their bets, consisting of fishing tackle and anything loose (portable), held in trust by a neutral rich person until one side had won it all. Each community had a professional "lucky" gambler, who would make the wager for all. Even if the chief sat in, the gambler, as specialist, still led the betting of his town. If his luck ran out, he appointed a successor. Once, Puget Sound Indiens banded together against visiting Yakamas to gamble for their horses and almost "broke" them, taking all their horses except for those needed to ride back home. On many occasions, people were invited just to gamble and, in hopeful jest, were asked to bring along lots of "money."

Commoners came along to the fishing camps with their village nobles and leaders. As they worked to meet their own needs, they also tried to add to the stores of their chief and his (or her) family <A81>. They prepared and cooked food for them to serve visitors, as well as brought water and firewood to keep the fire going all the time. Women cooked for these leaders. In ordinary times, everyone cooked and got wood for his or her own needs. But in this very public setting, commoners helped because their leaders were busy entertaining guests, managing the camps and fishery, and making future plans. They placed bets during gambling games, and helped serve food. All foods were shared in common to sustain this sense of fellowship that was so encouraging of hard work.

Only the rich owned nets because hemp (*qa'qewlx*)[209] was so scarce it often had to be purchased with slaves <A90>, a high prestige "commodity" or "currency." Carefully tended in special plots, nettles grew eight feet tall, then had to be dried, cured, and shredded to produce long fibers with a red brown color like cedar bark.[210] The mesh size was carefully calculated

---

207 Jerry's exact words, unfortunately, were that the fish "was not eaten but wasted," indicating his estrangement from this very traditional act of connectedness.

208 Presumably this release of fish somehow fed or benefited the dead, who then made fewer demands on the living, including "taking away" their lives.

209 Indian hemp (*Apocynum cannabinum L*) was a crucial trade item from interior tribes to coastal ones, who augmented it with fiber from their own nettle gardens.

210 Tending of such nettle gardens continued from prehistoric times, but the practice is not well known so details have been added to clarify Jerry's notes. BIA Agent Charles Willoughby (Indians of the Quinaielt Agency 1886: 271) reported "Formerly the twine of the net was made by the Indians from the fiber of the common nettle, which in some localities here has a luxuriant growth and is a good substitute for flax. All the fish nets of these Indians were once

according to the size and motions of the intended prey, whether salmon, ducks, or deer <A90>.[211]

Managers like Walisx^{w}ai, Kits'ap, and KoyopqəD knew how to make these nets and netting. At Minter, Gizmo made all the netting <A91>. Such leaders "bossed" the younger men so they could learn. When building a weir, a manager assigned a team of five men to each tripod. At Stuck, Walisx^{w}ai really "owned" the whole trap, but other leaders often determined the sequence of usage. When Kits'ap and the other managers had their nets set at separate stations, they would indicate the person who could use or borrow it next in turn and for how long a period of time. Since these leaders were experienced about conditions at those stations, following their directions and advice made things easier.

When the owner of the net was nearly out of fish, the borrower of his net wisely left enough of the catch for the owner's daily needs. While a polite gesture, it also made sure they would not be denied future use of the gear. Walisx^{w}ai had several of these nets, but only one was used at any time by the Stucks <A92>. The others were kept in reserve as a precaution. Visitors who helped put up the trap and stations used their own or borrowed nets to catch their share of fish. All shared access and bounty; otherwise the salmon would be offended by lack of generosity and stay away from fishers.

Members of each visiting household brought their own dip nets. Some fishers asked to borrow nets, or its owner politely loaned it to those in need without charge. But such sharing only took place after these owners had gotten their own fish for the day. When the fish run lessened, the catch was shared equally among everyone who happened to be there at the moment of distribution. After Walisx^{w}ai and Kits'ap got too old, Labluptəd took over as manager during Jerry's time <A77>. No one followed him and all of the fish traps finally washed away. No one else ever assumed the authority to coordinate all this effort.[212]

Two men could each fish with a net at one time, and the scaffold along the top of a weir could store 20-30 salmon <A82>. While the dip netting continued, others would take the catch to shore so these fish could be divided up by the leader's wife among all the women working to process them while still fresh. At Stuck, for example, this apportioner was Mrs. Walisx^{w}ai. She would divide the fish for cleaning, cutting up, and drying among the women of her own village – first giving some to women of the leading house, then to the poorer peoples, and, lastly, to outsiders <A83>. Leaders needed more fish because they shared more meals with families and visitors.

---

made of this material; at present seine twine is used." These plots, according to modern elders, benefited from urine.

[211] Complexities of this net technology, successfully deployed on land, sea, and air, need more research. An air net once stood near today's Seattle Center, as shown in its bus stop artwork.

[212] Again, Jerry was too polite because state fishery officers, under the regimes of Leslie Darwin and others, were notorious for decades before and after 1900 for blasting away weirs and arresting their builders, who paid stiff court fines. Big John at Muckleshoot was fined for blocking the Green River with a weir in 1892.

Everybody ate the first night's catch at a public feast (First Salmon) that included the poor. The fish trap builders had the honor of eating first.[213] When everyone stored enough dried fish, they moved on to their usual berrying and fishing grounds.

At Stuck, Walisx^{w}ai designated the men and work shifts for each night. The first catch was divided among his own house group, with any excess given to poorer people to dry <A85>. At the same time, everyone (including the poor) was also given fresh salmon to eat at their daily meals. One big summer salmon, cooked with dry berries, could feed 30-35 people. The poor would fish only for themselves, with the expectation that their end-products would be less palatable [and morally tainted], and so their catch was not divided up to share among families as was done with those of leaders.[214]

Being "poor" was a matter of ability, not property, because a slave [such as Dr Simon] could and did accumulate property (though it went to his master until he became free). Ability was a leadership trait confirmed through successful contact with a spirit power, much like a man with a higher education. The poor were often too lazy to train and wash [bathe] to get such a spirit, earning productive abilities that went with it <A93>.

After two weeks fishing on a large weir, where four distinct platform stations could be used by each of the four communities [probably Stuck, Fife, Alderton, Orting], outsiders from more distant communities were invited to fish at the very end of the salmon run. They arrived after the local poor (who were allied with the fish trap builders) because these were often Sound natives who followed fish runs upstream to these traps <A88>. Though outsiders, they could have any fish free for the taking as long as they did the work to haul them out.

These visitors stayed a week or ten days, then moved on to berrying grounds for the month of September, traveling in small groups that might meet up again at convenient berry patches and clam beaches, such as Quartermaster Harbor. Puyallups and Gig Harbors camped at Point Defiance before paddling across the Narrows to this deep and treacherous inlet <A89>.

Poverty and starvation were prevented by a fair division of all foods. Leaders were always ready to give something to anyone who did not have enough. Nobody ever went hungry <A69>. Anyone moderately able-bodied could always get something fresh to eat. Jerry never heard of any Indians starving to death, though this happened after diseases ravaged homes. All kinds of dried meats, fish, berries, or clams were kept on hand by the wealthy, and one could always get something fresh, though it might take hard work to get a mouthful, as with clams.

Overall, like migrating salmon and other species following their natural rhythms, Minters timed their efforts according to a keen sense of local conditions. At certain moments and months, they were engaged in predictable events. By knowing when and where they would be,

---

[213] I assumed that Jerry was carefully skirting discussion of the First Salmon Ceremony here because of his Presbyterianism, but careful rereading of these notes makes me suspect he had a Salmon spirit ally and so was being cautiously respectful. Indeed, the vision on Clay Creek of such an immortal, as described to Marian Smith (*The Puyallup-Nisqually* 1940: 63), wearing a pointed fur cap, black fur coat, and carrying a fish spear was probably Jerry's own.

[214] Again, the sense was and is, "You are what you eat." Everything about the food, the cook, and the cooking influenced the eater. For this same reason, human babies should not be given cow's milk because it makes them bovine and stubborn.

homesteaders could burn native houses without immediate consequences. Guns and enforced homestead law protected the claim, and Minters quietly (if sullenly) found other havens nearby.

Minter Hatchery

Today's use of Minter Bay for a state hatchery bespeaks its past high productivity. Indeed, the native fishery at Minter did not end with the 1874 torching of the native village, since families continued to visit and fish there. Since the land was taken over by gyppo loggers not by entrenched farmers, Meekers and others continued to return to fish at Minter and Glencove, storing their take in the Minter tree stump. By name, the most important species at Minter Creek are salmon (chinook, chum, pink, coho), cutthroat trout, and steelhead (a seagoing trout).[215] Some sockeye salmon appear occasionally, spawning in beaver ponds.

Apt testimony to the past and present abundance of Minter is the present-day management of its fishery by the state and tribes. Recognizing the quality and quantity of its freshwater, Minter state hatchery was built in 1936 to research and increase the viability of artificially raised broods. [216] Using fish eggs from other runs (in nearby Hood Canal), their efforts, however, threatened indigenous fish stocks. This issue is vastly complicated because of the potential genetic effects of these foreign introductions. Remodeled in 1992, it is now entirely devoted to salmon production. Sterile conditions are enforced throughout these areas to prevent disease outbreaks.

All of Washington State has 435 naturally reproducing ("wild") salmon and steelhead stocks in 40 basins, with 209 stocks within Puget Sound and Hood Canal. In the old days, stocks were identified by geography and appearance, but now genetic stock identification (GSI) has sorted out 76 stocks in Hood Canal and the Straits of Juan de Fuca, and 133 in Puget Sound (71 in the north, 62 in the south).

In the South Sound, Carr Inlet is itself distinct from the other five inlets because it drains the Kitsap instead of the Olympic Peninsula, and is fed by small, low gradient streams. "Minter and Lackey creeks are classic chum/coho/cutthroat streams; the same species that are currently present."[217] Flows for spawning occur from mid November to early January, and are particularly favorable for the return of fall chum. Overall, these stocks are healthy but indigenous runs have clearly decreased in numbers.

Today, in May, Minter Creek is blocked so that returning salmon, varying by species over succeeding months, can be penned by staff. These are spring chinook in May-June, fall chinook in August, coho in September-October, chum in December, and late chum about Christmas. When large enough numbers are gathered, eggs are collected and spawned artificially using milt from several males to assure genetic diversity, and the run is given free

---

215 Washington Department of Fish and Wildlife and Western Washington Treaty Indian Tribes, 1992 Washington State Salmon and Steelhead Stock Inventory (SASSI). Appendix One, Puget Sound Stocks, North Puget Sound (NPS) Volume - 418pp, South Puget Sound (SPS) Volume – 1994: 1-371.

216 Technical and editorial help with this section and the whole was provided by Kurt Reidinger, along with Hanz Fronz Jens O'Magonaghal.

217 James Ames, E-mail on Friday, 27 October 2000.

passage up the creeks to spawn naturally. A room filled with stacked trays, each holding up to 60,000 eggs, can hatch 2.5 million eggs. A month later, the hatchery eggs are sorted so only those healthy and fertilized are placed in vertical trays flushed with well or spring water, which is more disease-free. After a second month, the fry hatch and are held until they absorb the egg yoke. They remain in cement ponds for about three months – fed and medicated. While still young, the adipose fin of a fish is clipped to mark it as a hatchery product and a coded wire is implanted in the head. Just before release, creek water is mixed into the pens to begin acclimating the fish to their new abode.

Each year, Minter hatchery workers collect over 19,000,000 eggs, release 5,400,000 smolt, and welcome back 48,000 salmon adults. From most to least abundant, these are chums, cohos, fall chinooks, spring chinooks, and pinks (in odd years). Records track species, broods, and runs.

In the decade before Judge George Boldt affirmed the native right by treaty to half the allowable fishery, Puyallup fishers, as well as other Medicine Creek Treaty tribes, asserted their rights at Minter. Local land owners and the oyster farm were distraught, but the hatchery, to its credit, negotiated workable solutions. After the Boldt decision, as an expression of their tribal sovereignty, Puyallups built a chicken wire trap (an updated weir) at the Minter bridge, graciously returning any "surplus" to the hatchery. Eventually Puyallups let the hatchery handle the runs, in return for any "surplus." Today, working through tribal fisheries officers, Minter even schedules natives to fish out particular runs to prevent "genetic bottlenecks" from excessively large returns of fish with limited parental diversity.

The Minter Hatchery Complex has also been closely involved in the rescue from extinction of the White River spring chinook.[218] They ran from late May to mid October, peaking in September. The few survivors were kidnapped to a new facility, built at Hupp Springs (a Minter Creek tributary) in 1980, that has served as both laboratory and incubator.

In addition to the engineered redirecting of the whole White River, habitat destruction harmed the prospects of fish runs. "[R]educing the flow of water by over half [thereby] dried up the biologically important marshlands at the mouth of the Duwamish. Removing and burning over 60,000 cords of wood from the upper White [River] log jams removed ideal fish habitat."[219] Such riparian trees, marsh, and brush serve to shelter many land animals, as well as insects that fish eat. Their roots anchor the stream banks. Grasses comb out particles and slow runoff. Large woody debris (LWD) is important for stabilizing streambeds, cooling water temperature and providing a shadow cover. Gravel bars slow and braid the flow. Logging debris and eroding logging roads have added excessive, smothering sediment, and businesses have discharged pollutants. Gravel is scraped up by a process called, with ironic overtones, 'scalping'. Straightening the lower Puyallup to flow through concrete walls shortened the length of the stream and provided another hard surface to hurt the fish.

Increasing efforts to control Green River flooding produced more dams. In 1911, Puget Power finished a dam at Buckley (11 feet high and 352 foot wide of wood and concrete, after

---

[218] See Appendix F for the fierce battles between King and Pierce County, via farmers, engineers, and officials, to send the Stuck and White Rivers into either the Duwamish or Puyallup drainage, showing that hostilities were not limited to local natives.

[219] Patricia Cosgrove, A Great Diversion, White River Journal 2001: 1.

35,000 chords of LWD from a five mile stretch through Auburn were hauled off and burned).[220] An 8-mile canal diverts 64% of the flow into Lake Tapps, then through four steel penstocks dropping down 488 feet into the Deiringer Powerhouse before it returns into the White River. Fish formerly had no safe outlet from Tapps because what were called fish screens on the intakes served more like blank walls to "splat" the fry. Ramping, or surges in outflow, also smashed fish. Mud Mountain Dam was built by the Army Corps of Engineers (US ACE) in 1948, and Howard Hansen Dam was built at Eagle Gorge in 1962, and now threatens to crack open.

Hupp escapements averaged 137 White River salmon from 1978 to 1991, with a range that fluctuated between 10 and 500. Unfortunately, by using so few available spring chinook to start this rebuilding program, the state "may have created a genetic bottleneck."[221] Since 1987, the South Sound Net (SSNP) complex near Olympia, managed by WDFW and the Squaxin Island tribe, has produced the majority of these fish. Others are raised at a hatchery on the White River itself, a mitigation facility built by Puget Power (now Puget Sound Energy) and operated by the Muckleshoot Tribe. Following a recovery plan, when specific numbers are reached, Hupp will phase out of these efforts, with tribes increasing their own efforts.

Today, as for millennia, Minter remains intertwined with salmon, and with people; its bay provides the brand name for local oysters, and its importance for the understanding of the true history of Puget Sound is being restored, like the White River Chinook.

---

[220] Patricia Cosgrove, A Great Diversion, White River Journal 2001: 1.
[221] SASSI, SPS Appendix 1994: 133.

8 SUFFERING SLAVERY

The most traumatic reversal of fortunes any Northwest Coast person could endure was to suffer the dehumanizing fate of a slave. Usually reserved for captured children and women, after older males were killed, slaves lost control of their own lives and claims to their efforts. Each lost any identity, becoming known by a generic term, such as the name of their original tribe or town.[222] They occupied physical but not social space because slavery was a matter of interpersonal contrasts, prestige, and economic advantage.[223] Slaves were property (never persons) that had been captured, traded, and sold far from home or born of slave parents.[224]

> Endemic raiding supplied the richer villages with slaves, a workforce who could neither withhold their labor nor demand a large share of the harvest and who thereby undercut the power of free people to withhold or transfer their allegiance.... Certain scarce non-perishable items – disk beads, dentalia, baskets, canoes, blankets, and slaves – were used as a special currency for the potlatch system.[225]

Foreign women and older children were preferred, performing tedious and laborious food getting. They might be wagered as bets in gambling games by their master, along with his own wife, but never his canoe. A slave, if well treated, had a nickname and used fictive kin terms with the master's family and household, but they were also called by the name of their original

---

222 Colin Tweddell, A Historical and Ethnological Study of the Snohomish Indian People 1974: 475-694, 120. Indeed, as a Snohomish, given the N ~ D and M ~ B blendings, Dr Simon, with a Metis French pronunciation, sounds like their tribal name of snehomš ~ sdehobš.

223 Enslaving natives motivated much of early American history, especially in the East, as it has World History. Revealing studies include Alan Gallay, *The Indian Slave Trade ~ The Rise of the English Empire in the American South, 1670-1717*, 2002; James Brooks, *Captives and Cousins, Slavery, Kinship, and Community in the Southwest Borderlands* 2002. Overviews appear in Yasuhide Kawashima, Indian Servitude in the Northeast, *History of Indian – White Relations*, Handbook of North American Indians, Volume 4: 404-406 1988; Peter Wood, Indian Servitude in the Southeast, *History of Indian – White Relations*, Handbook of North American Indians, Volume 4: 407-409 1988; Albert Schroeder and Omer Steward, Indian Servitude in the Southwest, *History of Indian – White Relations*, Handbook of North American Indians, Volume 4: 410-413 1988; Robert Heizer, Indian Servitude in California, *History of Indian – White Relations*, Handbook of North American Indians, Volume 4: 414-416 1988.

224 Jay Miller, Back to Basics: Chiefdoms in Puget Sound 1997: 375-387; Astrida Blukis Onat, The Interaction of Kin, Class, Marriage, Property Ownership and Residences with Respect to Resource Locations among Coast Salish of the Puget Sound Lowland, 1984: 86-96; Wayne Suttles, *Coast Salish Essays* 1987, *Northwest Coast* 1990; Hermann Haeberlin and Erna Gunther, The Indians of Puget Sound 1930.

225 Pamela Amoss, Hair of the Dog: Unraveling Pre-Contact Coast Salish Social Stratification 1993: 8, 16.

community as a denigration, and, if they highly offended, were bluntly called 'slave' (*studəq*) a dire insult, that among the freeborn led to the murder of the insulter, directly or by ambush.

Little is actually known by the public about native slavery, since it was and is embarrassing and potentially dangerous, though legally suppressed 150 years ago. The lives of slaves were supposed to be filled with dull drudgery.[226] Today, native elders continue to use the native term for "slave" as a dire insult against members of other families, always phrased as gossip never in direct reference. Lushootseed lacks real obscenities so this word has great emotional potency.[227]

They became place markers rather than humans. After death, birthplace determined fate. Souls of slaves captured in raids went to their own ancestral afterworld, while those born into slavery remained in bondage in the afterworld of their owner.[228]

> "The one great difference in their status lay in the fact that slaves were outside the social struggle for prestige. They could be respected as individuals but they could not translate that respect into influence over other members of the society. Their word was forever without authority.... The only child really at a disadvantage was the child of a slave. He was not himself a slave, yet he was always open to insult. If he had no ambitions no one bothered to apply the insult. On the other hand, if he spoke with authority and assumed a right to do so, the insult could be applied – at the risk of open enmity as an invitation to conflict which was fought on the same basis as any other struggle for prestige."[229]

In historic times a leader sometimes took it upon himself to redeem any members of his community from slavery, either confronting the slavers, fighting back, or ransoming the captive. At Puyallup, such was a leader named Zachias; at Minter, he was Broken Tooth, and at Steilacoom (Chambers Creek) Cecolquin, father of the first husband of Jerry's mother Sally.

Taken and regarded as children, some slaves remained childish their whole lives, and some were assigned as personal attendants to care for an elite child. They were clothed simply by the family of their master, and their hair was kept short and bobbed. Lummi regarded orphans as slaves because they were dependent on others, and similarly unprotected.

> The master does not talk to the slave unless he is giving orders and the slave may not look at his master too much and must be very humble and servile. When a male slave, captured as a child, grows up, he is still referred to with diminutive kinship terms even by children many years his junior. Masters although always discriminating against them are careful not to mistreat slaves too cruelly for fear that a slave in a depressed condition might obtain a spirit power enabling him to secure revenge, for a slave has nothing to restrain him from killing. They are given the

---

226 Leland Donald, *Aboriginal Slavery on the Northwest Coast of North America* 1997: 126-138.

227 Colin Tweddell, The Snoqualmie-Duwamish Dialects of Puget Sound Salish 1950; also *LD*.

228 Jay Miller, *Lushootseed Culture and the Shamanic Odyssey* 1999: 23.

229 Marian Smith, *The Puyallup-Nisqually* 1940: 52-53, 160.

> worst food, cheated in the games of the children, restricted in associations and forced to do the drudgery of the household.[230]

A slave who escaped or was rescued by family often suffered a taint that denied their continued honesty and reliability,[231] unless they quickly hosted a feast and give away as "proof of ability to exercise an expensive upper-class prerogative."[232]

> While any leader was usually too busy to hunt and fish, his wives harvested roots, berries and clams. His slaves did the fishing and hunting if they were young; older slaves made [carved] canoes and utensils for the family.
>
> While a family might have a slave or two, a chief always had more than two. Slaves had to do at least as much work as their masters, so most worked long and hard. Master and slave sometimes worked together, but a valued slave always made more effort. If the master got angry, he could beat or kill the slave without consequences. Usually, instead, slaves were scolded or set difficult tasks to punish them. Often, a kind man was asked by slaves to purchase them from a harsh master.
>
> In the plank houses, slaves did all the cleaning, and got basic supplies like clams, drinking water, and firewood. In camps, slaves lived in a separate mat hut. Regardless of abode, slaves always ate after everyone else was finished.
>
> Only slaves captured from other areas had naturally rounded heads, which were considered ugly along the central coast. Closer to Alaska, however, captured freeborn Salish stood out as slaves because of their shaped heads.[233]

Slaves performed special services for their owners. The slave of a shaman listened throughout the community to learn who was sick or in need of treatment. They acted on orders behind the scenes for social control, revenge, or profit. Slaves administered poison or killing blows for their masters, acting as covert henchmen involved in the dark arts or doing the dirty work.[234]

Slaves bore the brunt of early history in this region. They were sent out to meet strangers and to taste-test exotic foods. Ruth Sehome Shelton,[235] wife of the leader on the Tulalip Reservation and daughter of the founder of a present Bellingham suburb, mentioned how slaves at S'Klallam and Quinault served as such food tasters. Since they were expendable, they became the first to try European "gifts" of alcohol, rice (looking like maggots), potatoes, and molasses (looking like corpse discharges).

---

[230] Bernard Stern, *The Lummi Indians of Northwest Washington* 1934: 74.

[231] June Collins, *Valley of the Spirits* 1974: 127-128.

[232] William Elmendorf, *The Structure of Twana Culture* 1960: 346-347.

[233] Jay Miller, *Lushootseed Culture and the Shamanic Odyssey* 1999: 92-93, 115.

[234] Leland Donald, *Aboriginal Slavery on the Northwest Coast of North America* 1997: 83-84, 127. Of note, such slave henchmen used the names of powerful spirits, adding to the aura of these supernaturals.

[235] "Gram" Ruth Sehome Shelton, *siastenu* 1995.

Slavery

With the fur trade, slavery became an asset, since money from their wages and labor belonged to the master. Males hunted furs or were hired out to log or farm; females prostituted, cleaned houses, cooked, or worked on farms. Slavers from north Puget Sound, while living securely upriver, raided communities in the south. Hebał and his six sons of the Skykomish were notorious slavers until the father was killed at Old Man House and his wife enslaved. The sons and their families then scattered for their own safety, depopulating the Skykomish area. Jerry's father and uncle were among them, though these brothers had no known connection with slavers.

The regional native emporium for slaves, pulverized "salmon flour," and other commodities was at the Dalles of the Columbia River, though smaller trading hubs flourished at Coupeville, Port Hadlock, and elsewhere. A Skagit slaver fortified his house at Burton, near Puyallup inlaws, Duwamish victims, and European traders at Fort Nisqually.

Skagit Fort

During the early 1800s, the value of slaves in fur trade production and chiefly rank encouraged both predatory raids and defensive fortifications at strategic locales favored by active slavers.[236] Buried in the monograph and fieldnotes of Marian Smith are references, all or largely from Jerry Meeker, to a nearby defended house built between Maury and Vashon Islands at Quartermaster Harbor by a Lower Skagit warrior. He belonged to a prominent but not noble family whose most famous member was Goliah, an influential English speaker for the Lower Skagit on Whidbey Island, US-appointed "chief" of the northern Lushootseeds, and signer of the 1855 treaty at Point Elliot. Trusted to carry documents and written messages, Goliah appealed to American authorities.[237] His brother *sadsəhədix*^{w} was war lord ~ champion of a fort on the south Sound island, with crucial access to Fort Nisqually. Much alike, both Penn Cove, the Lower Skagit homeland, and Quartermaster Harbor were deep bays sheltered within islands that were more easily defended.

In Marian Smith's book, only the place name is given. It was "14. tsugwalɛ' … at Quartermaster Harbor." The founder married into neighboring native (Puyallup) communities, though someone there also had a Skagit wife. Because he raided the Duwamish for slaves, the fort was under constant threat so "when its founder became old this village moved to Gig Harbor. The movement took place not long before the treaty."[238]

In Jerry's notes, the man is named "*sadsəhədix*^{w} (brother was *gelai'a*)" with "a winter house on Maury Island … when Duwamish got after him strong he moved over to his people on Gig Harbor for greater protection. Jerry thinks there must once have been

236 These forts were typically the work of "war lords" colonizing (asserting footholds) into the lands of others around the globe; for Salish Sea names and locations, See Jay Miller, First Nations Forts, Refuges, and War Lord Champions around the Salish Sea 2011.

237 Though Goliah's role was brief since he died in February 1857, see NARA M234 Reel 907, frame 1361.

238 Marian Smith, *The Puyallup-Nisqually* 1940: 11.

forts because when he was interpreting once an old woman (?) referred to *sadsəhədix*^{w}['s] house on Maury Island as his "fort." Knows no details."[239]

Combining these references adds clarification that *sadsəhədix*^{w}, brother of the Lower Skagit spokesman Goliah, had a fortified large winter plank house on Quartermaster Harbor between Maury and Vashon Islands, an important portage in the south Sound. Members of the important Sneatlum family of Penn Cove also used it, particularly a man named George.[240]

Moreover, a clearer view of the international and intertribal complexity of the region is shown by the ability of important families to set themselves up in foreign territory to take advantage of slaving upon locals and trade at the British fort. Such vigorous, aggressive warriors protected their home locations, while visiting widely to raid, trade, and compete. Throughout this region, competition took many forms, not all of them involving weapons and warfare. The Minters themselves became famous by gorging on foods.

While a few slaves were freed in response to Lincoln's 1862 Emancipation Proclamation, most had already been freed in the treaties forced by Governor Isaac Stevens during 1855, which insisted "The said tribes and bands agree to free all slaves now held by them, and not to purchase or acquire others hereafter." A few finally benefited from their own hard work, becoming prosperous by selling clams or lumber in the city of Seattle.[241] They also benefited from the settlers and money economy, buying their own freedom and taking on new jobs. Uniquely detailed, the role of Simon at Fort Nisqually well illustrates the embracing of these new conditions.

Dr Simon

Two tiny houses at Minter were the homes of slaves belonging to Damasq. We know very little of the woman, but the life of the Dr Simon[242] is detailed by Jerry Meeker at the end of

[239] Marian Wesley Smith, Microfilm Roll 3 (Reel A1738), British Columbia Archives, MSS 2689, Box 6, Folder 9 (Houses 26); Royal Anthropological Archives MSS 2794, Houses p26. Since Lucy Gurand lived at this selfsame Quartermaster, she was probably the woman Jerry interpreted for.

[240] The one lead that has been found suggests a link with a Tuttle family. In the 1919 Roblin Roll for Skagits, Folder 115, File 4, James Tuttle says he was half Skagit born at Quartermaster Harbor on 9/12/[18]71. Using kin codes (p170), his M Annie = Quio-litza was about 80 years old in 23/3/[19]17, his MF was Swut-kadub ~ Kwuss-ka-nam = George Sna-lum and his MM was Tyee Mary ~ Tupt-aleut, a Duwamish Snoqualmie Yakima, who died at Cedar Mt in 1890. *Tyee* is the Chinuk WaWa term for a leader and member of the nobility, indicating her high rank. Sneatlums of Penn Cove were especially prominent during the fur trading era, with extensive marriage and trade contacts, but Swut-ka-dub {sx^{w}ətkadəb} is not the same name as Sad-sə-hə-dix^{w}.

[241] Jay Miller, Suquamish Traditions, 1999a. Many but not all African American slaves in the Northwest were freed in response to Lincoln's 1862 Emancipation Proclamation. The most famous case involved Charlie – the slave of James Tipton, first regent of the University of Washington – who escaped to abolitionist British soil at Victoria.

[242] Jay Miller, Dr Simon: A Snohomish Slave at Fort Nisqually and Puyallup 2002.

Notebook B just before, in obvious contrast, he gave his own boastful biography of the first half of his life to fill the pages of C. This enslaved Snohomish at Minter quickly acquired the English name of Simon after he was redeemed at Fort Nisqually by Dr William Fraser Tolmie.[243] Simon progressively become slave, curer, Fort Nisqually teamster, and Puyallup farmer. At Puyallup, "Although one of the four slaves remembered had come of a wealthy Snohomish family, no attempt had been made to redeem him. Slaves could be gambled or sold but here, again, no instances were known."[244] Based on his subsequent career, that Snohomish was likely Simon, whose native name was *dak^{w}iłał*, and he does indeed provide an instance. He had been captured, lost in a gambling bet, sold to the Minter headwoman, ransomed at Fort Nisqually, and allotted on the Puyallup reservation. The verbatim notes say:

> Simon – Snohomish slave at minter – came when 12 or 14. he got his power right here at Gig Harbor.
>
> Woman from lummi was a nisqually slave.
>
> Dr Toldman or Tully [Tolmie] brought <B51> *dak^{w}iłał* the slave man from them. He was Hudson Bay Co head. He paid so many blankets for him + had him work for him at fort Nisqually. He kept him there until he left for Vancouver [Victoria]. Then let him free.
>
> tsidəwtəwlq ~~owned~~ brought him k^{w}itsa'qs – original master. His power (twida'B [x^{w}dab]) was doctor[ing]. He [Simon] got rich over his doctor power after he was set free. Got many horses, money, clothing. I've seen older dr [doctors] dr [doctor] a lot of Indians. He used to use lots of erbs [herbs]. Wild roots + cedar seeds. Nettle roots. Made tea from them. Also chutum wood bark – made people <B52> drink it. He used them {not with his power} for curing. Diff[erence] between power sickness + regular physical sickness [religious vs medical illness].
>
> They knew he was good (when at Gig Harbor) + called him to help [cure] them even though a slave. "Seems funny doesn't it." [Jerry mused]
>
> He worked for his master all the time, even if he was a doctor.
>
> Sometimes slave goes out by himself to hunt. But usually went with master to help fetch things + go in canoe to[o].
>
> k^{w}itsa'qs was original master of the slave man and captured him. But he sold him <B53> or rather gambled [him] away + then got him back. Then sold him to Hudson's Bay man [Tolmie].
>
> k^{w}itsa'qs family was very nice + treated the slave like one of their own family. He received little gifts from people he cured before he was sold to Hud[son] Bay man + freed, then became rich through his curing. He was about 50 [15?] when sold to H.B. man. He broke + rode horses, farmed for Hudson's Bay company (Had big farms where H.B. Co raised wheat, barley, oats, peas. <B51-53>

---

243 Cecelia Svinth Carpenter, Fort Nisqually 1986; William Fraser Tolmie, *The Journals of William Fraser Tolmie: Physician and Fur Trader* 1963.

244 Marian Smith, *The Puyallup-Nisqually* 1940: 52, Dr Simon is indeed an example of someone gambled away, repeatedly.

Throughout Puget Sound, as noted, a chief was expected to have two or more slaves to meet obligations of prestige, abundance, hospitality, and generosity. During the mid-1800s, Simon belonged to the woman leader at Minter. Of note, though, she cooked all meals. Thus, while some of the food was provided by Simon and the slave woman from Lummi, its final preparation and cooking was done by this high class woman. Slavery carried with it a moral taint that could spread by contact and proximity.[245]

Once Simon was free and working at the fort, his own shop purchases are on record. While bulk commodities of tea, flour, and sugar are not exceptional, a padlock, brogans, lady's shoes, mirror, and fine clothes suggest Simon was a dandy. This is in keeping with his confident and prosperous role as successful shaman or Indian doctor. Chiefs and others were expected to be inconspicuous because their own social prominence put them in danger from sorcery or malevolent magic motivated by envy, jealousy, revenge, or resentment.[246] As powerful individuals, shamans attracted attention both by bravado to assert their own abilities and to advertise for patients.[247] In the native view, Simon's own knowledge of plant medicines also contributed to his ability to handle herbivorous livestock as a teamster.

Moreover, as a former slave, Simon should not have an official spouse, yet he did, named Lucy. No children are specifically mentioned,[248] though the purchase of boy's shoes suggests the couple was raising at least one youngster. Again, fostering was an expected practice among prosperous families, where a career was passed on by a life-long apprenticeship.

In 1871, the Bureau of Indian Affairs Superintendent for Washington Territory officially banned "Indian doctoring," firming up government control after the Civil War and the final departure of the Hudson Bay Company. Since they continue to heal in local native communities, these curers had to become more careful and less public. Since there was a local agent stationed at Puyallup, Dr Simon and the others must have been especially circumspect.[249]

During the hearings into the allotment and sale of Puyallup lands, Dr Simon Hogalcut is identified as a Snohomish and former slave. Moreover, he was implicated as an ally of Judge James Wickersham[250] in the testimony of Thomas Dean, who was attacked by both Jim and Jerry

---

[245] This moral concern with food is most telling in terms of Untouchables in India, where vegetarianism remains a mark of high caste and public cooking is carefully regulated by Brahmans themselves to prevent contact with meat eaters.

[246] Brad Asher, A Shaman-killing Case on Puget Sound 1873-1874 1994/95: 17-24; William Elmendorf, Skokomish Sorcery, Ethics, and Society 1970: Chapter VI, 147-182; Jay Miller and Vi Hilbert, Caring for Control: A Pivot of Salishan Language and Culture 1993: 237-239.

[247] Jay Miller, *Shamanic Odyssey* 1988, Native Healing in Puget Sound 1992: 1-15.

[248] Periodic checking of census records eventually showed a 30 year old daughter, Annie, in 1891, when Simon was listed as 60 years old and Lucy as 65.

[249] Erna Gunther, The Shaker Religion of the Northwest: 37-76; Marian Smith, *Indians of the Urban Northwest,*1949: 41; Edwin Chalcraft. *Assimilation's Agent* 2004: 27-49.

[250] James Wickersham, Pueblos on the Northwest Coast 1896: 21-24; Nisqually Mythology, Studies of the Washington Indians 1898: 345-51; Notes on the Indians of Washington 1899: 269-375.

Meeker.[251] Simon's sister was listed as Somanalish, his wife as Lucy, and her brother as John Quol-ol-i-eish.[252] Since a slave has *no* "family," this sister may well have been the fellow slave at Minter taken from Lummi, though Jerry's notes explicitly say she relocated to Nisqually.[253]

Simon was never a typical slave, as described in the available literature, since his work involved little drudgery and much excitement.[254] Relying on a natal noble rank, he earned a successful and profitable power that allowed him to work hard and dress well. Glimpsing into the life and exceptional career of an industrious slave in Puget Sound vastly expands our understanding of the complexities of native society and notes a "redeeming" virtue of the fur trade based at Fort Nisqually. Moreover, confirmations of these people and events in other documents prove the worth of the Meeker notebooks.

---

251 James Wickersham writing as A Boston Tillicum, A Plea for the Puyallups 1892: 9, 16, 21, 31.

252 Puyallup Land Commission Report 1903: 13.

253 Certainly, the unambiguous M and N sounds in her name are distinctive of Straits Salish branch, which includes Lummi and Klallam but not the Lushootseed branch.

254 At Suquamish, freed slave John Kettle became prosperous selling shellfish to the Seattle market, transforming former drudgery into personal profit, See Jay Miller, Suquamish Traditions 1999a: 130.

9 JERRY'S KIN

Following the brief biography of Dr Simon, Jerry filled the last notebook with an account of the first half of his own life. To understand what is and is not in these notebooks, as well as the mysteries of where they have, can, and do lead, we now focus on the career of Jerry Meeker (1862-1955),[255] reviewing some details already considered but now providing a better and fuller context for them. Notebook C provides the start of his version, but his regional fame and controversy came later as he dedicated his life to turning the ill fate of his parents into good fortunes of his own – dealing profitably in contested lands.

Steilacoom was an early seat of American activity.[256] Its settlement in 1850 attracted many people, including native Skykomish brothers Jim and William (Bill).[257] There, Jim met and married a widowed Sally, and their family took the name of Meeker because he became the "favorite Indian" of his employer Ezra Meeker, the "Hop King." When visiting Steilacoom to shop and to sell their timothy seed as a cash crop, the family slept in their canoe, forbidden by town laws from using the beach.

Both of his parents had relocated. With the end of the Oregon 1818 joint-use treaty between the US and Britain in 1846, his mother Sally relocated from Minter to the Puyallup Valley. Her first marriage was to Ce-col-quin, son of the leading family at Steilacoom (tctilxum > tštilx̣um, Chambers Creek),[258] but that husband died after they had one son, John (aka Steilacoom John).[259] Her father-in-law gained community goodwill by actively redeeming any

---

255 Jerry's tombstone in the Puyallup cemetery has him born 6 April 1862 and die 4 April 1955, two days before he would have become 93.

256 Joan Curtis, Alice Watson, Bette Bradley, eds, *Town on the Sound*, Stories of Steilacoom 1988: 7, 18, 85, 165.

257 Steilacoom was first homesteaded by three men of the British crew of the *Albion* after she was seized at New Dungeness (Port Townsend) for (a trumped-up US) revenue violation. Lafayette Balch sailed from Portland, Maine, with a pre-fabricated house, intending to reassemble it at Olympia, then called Smithfield ~ Smithter. Fearing competition, Edmond Sylvester and Michael Simmons so inflated land prices that Balch was forced north to found Port Steilacoom, as George Gibbs, dedicated ethnographer and local homesteader, taught everyone to spell it. Soon J. B. Chapman, who had failed at towns on Gray's Harbor and on the Chehalis River, founded the rival Steilacoom City. Today, Union Avenue to the local ferry terminals marks what was the boundary between these former towns, forced to unite by the first state legislature.

258 Michael Avery, Martha Gray, and Linda Perez, Chambers Bay, A Historical Perspective 1983; Michael Avery, Fred Crisson, and Todd Tucker, Archaeological Investigations of Chambers Bay 45PI50 1984.

259 Puyallup Land Commission Report (p20) refers to him as John Meeker, with wife Elizabeth and daughter Margaret, though Joseph and Annie were born later. Annie seems to be the name of both a daughter and a wife. John's mother Sally and his own wife Liz ~ Annie had a bitter falling out 6 February 1883 (Puyallup Agency, Police Case Records and Accounts, 1880-1886, Edwin Eells, Box 3, Folder 10B, #11 WSHS). The 1905

of his villagers enslaved at Lummi and Tulalip <B50>. Although their labor remained vital to the development of this early US town, named for the resident (now federally unrecognized) tribe, native homes and camps were banished from the beach front. Town leaders, though, acknowledging his local importance, built a floathouse for John and his wife Annie so they could cast off and quickly move out of harm's way.

Over time, Jim and Sally had 4 children, though twins Joseph and Fred, and a daughter died young.[260] Only John and Jerry, half-brothers by Anglo kinship, lived to become adults and marry. Jerry's link to Minter was through his mother Sally,[261] whose family provided Jerry's own Indian or "real" name of *ləhaldx*, inherited from his mother's brother William, through his mother's grandfather (a first cousin of the famous Nisqually war leader Leschi). That grandfather's father was probably Klickitat,[262] a division of Sahaptin-speaking Yakamas living along a Columbia River tributary east of the Cascade Mountains. Acquiring horses and needing pasture, some Yakamas moved and married to the west across the mountains into the upper Cowlitz, becoming known as the Taitnapam. They also became slavers, trading captured children for horses at markets along the Columbia River.[263] Minter suffered from their raiding, though intermarriages later provided a kind of diplomatic truce.

As a boy, this grandfather married at a public "Wedding" dance at Nisqually (in the village of skʷaliaybš)[264] when he deliberately placed his hand on a girl's shoulder and she let it remain there. These dances were a local aspect of the Prophet Dance sweeping the Northwest in the early 1800s.[265] Apparently, one maternal grandfather (ləhaldxʷ) was Nisqually and the other (unnamed) was Puyallup, based at Minter.

---

stereograph image #527 by J. A. Blosser of Snohomish (Seattle Historical Society #19,058 at MOHI) depicts both Steilacoom John and Annie seated on the porch of their floating house and names his father Ce-col-quin as a signer of the 1854 Treaty of Medicine Creek. The suffix *–qn ~ –qd* appropriately is the lexical for "head" and often ends chiefly names.

260 Puyallup Land Commission Report (p8) refers to these boys as Jake and Wash, who died as minors.

261 Jim Meeker and four young men helped Ezra make the first survey plat of Tacoma (Ezra Meeker, *Busy Life of Eighty-Five Years* 1916: 221).

262 Klickitat derives from their name in Chinookan, their own ethnonym translates as Bluejay (Stellar's Jay) People.

263 According to George Gibbs (1855: 189), "Dr [William] Tolmie informs me that the course of the slave trade has always been from south to north; the only exception in his knowledge being that the Kowlitz Indians, formerly a very strong tribe, used to make forays on the Sound and carry their prisoners [north to south] to the Columbia river.

264 Marian Smith, *Puyallup-Nisqually* 1940: 12 #20, says this is not the name for the main village at the mouth of the Nisqually River, as expected, but for an upland group and thus closer to Sahaptins.

265 Wayne Suttles, Plateau Prophet Dance among the Coast Salish, *Coast Salish Essays* 1987: 152-198. Such public touching (PDA) violated traditional modesty and, soon, Klallams, probably enforcing "academy" elites, stopped the spread of this dance because it mixed classes and ranks promiscuously.

Jerry's mother Sally was named də'at.[266] She was Puyallup and first cousin to tšiałitsa, the Minter "chieftess" Damasq, whose grandson (DS) was John Hawk at Skokomish on Hood Canal.[267] Later in these notes, Jerry intimated his mother[268] Sally kept track of her menstrual cycle {"period"}, each full moon, by tying a new string on her finger <A57>. On one occasion, as noted (Chapter 6), she saw strange faces reflected on a water surface and was able to give warning before a Haida raid <A117>.[269] Pursued and defeated in Quartermaster Harbor, one of these enemies escaped overland to Arletta, where he was stoned to death. Such stories were integral to the history of Minter, and may collapse the time frame such that various events involving the same hereditary name held by a series of people became attributed to Jerry's immediate family members.

Sally had five living siblings. Her brothers were William (holder of the Nisqually name ləhaldxʷ), who married a Puyallup woman called tʷadabšab; Charlie (wilq̓); and another brother named tšu'kbid living with the Nisqually. Her sisters were *tsəłtsi* (*tsəltsi*), who married Gig Harbor Joe, and Mary [Cf L2 on the house diagram], who married a man named Sloane and had a son named George, whose wife tsa'elab was related to Joe Moses of Renton. George Sloane's children were Charlie at Fife, just north of Tacoma, and Mary.

Jerry's father James (Jim) was named skayłk̓ (skay'ək̓) and came from the Skykomish River, in the Wallace-Gold Bar (sqəx̣ʷbš) area. Jim's brother, William (wa'šux̣, Bill Washux), married three times.[270] The first wife (xʷəlxʷilt̓ən) was a Nisqually, and the second (Minnie) was a Stillaguamish. The third (Mattie) was the Puyallup daughter of Chehalis Bill,[271] but their four children (three boys, one girl) all died young. Their home was located above Cushman Hospital on Puyallup lands in Tacoma.

Jim's sister was key'solaytsə, who married John st'so'os, a renowned Skykomish fisherman, and they lived at Tulalip. He had gill nets, trolling lines, and much more equipment than most other fishers. John had earlier been married to his wife's aunt (Jerry Meeker's father's mother's sister). Sharing his success, he and two others hosted the biggest "doings" (sgʷigʷi ~ "invitational, potlatch") that people could recall. Later Jerry Meeker's daughter Maud inherited this name of key'solaytsə, but her own children treated it as a kinship term like "grandma" and lost any sense of it as a prestigious hereditary name that would have been much desired in any Lushootseed community. According to a direct notebook quote, {"These were famous names,

---

266 One obituary and the middle school now named for him have confused Jerry's mother's native name with his own native name, a true failure in intercultural understanding but consistent with the present degree of local knowledge.

267 John (Johnny) Hawk, though mislocated at Skykomish in the notes (by the scribe's mishearing?), long lived at Skokomish, where he often hosted Jerry, as well as many fieldworkers, including Ethel Aginsky, Erna Gunther, and Marian Smith.

268 This attention to menstruation briefly led me to think that the scribe was a woman.

269 As noted, versions of this story dating to much earlier times probably involved her ancestral namesakes.

270 Puyallup Land Commission Report (p130) lists Bill Meeker married to Mattie Bill, with children Peter, Willie, and Baby – all dead. Mattie later married McKinney Polsoval at Skokomish (NARA Seattle).

271 Chehalis Bill died 1 June 1898 and is buried in the Puyallup Cemetery near his daughter's home.

and one knows … the exact village the name comes from … to differentiate them from the other [commoner] people" <A43>).

The Chambers and Minter headmen attended the Treaty of Medicine Creek in December 1854, where Tyee Dick of Minter signed it as E-la-kah-ka, 24th on the list.[272] During the subsequent Treaty War, Indiens not already on south Sound reservations, such as Minters, were confined to Fox Island. At a special consultation there with Gov Stevens, Indien leaders demanded four reservations, including one at or near Minter. Nothing became of this proposed location. The Muckleshoot reservation of tip-linked diamond-shaped townships[273] came out of the Fox Island meeting, founded under the Medicine Creek Treaty on land ceded by that of Point Elliott, to keep hostiles under watchful eyes at that US Army fort. Governor Isaac Stevens also proposed wording for Executive Orders to expand the sizes of the Puyallup and Nisqually reservations, allowing for much needed horse pasture and elbow room. An agent was put in charge of each one, assisted by a white police chief, a native police captain, and four policemen.

In 1862, Ezra Meeker settled at Fern Hill, where his favorite Indiens Jim and Sally gave birth to Jerry Meeker,[274] who later decided to take as his first name that of a neighbor.[275] Minter continued to be a seasonal base for the family until the mid-1870s, when their last houses were arsoned, and they continued to fish and visit there by canoe.

> When I was 10-12-13, the big house at Minter was destroyed by whitemen who took up land around there and built their houses right where our houses used to be [1872-5, actually 1874].

Until Jerry was about 18 [1880], August was always spent camping at Minter to dry salmon, and store it in a hollow tree <C3>.[276] Nearby Glencove remained their prime fishery, [277] after native Minter was burned down[278] and its community life ended. A

[272] Charles Kaeppler, *Indian Treaties*1904: 664. This Tyee Dick was not the son of the Cowlitz high chief who became an intertribal leader and is buried in the Puyallup Cemetery.

[273] Here again, George Gibbs seems to have provided the spelling if not also the name of this fork.

[274] *Tacoma Times*, 6 April 1944, reported of Jerry, "His father was from the Skykomish lands up north on the foothills of the Cascades. His mother was born and raised at what is now known as Minter on Henderson Bay, known to the Indians as Posseholcums. 'Spell that if you can, challenged Meeker'." Later he added that the 1862 winter after he was born was so cold, snow stayed on the ground for three months. (For traditional Lushootseeds, notable or special births are believed to coincide with unusual weather.)

[275] This squatter homesteader was Jerry Stilly (Ezra Meeker, *Busy Life of Eighty-Five Years* 1916: 352).

[276] Necessarily reinforced again and again, Minter was their home and belonged to them even when they were not in residence because its foods sustained them constantly, as its stored bounty nourished them throughout the year both at home and traveling.

[277] A Glencove native house built in 1870 must have preceded the larger one built after Minter was burned out in 1874. Each of these "commuter stations" with a plank house had to be renewed or rebuilt periodically, and some native planks may have been reused to build a homesteader's smokehouse, as mention by a witness for homesteader William Gaines.

decade later in 1884, ready access to the Glencove fishery ceased with the burning of that house by a homesteading family.[279]

In keeping with expectations of constant industry by natives of high rank, both parents worked hard. Sally cleaned and washed for Ezra's hired men. Jim worked on Ezra's farm, as well as his own, renting 300 acres of Ezra's land in 1870. They took their wheat and grain to the Steilacoom Creek gristmill, one of the first American enterprises in the Sound. Run by the Chambers family, the mill and creek soon took their name.[280] The Puyallup area had its own stores by 1872, and Old Tacoma was founded in 1878.

Ezra Meeker,[281] shamelessly paternal, enjoyed his mentoring of Jim ~ Sky-uck, without "a lazy bone in his body [taking] pride in doing his work well and learning the ways of whites" while also noting his wife Old Sal "was not as intelligent as many others of her class nor as good natured" without mention of her pedigree.

In response to Jim's death notice, Ezra[282] wrote Jim "came to my house an orphan boy when a lad of some ten years, in the autumn of 1855" and was faithfully employed for twenty years, trusted as one of the family "with the key to the house" and "money to make purchases." During the Treaty War hostilities, feeling vulnerable, he left for his own safety for most of a year. He was married four times, always to Sally, first by Indian custom, second by justice of the peace, third by Presbyterians, and fourth by Catholics, for whom marriage is a binding sacrament. The couple picked the first box of hops, earning income ($1/box) by their own efforts instead of by the day, as previously. Eventually Jim had his own farm, worth $20,000 with five white laborers.

While she lived, the headwoman Damasq (tšia'łits'a) hosted traditional winter dances, contests, and rituals. These ended when she died and her "daughter married into Nisqually and never did come back."[283] The Minter headwoman probably died about 1876 and her son in 1878, when Jerry began Puyallup public school at 16 years of age.

Rev Mann

Rev Matthew G Mann (1842-1945)[284] arrived at the Puyallup Reservation in January of 1876, and was appointed superintendent from February to July, when the school closed at the

---

278 Minter Point(e) itself consists of eight feet of human midden. The final E on Pointe has been added recently as local waterfront property values sky-rocketed.

279 As a boy in 1906, Oles (1986: 50-51) helped natives seining at both Glencove and Minter.

280 Thomas Chambers helped convince the Denny Party to settle at what became Seattle when they met in Portland in 1851.

281 Ezra Meeker, The Tragedy of Leschi 1905: 21, Chapter 3, Primitive Peoples, including a subsection "Medicine Creek Treaty Caused the War."

282 Ezra Meeker, Indian Jim Was True, *The Tacoma Daily Ledger*, 30 June 1890: 3.

283 If married to John Hawk, this means the place on the delta not the tribe.

284 Mann had been born in Germany, brought to Newark, New Jersey, at the age of two, graduated New York University and the first class (1871) at Union Theological, with additional study for the ministry in Berlin, and was ordained by Presbyterians in 1873. He served in Astoria (Oregon) until, in 1876, he became superintendent of instruction at the

end of the thirty years of funding as stipulated in the treaty. During that year, Mann legally married "three-fourths of the couples on the reservation."[285]

Mann also baptized Jerry Meeker, aged 14, that same year. By then, his native family was involved in both reservation and town affairs, sometimes in prominent roles. The Jim Meeker home was near what became the Western Washington Fair Grounds in the town of Puyallup. In September 1878, Jim won the election for county surveyor because of name confusion with Ezra, but resigned because he could not read nor write.[286]

> The missionary [Matthew G. Mann][287] was important as head teacher when I went to school here. He lived to be 103 years old, and just died a short time ago.[288] He went back to Germany before I WW and couldn't get away [out]. He married a German woman, and came back after I WW <C25>.[289]

Mann undoubtedly taught Jerry Meeker the woodworking skills that later earned him income and regard in Tacoma, as well as motivating him to oppose "impertinent official interference with the rights of Indians."[290]

While the Meekers became Protestants for a time under the influence of Ezra's family, other Puyallups were Catholics, including some of Sally's close kin, such as brothers Jim Coates and General Spott.[291] At least one family at Minter, Gig Harbor Joe [B1], was married by a priest.

Catholics were served by Fr Casimir Chirouse at Tulalip, with General Spot as local catechist between visits. The church stood on the allotment of James Coates, who never legally transferred it to the congregation. At his death, the land was sold to the Tacoma Meat Co, which built a slaughter house beside the church. When the meat company failed, Jim Cross bought the land around the church, but not the slaughter house. In time, health conditions forced the deconsecration of the church, and nominal renting of the building to the slaughter house. Mass

---

Puyallup Reservation. His mission included instruction in carpentry, blacksmithing, and farming until dismissed, as explained in Appendix D.

285 Elizabeth Shackleford, History of the Puyallup Indian Reservation 1918: 46, 60.

286 *Tacoma News Tribune*, Sunday, 24 September 1878.

287 As noted, Matthew G. Mann died just before he would have turned 104. Because of the holidays, most people did not learn of his death until after the New Year.

288 This sentence is the most useful in all the notebooks for internally helping to date them to 1948, though this "just" refers to two years instead of a few months, as I first thought.

289 The time until World War I was remarkable for the close ties between natives and Germans in the Northwest and Washington State, where both Franz Boas and his premier student Herman Karl Haeberlin assembled voluminous native data.

290 *Tacoma Times*, 8 January 1937 [in TPL computer file on Mann].

291 Everything in the written record emphasizes Jerry as a staunch Presbyterian, so it was startling for me to learn from his granddaughter that her mother, Jerry's daughter, was Catholic and her father Methodist. Even though he seems to have abandoned his family, Jerry's first father-in-law was Irish and left the imprint of his religion. Jerry's father Jim, at least, was buried as a Catholic.

by Tacoma clergy was held at the school.[292] In time, Fr Peter Hylebos (27 December 1848 to 29 November 1918), combining his own family funds with donations, established St George's boarding school (1888-1936) for native students. Those buildings are gone, the last in 1971, but a large cemetery of young graves remains.[293]

Jerry had gone through traditional training under the supervision of Lashibiya to fast, thirst, pray, and quest until puberty because "my parents ... wanted me to get an Indian power. I never got one though, poor luck,[294] poor devil [me]." However, Jerry had begun his training for initiation into the Growlers, as well as questing for spirit help, which he publicly denied ever achieving. As a staunch Republican and Presbyterian, Jerry often skirted personal issues of native ritual and religion. Close rereading of these notes, however, suggests he did gain a Salmon spirit ally. Indeed, Marian Smith's mention of a vision on Clay Creek involving such an ally, wearing a pointed fur cap, black fur coat, and carrying a fish spear was probably Jerry's own.

From 1880-83 Jerry attended Forest Grove federal boarding school in Oregon (26 miles west of Portland), whose first class was entirely made up of displaced Puyallup students. His assignments included actually clearing land and building the school and dormitories – learning to build the buildings and then learning inside them, as he once phrased it. In 1883, he started an Indien musical band, and married his classmate Eliza O'Dell on Feb 3rd, 1883.

Eliza was from {Latcheh <A38>} (Lackey Bay, prior name for Witcher Bay), one of two daughters to survive from her mother's marriage to an Irish settler named O'Dell.[295] After her mother next married a man of the Suquamish, described as {"Duwamish living across from Edmonds"}, Liza was brought up working for the Henry family at South Bay near Olympia until she went to the federal school and met Jerry.[296]

Two of Jerry and Eliza's four children (two boys, two girls) lived to become adults. These were Silas (12 June 1886 – 22 March 1957) and Maud B. (1 January 1890 - ?). Silas married a widow named Arkette with three children, two sons and a daughter.[297] Maud married Stanley P. Hawthorne from Ohio, who came west for gold, and they had three children.[298]

---

[292] Elizabeth Shackleford, History of the Puyallup Indian reservation 1918: 66.

[293] The interplay of global events is acute in this history since Fr Hylebos died on Thanksgiving Day as a casualty of the great influenza epidemic, while his school was closed by forces of the great Depression.

[294] To indicate the difficulties involved in deciphering this handwriting, "poor luck" first looked like "roast duck." His claim not to have a power, moreover, protests too much, Cf Marian Smith, *The Puyallup-Nisqually* 1940: 63. Such an ally also aided the success of his Brown's Point salmon bakes, which indeed continue to this day.

[295] A land sale indenture dated 7 August 1875 of James O'Dell was kept by Edwin Eells (Box 3, Folder 10B WSHS). Eliza was either named welatšit or her mother was from Wollochet.

[296] This Forest Grove federal boarding school later relocated to become Chemawa near Salem, Oregon; See SuAnn Reddick, Chemawa Indian Boarding School 1996; Jay Miller *Lushootseed Culture* 1999: 151 #3; Edwin Chalcraft, *Assimilation's Agent* 2004: 114-125.

[297] By name, Donald, Gordon, Naomi.

[298] Jerry Meier Meeker Hawthorne, Ramona Hawthorne, Franklin Hawthorne. Only Ramona was alive in 2014 as "last of the line" and said her father Stanley came from Ohio for the

Newly married himself, Jerry farmed and hired out as a carpenter. He was proud of his involvement in the tribal politics that replaced hereditary leadership with elected officials. In late 1883, he was voted onto the new tribal council that displaced the hereditary Puyallup chiefs, insisting "No woman could be chief."[299] The new political parties were Republicans ("young turks") or Democrats ("old guard"), who called themselves the "barefoots." Each slate had five candidates, a chief and four district sub-chiefs, who also served as court judges. Jerry ran and won as a Republican.[300]

Jerry was instrumental in replacing tribal judges with a police court, side-stepping fairness and impartiality. Indeed, federal Indian policy was ironically "immune" to American ideals, such as balance of powers, civil rights, cemetery protection, and freedom of religion.[301]

During October work on road improvements, Jerry was supervisor of the lower reservation. He worked on the agency farm, 1883-6, and, in 1884, joined with others to buy their own thresher instead of renting the machine of a neighbor. The agent appointed him a tribal judge, 1884-5, and police captain, 1884-88, before he worked for the agency school. Pay was $5/month as police or judge, and $8/month for captain or head judge.[302] For alcohol-related crimes, Jerry both arrested as police and fined as court judge several familiar people, including Napoleon (28 October 1884) and "Jimmie Hom-al-good," for a first offense with a light fine ($5) because he implicated the white bootlegger.[303]

Tycoon

In 1890, Jerry and fellow Puyallup Rev Peter Stanup[304] (1857 - 1893) began working for the Northern Pacific Railroad to get a right of way signed off from other

---

1898 Alaskan Gold Rush. He is buried down the slope from Jerry at the Puyallup cemetery.

299 An erroneous statement since the default leader at Minter was indeed a kinswoman <A52> while Jerry was a child. More likely, he was referring to the head chief of the tribe, who was invariably a man who led in partnership with his senior wife, and had to meet with the approval of the federal Indian agent.

300 Abraham Lincoln took the Republican Party in national politics, becoming their martyr.

301 Indian police were intended to provide a sort of law and order, enforcing official policies to discredit and harass chiefs and traditional leaders, and replace them with new leaders duly elected by "the people." See William Hagan, *Indian Police and Judges* 1966.

302 This was the federal rate. Personal clout, spiffy uniforms, and prestige (not salary) attracted native policemen since, on the Plains, scouts earned three times as much and teamsters six times, See William Hagan, *Indian Police and Judges* 1966: 43.

303 Jerry Meeker is listed as Puyallup police captain from July 1884. He was 22, married, 162 pounds, 5 feet 10 inches tall, with uninflated chest of 38½ inches and inflated of 40½ inches. Sergeant was Joe Taylor, 28, married, three children; and Privates were John Morris, 31, married, one child, and John McLeod, 30, married, three children. Local teacher, AR Campbell, was Chief of Police. (Edwin Eells Collection, Box 3, Puyallup Agency, Police Case Records and Accounts, 1880-1886, bound page 68, Washington State Historical Society (WSHS), Tacoma).

304 See his biography and photo in Castille, *The Indians of Puget Sound* 1985: 249, 358.

Puyallup tribal members. In 1893, they went to DC to lobby for a federal allotting bill. Instead, Senator Henry Dawes's infamous Severalty Act "to pulverize tribal unity" and allot reservation lands to individual members became national policy, producing nearly 100,000 acres of "surplus" land to be sold to homesteaders.[305]

In 1894, three land commissioners arrived at Tacoma to begin dismantling the Puyallup reservation. Rev Stanup[306] had died under suspicious circumstances,[307] and Jerry became guardian of his wife (Anna) and surviving daughters (May, Grace). Later, after his first wife Eliza died, he wed Peter Stanup's widow.[308]

> That fall in 1893, Peter was killed. He was out drinking with a gang and he was taken home…. There was some foul play there somewhere. His neck was broken [next in pencil >] and they found his body in the river. <C51>

On 19 February 1901, early in his real estate dealings, Jerry supported ("spark plugged") an election to shift land from King to Pierce County beside burgeoning Tacoma. The annexation of this six- by two-mile rectangle – including Brown's Point, Dash Point, Northeast Tacoma, and "a good portion of that lovely tax-paying industrial land on the tide flats" – was decided by ten unanimous male-only votes. Six natives and four whites voted at the home of William Fife along Hylebos Creek, open between 9am and 7pm. Jerry personally hired a vessel from Foss Launch[309] to fetch several natives off their fishing boats to get them to the polls. The Seattle Chamber of Commerce later challenged the right of natives to vote, but the election held.

---

305 "Stanup, in particular, caused a sensation at the [US] capitol where the prevailing idea of an Indian was a chap who dressed in paint and feathers and went about brandishing a tomahawk and saying 'How.' It was a revelation, therefore, to hear Stanup and his associates [Jerry] talk the white man's language and to present their case in a logical manner." *Tacoma Times*, 8 January 1937.

"[Senator Henry] Dawes <C49> said, 'Do you mean that those Indians can go anywhere in the U.S. and not get lost?' Peter Stanup answered him and said, 'I've been in Chicago 3 times and always came out.' We were citizens and were capable of handling our own money."

306 Edwin Eells Autobiography (Book V: 248-51, Folder 9, Box 3, WSHS) describes an unnamed full blood married to a mixed Kanaka (Hawaiian) woman, who rose among the clergy until five of his children quickly died of measles and whooping cough and he took to drink. A check of TPL's Puyallup cemetery record shows the deaths of five Stanup children, especially in 1888. Lula lived 6 months in 1883, then February 1888 swept away Lottie (age 9) on the 3rd, a baby born and died on the 5th, Clara (age 2) on the 15th, Calvin (age 7) on the 26th.

307 Rev Mann, his mentor, conducted Peter's funeral, proclaiming, "He educated his people up to a higher manhood."

308 Puyallup Land Commission Report, 1903: page 146, patent 129 (NARA Seattle).

309 A family member of this company served as the inspiration for Tugboat Annie of films and stories.

Nearby Tacoma immediately began building a road and bridge into this area along the north edge of its own bay.[310]

The Puyallup Reservation and government legally "vanished" in 1903, except for an accounting error that later became their salvation in1936. In 1904, when the Puyallup Act ended, Jerry, George Taylor, and Frank C. Ross formed the Bethel Real Estate Company. For four years, he and Clinton A. Snowden[311] sold reservation bonds. Until 1914, Jerry actively engaged in marketing lands, negotiating his own terms, avoiding administration fees, and receiving immediate returns, unlike other Puyallups who had rarely received payments. His foresight and political connections enabled him to transform "his land into capital ... to become involved in entrepreneurial ventures."[312]

Over time Jerry helped plat the Tacoma additions of Brown's Point, Northwestern, Tacoma Valley, and Garden. A booster biography identified Jerry as a Woodman of the World, Presbyterian, Republican,[313] authority on local Puyallup history, and fluent speaker of Lushootseed.[314] In 1905, he built a cabin at Brown's Point using locally-cut timbers, and in 1906 bought a large timbered home on the bluff above that yet remains in the family. In 1913, he paid $4,500 to build the first dock there, later giving it to the county for one dollar ($1).[315]

Before and after 1912, when Jerry settled full-time at Brown's Point, he presided over festive summer bakes in the public park next-door behind the lighthouse. Jerry at first served steamed shellfish purchased from a man who rowed over from Vashon Island, standing up because the boat was filled with wet gunny sacks filled with butter clams. Ed Newcome, who lived in direct sunlight up the hill, provided the fresh corn that was served. Later, Jerry switched to salmon after the shellfish beds were destroyed, ironically, by pollution from "development."

Skykomish

Jerry maintained helpful ties with his own kin and communities, including his father's people from Skykomish, a branch of the Snohomish and Snoqualmie River system whose name

---

310 *Tacoma Sunday News Tribune and Ledger*, John McDonald, How Pierce County Took Part of King Co. [TPL file, missing 1900 date supplied by clippings]

311 Clinton Snowdon, a Puyallup Land Commissioner, authored a history of Washington State. Ross was the mother's father of Richard Daugherty, the famous Northwest archaeologist.

312 Kurt Kim Schaeffer, A Bitter Pill: Indian Reform Policy, Indian Acculturation, and the Puyallup Act of 1893, 2010: 17, 24.

313 Herbert Hunt, *Tacoma* 1916: 39, 40, 509-510.

314 Jerry Meeker listed the succession of Puyallup hereditary chiefs as Klapasha to Squstahan to Tyee Dick (Sinawah) [aka General Spot] to Joshua Sitwell (Sitwulch) to Tom Thompson (Za-qua-la-co) to Sitwell (again) to Tommy Lane (Quayupyet), the half brother of the Puyallup sharing the famous name of Kitsap. Arthur Ballard's notes, as mentioned, indicate three men named Kitsap: the famous Suquamish leader before Chief Seattle who provided the name for the Kitsap peninsula; a Yakama, who sometimes lived at Muckleshoot; and the Puyallup fishing boss.

315 *Tacoma News Tribune*, 15 April 1938.

derives from the Lushootseed word for "uprivers" (sq̓ixʷəbš).[316] He wanted them also to practice what he was preaching about progress and the Protestant ethic.

As a "Skykomish-Puyallup" aged "59 years," living "at Browns Point, Tacoma," Jerry served as interpreter for Jennie Davis Johnson in a routine Bureau of Indian Affairs (BIA) hearing to determining the heirs of Sarah Wallace (Huh-lah-lit-sah), as well as testifying himself about his father Jim's homeland.[317]

Sarah, a widow who died in 1891, had homesteaded 160 acres near the town of Startup where the Wallace River runs into the Skykomish River. Sarah's own ancestry included Wenatchee, Snoqualmi, and Duwamish, but her link to this namesake locality probably had been her husband Joe Wallace (Kwahsylsh). This is the only instance on paper where Jerry speaks in his own father's dialect, Northern Lushootseed. He was brought in to interpret because Jennie spoke the same variant of northernmost Lushootseed as his father. Since he also knew Sarah and her family over many years, this suggests visits to the region and probably kinship with the husband Joe.

When Sarah was allotted in 1890 under the 1884 Indian Homestead Act, the land went into trust for 25 years under BIA supervision. Soon after, and all too typically, Sarah, a daughter, and a grandson died. Jennie became sole heir, along with two minor grandchildren, Mary Anne Shelton and George Sneatlum. These are the names of prominent families, indicating that the Wallaces were themselves of high rank.

Jerry became involved because the BIA filed suit on behalf of these minors against the estate administrator, Edward Mills, and the Dickey Woods Lumber Company of Everett. Mills, of note, was a Republican state committee man who blithely went through the probate court, ignoring the BIA trust, to sell off the homestead's timber. The BIA asked for triple damages (over $6000) when the case went to court in 1923, but the court's final decision has not yet been located.

Jerry long continued to give Winter weather predictions in the local papers. Many reported his own passing on their front pages, when, on 4 April 1955, just before his 93rd birthday, Jerry died at home on Brown's Point, on ancient Puyallup tribal lands that he had helped to put into private hands.

> Meeker, knowing he couldn't beat 'em, joined 'em. He went into selling real estate. Many a white man was startled to be met by an Indian selling him a choice

---

316 Skykomish were to move to the Tulalip Reservation near the mouth of the Snohomish River, but many scattered, like Jim and his brother. Explanations are vague, but a key feature was hostility toward a famous slaver (Hebał) with many sons raiding from this upriver location. The Twana called xebał a "low class bully," See William Elmendorf, *Twana Narratives* 1993: 92, 305. Skokomish shamans tried to kill him by "poisoning" his land, but instead killed many Skykomish while he escaped alive. This is a uniquely native view of the epidemics depopulating this region: a fatal by-blow from shamanic good intentions.

317 Jerry Meeker, 3 August 1921, Sarah Wallace Heirship Hearing, Tulalip, BIA Realty Records. Family copies.

waterfront lot. Meeker, who adopted the white man's ideas fast, was trading lots for money, not beads or trinkets.[318]

A few months later, the Brown's Point Improvement Building was dedicated above the beach beside his home. He had worked hard to get it built, and he was eulogized at its opening, and continues to be at today's Salmon Bakes. Yet the point itself remains contested territory, with occasional flare-ups between the light house historical society, the Improvement Club, and the chain-fenced Meeker property.

Over his long life, Jerry moved from a life *on* the land, based at (and fed from) Minter, to a life *from* the land, alienating it from his own people for sale to in-coming settlers from far and near. Eventually knowing what had happened not once but twice to his own family and native community leads to an appreciation of his real estate dealings. As acts of defiance, if not an outright effort to fight back against the grasping forces of Anglo history, Jerry, as a real estate promoter, could schedule land sales to his own advantage, without having to flee suddenly from malicious flames.

Continuous generosity and hospitality earned the respect of his (native and white) neighbors, while charity to kin and others benefited the Puyallup during his lifetime. He was a complex and involved person, whose voice provided the means to restore native Minter to its former significance.

His tombstone reads:

OUR DAD

JERRY MEEKER

BELOVED BY ALL

Apr 6 Apr 4

1862 1955

[318] *Seattle Post Intelligencer*, 1 June 1952, Brown's Point Gets Forecast.

10 JERRY AS EXPERT

Jerry willingly shared his knowledge with many casual visitors, as well as newspapers and academics. Some of his most detailed information was offered from the witness stand during land claims and other trials. Judges and lawyers are not ethnographers, however, and Jerry's testimony was sometimes cut short before he could finish a full account, especially of plant usages.

Thelma Adamson (1901 - 1983)

Thelma Adamson[319] worked with Jerry at Skokomish in 1926, probably at the Hawk homestead, writing down Puyallup tales called The Contests, The Spirit of Wealth, Star Husband, and Moon and Sun. A special feature of his recitations is a series of five sisters, using the pattern number (5) that is a characteristic of Whulshootseed culture in the south, in contrast to four (4) in the north.

Jerry told Thelma about a wealthy community distressed over two "lazy" boys, who secretly quested to gain the spirit named *Tuołbəx̱*, who provided *yabedib* "Riches" power. Jerry specified these events "took place long before the flood, when Indians were almost animals – before the Transformer came."

For the epic which established the chiefly lines of Puget Sound and their dicta, Jerry's strangely divided Star Husband from Star Child as though they were two different unconnected stories instead of those of father and son. Each featured five sisters, with the middle one the mother of the twins fathered by Stars. Toad is their blind grandmother.

According to his version of the story, in honor of Moon's birth, festive contests were held at swimming, foot racing, spearing, archery, and, especially, swinging. Toad was babysitter while the sisters attended the big swing contest on the fifth day. In the excitement, Moon was kidnapped by five sisters who lived in the underworld. Grieving, the oldest of the sister-mothers took Moon's diaper to wash out and, in the wringing of it, produced a brother twin: "cross-eyed Sun." Meanwhile the athletes went after the stolen child, but none could get beyond the clashing blade that blocked the route until Bluejay rushed under it, though it bent his top tassel. Bluejay searched for years in the underworld, asking at four far-removed houses until he found Moon making hard baskets with an awl in the fifth house. Irritated, Moon dashed water into Bluejay's eyes, discoloring them to this day. Sorry, Moon listened and decided to follow Bluejay back to the upper world. Traveling separately to avoid witchery by the underworld people, Moon advised Bluejay to pass under the left side of the cleaver, since it was much slower. But Bluejay did not return the favor by telling of the dangers along the return route.

Powerful, sharp-eyed Moon began to change things on his way back. He provided a stone maul to a man who was using his own head as a hammer to make cedar planks. He

---

319 Thelma Adamson, *Folktales of the Coast Salish* 1934: 351-361 [reprinted 2009]. The delay in publication had to do with Adamson's admission to an asylum for the rest of her life. See William Seaburg, Whatever Became of Thelma Adamson? 1999.

instituted wooden tripods on fish weirs in lieu of three-men acting as a derrick to hold up the weir walkway. He strengthened Heron's legs to make a bridge across a river. Lastly, when five children with potbellies sang an alluring song that caused a roaring prairie fire, Moon asked various trees and rocks to save him until Trail protected him from the flames.

When he got home, people gathered in council to remake the world. They asked Moon to light the day, but he was much too hot, so Sun shines during the day and Moon at night. Toad went to live with Moon.

Taken all together, Jerry sequenced his tales in such a way that they convey a sense of redemption. Bluejay first appears amidst hilarious and unnatural incongruities. By the last story, however, Bluejay does best what is now a species characteristic, and scoots through a door (though his topknot, a tassel made from the pubic hair of his own grandmother Mouse, is clipped) to rescue Starchild, the founder of chiefly lines in Puget Sound. Thereafter bluejays (as birds) become a swift and colorful species. Considered in their published order, these stories are a brilliant interweaving of actors and events still significant throughout the region, but given a particularly Minter twist since the last ordeal explains how to survive a destructive fire. Jerry never provided full stories after 1926 <C1>. During later fieldwork, Marian Smith reviewed this work by Thelma Adamson with Jerry (below).

Land Claims I, 1920s

On March 25, 1927, Jerry, identified as a 65-year-old farmer living at Brown's Point, was deposed on the Puyallup Reservation for their first tribal land claims case.[320] He was asked about Puyallup "historians," whom he called "professors" and listed Tyee Dick,[321] Linnanur, Washington Stykes, and Chief Sitwell. He insisted Leschi fought in the Treaty War because the size and location of the original tiny Puyallup and Nisqually Reservations did not provide enough horse pasture. Natives took good care of their lands, he insisted, renewing them by setting fires in March to nourish timber and berries with fresh ashes.[322]

He listed six buildings at Minter, including the "training house to train their young ones, and also there was a sort of secret fraternity among the Indians, and they used to train their young people into this secret fraternity" … what you would call, in English, professors, the ones that trained the children."[323] Trainers mentioned in the notebooks were the father of Tyee George and Gizmo, followed by Lashibiya.

He also pleaded for unpaid claims concerning the Northern Pacific right-of-way through the Puyallup reservation. His own knowledge of real estate was queried to evaluate reservation soils and tidelands. His linguistic skills were tested by a discussion of the limitations of the local trade jargon (Chinuk Wawa) to express legal and treaty complexities, stating his preference for

---

320 Jerry also testified for the Indian Land Claims Commission on 13 June 1952 in Seattle (below). See others' testimony on burned villages in the Finale.

321 Tyee Dick (Richard Scanewa 1814-1904), the oldest son of Cowlitz chief Scanewa, married a Nisqually and is buried at Puyallup. He long served as an intertribal leader. Presumably his was a diplomatic marriage to offset early Cowlitz slave raids.

322 Duwamish and Others1933: 630.

323 Duwamish and Others 1933: 628, 629.

the Wawa dictionary by the brothers Edwin and Myron Eells.[324] Later that same day, Jerry was recalled to clarify the limitations of jargon in terms of Article 6 of the Treaty of Medicine Creek, stipulating the President's right to relocate or allot a reservation.[325]

Cross-examination added the names of Wa-sach-alt, Quatsuk, John, Quick-shot, Jackson, and Spaim [Speym] as Minter historians. In describing their movements to and from the reservation, he noted that when his parents and family once went to Puyallup, they lived in the four-family home, forty by forty feet square, of Mrs. Dean's father, near the agency.

Jerry's home was so well known that it served as a landmark used by prolific local ethnographer Arthur Ballard in concluding a story, told by Burnt Charlie, a Puyallup, of how a legendary Changer-Transformer named Xode dealt with a foul-mouthed woman at Brown's Point, turning her into a stone with an open mouth that had power to bring rain.[326]

Merriam Report

A sea change attempting to improve US federal policy toward Indians began with the extensive research and report prepared by Lewis Merriam and his team.[327] In preparation, they toured the country gathering information and perspective. Chronicling these survey efforts, Merriam wrote a series of letters back to DC that includes high praise for Jerry.[328]

> We were very fortunate at Tacoma because Jerry Meeker, one of the leaders of the Puyallup Indians, called on us at the hotel on Sunday morning. Although he

---

[324] Duwamish and Others 1933: 636. Misnamed Byron in this record, but consistent with the Lushootseed M = B shift, confusing to English speakers.

[325] Charles Wilbur, a wealthy Swinomish farmer, and Peter James, Duwamish chief forced to Lummi, were asked (Duwamish and Others 1933: 689, 713) to back translate or comment on Jerry's efforts from jargon into English by both lawyers, Arthur E Griffin for Claimant and George T Stormont for Defendant, who insisted it could be done. The most telling exchange, however, is between Griffin and Jerry (Duwamish and Others 1933: 681) "You would not guarantee that the Indians would understand it, would you, Mr Meeker." "Oh, No, No."

[326] Arthur Ballard, Mythology of Southern Puget Sound 1929: 82. UW anthropologist TT Waterman later met Charlie at Wollochet Bay. This rock was probably obliterated during the construction of the Brown's Point Improvement Club on the beach next to Jerry's home. Rain was caused by rattling a stick inside the mouth opening in this rock.

[327] Lewis Merriam, *The Problem of Indian Administration*, Baltimore: Johns Hopkins 1928.

[328] Donald L Parman and Lewis Meriam, Meriam's Letters during the Survey of Indian Affairs 1926-1927 (Part I), *Arizona and the West*, 24 (3, Autumn) 1982: 253-280, 265. Emma Duke "was at Tacoma making a study of the conditions surrounding the Puyallup Indians who have been largely absorbed into the surrounding white civilization."

Their Footnote 33 mentions "Jerry (or Jere) Meeker was an industrial teacher at the Puyallup Boarding School from December 1, 1887, to November 21, 1889, at which time he was about twenty-nine years old." *Biographical and Historical Index of American Indians and Persons Involved in Indian Affairs* (8 vols, Boston: GK Hall, 1966) V: 437; Marian W Smith, *The Puyallup-Nisqually* 1940: xi-xii.

> has had very little formal education, he is a man of very great native intelligence and ability. He spent several hours with us and then stayed to dinner with us at the hotel. I wish you might have seen him. He is a man of about sixty seven years of age, who has made his living as a carpenter and a farmer. He possesses to a marked degree that dignity which we have learned to recognize as characteristic of the better Indians. His vocabulary is a marvel to me, as he uses his words with exceptional precision. He combines with it a delightful sense of humor. He placed himself entirely at our disposal and on Monday last he gave the day to going about with Miss Mark and Miss Duke to visit the homes of different Indians of his tribe. My hours with him were among the most delightful that I have had on this trip. I suppose one reason that I enjoyed Jerry Meeker so much, was the fact that we had just come from Yakima, where the relationship between the whites and the Indians is very strained.

Jerry's willingness to help these researchers speaks volumes about his ready grasp of national and local politics, as well as his boosterism and people skills. That he devoted a Sunday (away from church) and Monday to committee members demonstrates his commitment to improving federal programs, though his own experience with them was decidedly mixed.

Marian Smith (1907 - 1961)

During her Puyallup-Nisqually salvaging fieldwork from October 1935 to May 1936, Marian Smith[329] relied heavily on "Jerry Meeker, Carr Inlet, village 15 sxotlbabc" (Shotlemamish; Shohtlbabsh), closely allied with 16 q'lba'ab't^{u} Glencove, and 17 t^{u}lelaq'le at the head of Burley Lagoon. Smith, a New Yorker sent out from Columbia by Franz Boas, had had polio and walked with arm braces, which quickly gained her sympathy among the elders. Smith[330] was privileged to share the first intensive and systematic work done with Jerry Meeker.

---

329 Marian Smith, *The Puyallup-Nisqually* 1940: xii, 12. Her Plate I after page 112 includes three self-posed portraits of primary Puyallup informants for River, Salt Water, and Prairie. Jerry Meeker (Salt Water but not named) stands behind his house overlooking the Brown's Point Lighthouse. In 1920, Thomas Waterman, who worked closely with Arthur Ballard, assembled a manuscript of Puget Sound place names that has been cited for information not available anywhere else. Ballard seems to have introduced Smith to Jerry, though, as many others have noted, Jerry was a local celebrity often quoted in local newspapers who made himself readily available to the public.

330 In these days before Xerox machines, Smith composed her publications by cutting up her fieldnotes and pasting entries onto color-coded paper. Since only two microfilms of the Smith collection have been allowed in North America (at Ottawa and Victoria, Canada), the colored background sheets are not obvious. A code indicates that the green sheets have Jerry's versions pasted on them. The manuscript for her 1940 Puyallup Nisqually ethnography has not survived, but other notes from that time, particularly a collection of myth texts, appears among her papers in London. She was particularly interested in house types, asking questions about design and layout over her entire career. By doing so, she got the first and best descriptions of the layout of Minter itself.

Marian had a copy of Thelma Adamson's 1934 folklore collection from Chehalis and asked Jerry about some of its material, including the five stories he provided. Because Jerry told texts to Marian but never again, I presume he did so from loyalty to her, in the expectation that she would publish his versions. Marian's surviving notes indicate that allusions to these mythic epics were ever present in their collaboration.

On the subject of mythology, Jerry said he learned many stories and much else when he stayed in the Stanup home, where the parents woke up about 2-3am to talk about family history and legends until it was time to get up.[331] Their son Peter never got them to reform, even after he was ordained. Indeed, it was just such conversations in bed by married couples that bridged the daily division of labor between the genders distanced apart by separate workloads.

Thelma herself was still well enough to be consulted by Marian, and she did the abstracts of the Puyallup texts included in these Smith files. A handwritten preface, presumably to Thelma's own lost thesis on Coast Salishan Transformers and Tricksters, begins by citing Jerry's Sun and Moon (Starchild) as the "offspring of the third of five sisters" in her own published collection. Marian reviewed the many Chehalis texts by Marion Davis with Jerry, who found them familiar, but he did not recognize some of the other Upper Chehalis stories.

Jerry provided comments on other versions of the Starchild epic. He insisted the Moon story is *tiotlbax* "rare" [*tiyułebax̱ed* = rich, treasured] because it involves the all-important "hex'' [dicta] that comes from the Stars. He thought that the stories about witch [basket ogress] and pheasant [other worldly] were not intended to change the weather, as was the result of telling other epics such as North Wind and Beaver. He also provided brief recollections of mythic incidents he had heard from others, such as the Dog Husband epic as a founding charter for a subgroup of Skagits.

He used the word $dsak^u$ [d^zak^w] to refer to the time when the world "capsized" due to the efforts of the Changer(s) to prepare for the arrival of humans, but noted that a place known as t^usabaq'ab in the Bay would not change. This is clearly Devil's Head at the end of the Key Peninsula and, indeed seemingly willful, the epicenter of the 2002 Ash Wednesday earthquake.[332]

He recalled encounters by family members with the Little Earths, the immortals who are believed by natives to own fresh springs and to guide shamans when these doctors went to the

---

Marian Wesley Smith, Microfilm Roll 3 (Reel A1738), British Columbia Archives, MSS 2689: Box 6, Folder 9 (Houses 26); Royal Anthropological Archives MSS 2794, Houses p26.

331 Jonas Stanup, from a chiefly family, was well connected to leading Tacoma families through their back doors: "And the Indian Stanup, purveyor to the first families, could have been seen almost any morning coming and going among the stumps, with his basket of vegetables and shellfish [lamenting that once] you could see a house here and there among the trees, now you can only see a tree here and there among the houses," Robert Walkinshaw, *On Puget Sound* 1929: 85, 88.

332 The explanation for this resistance is implied in typed pages that Arthur Ballard provided to Marian (MS 268: 8: 4, Reel 4) listing "TcAkwAp – Dirty buttocks, a point between Tacoma and Olympia. The whites call it Devil's Head." Its power, therefore, was alimentary and undeniable since the 2002 tremor.

land of the dead (the "deadline") to recover lost vitalities. They mostly live in swamps, but never in open ground. Jerry's mother once heard them when camping near South Tacoma just as she was dozing off.

Because her early fieldwork was in the south Sound, Marian was also keenly interested in the Indian Shaker Church. She collected accounts of its founding by John and Mary Slocum, as well as his life/death experience and return. In one of these reports, Joe Young says he himself reformed and was brought into the church by John Hawk at Skokomish. Before his vision, John Slocum asked General Spot (sXodAbqAd) to teach him how to pray like Catholics, but he could not master the required Latin.[333] He next asked for instruction from John Swan and the Presbyterians, with encouragement by Rev Mann.[334]

In her remarkable published study, Marian Smith produced a map and appendix of allotments that numbers and lists familiar names.[335] Recognizing divisions based on Puyallup terrain (I saltwater, II river, III prairie, IV inland), the first column specifies homeland, the second the affiliation of the spouse, and the third the predominant band, while the "X" signals a non-Puyallup (such as ex-slave Dr Simon, a Snohomish). People figuring in events at Minter are extracted below, glimpsing their meager paper trails.

		home	spouse	band	
32	Simon Hogalcut	X	I	I	
33	Jimmy Homotgood	I	X	I	
34	John Hote	I	X	I	
79	Bill Meeker	X	?	I	
80	James Meeker X	I	I		
81	Jerry Meeker	I	?	I	
82	John Meeker	I	II	I	
122	Mary Sloan	I	X	I	
136	Jonas Stanup	II	II	II	
137	Peter Stanup	II	*	II	* = blank
139	John Swan	I	II	II	

Dr Simon's property was almost an island at the mouth of Wapato Creek, while the Meeker allotments were in a bend further up that same creek. Mary Sloan [Sloane], a cousin, had lands both directly across from Jerry and near the mouth of Hylebos Creek. The Stanups

333 Confirming these notebooks, General Spott was buried from the home of Jim Coats, his full brother, at 12:30pm on Monday 21-1-03, Edwin Meany File, 86-14, Special Collections, UW. TPL Puyallup Cemetery list #338 is Marcellus (General) Spot, 15 Feb 1903 (65 years).

334 Joe Young to Arthur Ballard, MS 268: 8: 4, Reel 4, 12 April 1928: 9.

335 Marian Smith, *The Puyallup-Nisqually* 1940: 46, 327-330.

were directly north and south of the City of Tacoma, while John Swan, who led the attack on the Haidas when living at Gig Harbor, held the land directly to the east of the city on a creek that entered a sharp bend of the Puyallup River.

Family

Fieldwork sessions with Marian are still vividly recalled by Jerry's last direct relative, his granddaughter Ramona.[336] After Jerry's last wife (recalled as Lilly Arkett not Annie Stanup) died, his daughter Maud and family moved into the Brown's Point house that Judge Freemont Campbell had built in 1904. Jerry bought it in 1906 and then added two cabins below on the beach. During the summer, many Puyallups came to visit and Jerry started the goodwill clambakes, buying butter clams dug from Vashon Island (by Lucy Gurand ?) until these beds were destroyed, and he thereafter served salmon.

Marian Smith came everyday and worked with Jerry at the kitchen table. He always cooked lunch for her, except one day when she made lunch. Maud's children were in high school and had strict instructions to leave them alone and to keep very quiet. When her book was published, she sent a nicely inscribed copy to Jerry, who had provided consistent pronunciations for all the southern Lushootseed words used in it.

The Meekers enjoyed a reputation for generosity and kindness. Julia Hovick, a blind woman, came to live with them.[337] She made rugs from strips of gunny sacks after she tore them apart and Maud sorted them as light and dark for her to braid together.[338] The family observed many religions. As noted, Jerry was Presbyterian, his daughter was Catholic, and her husband was Methodist.

According to his family, Jerry did so well (for a "full blood Indien") that an unkind rumor said his father had been a cavalry officer, presumably at Steilacoom. As a final word, Ramona said, "Jerry was a person who was striking, dramatic, and intelligent. He was a good public speaker and he remembered everything."

A flurry of local newspaper stories for July 1946 indicate that, with the end of WW II, Jerry resumed cooking salmon at Brown's Point on 3 and 4 August, with special events from noon to midnight and meals served 1-3 and 5-7PM. Yakama dancers performed three times after 2:30, with camera photography allowed.[339]

In the early summer of 1948, on their honeymoon, John and Marcia Winterhouse, as noted, conducted an archaeological survey by land and water of southern Puget Sound in which

---

[336] Maud's dates are 1 January 1889 to 5 May 1973. Ramona was born 25 November 1921.

[337] The TPL Puyallup Cemetery list includes #245 Julia Hovick, without dates.

[338] They also had a large collection of baskets and artifacts that Ramona inherited along with the houses. But these were stolen by someone who knew her schedule – shades of the Minter torching. Those few hidden away were placed in storage, but the company moved and claimed to have lost them. Yet later events show that some artifacts had been in the keeping of a fellow church member ~ guardian, who tried to sell them until they were confiscated by tribal police; See R Roberts, Auction Artifacts Believed Stolen, *The News Tribune* 07/17/09.

[339] Puyallup Newspaper Clipping file, WSHS.

the deepest and most extensive site was located at the native town of Minter. John came with a gift bottle to ease the interview, and, in the privacy of the upstairs, Marcia took notes from Jerry on the back of the envelope that held their new marriage license.

From August to September of 1948, Jerry provided the material recorded in these three notebooks. My dating first relied on the internal reference <C25> to the death of Rev Matthew G Mann. Much later, the discovery of dated letters between Alfred Smith and Arthur Ballard in Robert Hitchman files clinched the date. That Smith was intent on stories for his novel is indicated by the off-hand remark,[340] "Stories told by my mother, I don't remember, except that when soldiers were stationed at Steilacoom during the [Civil] War, I was 4-5" <C 1>. As further corroboration of Jerry's willingness to share the information in these notes, "about 10 years ago … he wrote his own obituary."[341]

During August or September of 1950, Willard Rhodes of the Library of Congress recorded at Skokomish both Jerry Meeker and John Hawk singing a disk gambling song in Puyallup, along with Hawk's love, bone game, potlatch, doctoring, and Shaker songs.

On 17 August 1951 at Brown's Point, Jerry recorded two songs and two stories for Drs. Marian Smith, Melville Jacobs, and George Herzog, famous scholars of Northwest cultures, languages, and music. In commenting on his own disk gambling song, he noted that he should have been pounding with a long pole while singing, suggesting the long staff used by the son (Lashibiya [R6]) of the Minter headwoman Damasq when she sang her own women's power song.

On 14 November 1951 in Seattle, Jerry was interviewed by Donald Clark[342] for his dissertation on the role of forestry in settlement, with specific reference to the hazards of sawmills lit by wicks hanging from open cans of fish oil: "A more fire-hazardous condition could hardly be conceived." This bibliography lists "Meeker, Jerry. Brown's Island, Washington. Full-Blood Puyallup Indian, 90 years of age. Worked in earliest sawmills in the region, and knows from first-hand knowledge of early logging methods" [and fire dangers].

Land Claims II, 1950s

On 13 June 1952, Jerry at 90 testified before the Indian Claims Commission for the Puyallups (Docket 203).[343] Thirty years after his testimony for Sarah Wallace, he is clearly hard of hearing. Once again, lawyers did not allow him to elaborate on vital information. Yet this is the one known instance when he is clear on the importance of plant foods, otherwise missing

---

[340] Jerry's reference to these Civil War soldiers of his childhood suggests an ironic way to sidestep racist rumors of his parentage.

[341] *Seattle Post-Intelligencer*, 5 April 1955.

[342] Donald H Clark, An Analysis of Forestry Utilization as a Factor in Colonizing the Pacific Northwest and in Subsequent Population Transitions 1952: 63, 212.

[343] Jerry Meeker, 13 June 1952, Friday afternoon, Seattle, Indian Claims Commission (Docket 203).

from his record. For example, notes taken at the 1857 Fox Island meeting are the only mention of the large potato patch that was probably at Minter because of its rich organic soil.[344]

Other details are added incidentally. After saying he was raised at what used to be called Williams, in the valley just beyond Browns Point, he listed Puyallup villages and graveyards, indicating where his own relatives were buried. His sister was interred at Gales Creek; and his grandfather [MF] and father were at Minter. Later he added, "Minter was Puyallup. My mother belongs to Minter [but] There is no more Indians there at Minter." The pathos of this bare statement was lost on the court.[345] Jerry mentions the hunting of mountain goats and elk on Takoma (Mt Rainier, "Well, your ancestors renamed it."), geese on the prairies, and ducks on the tide flats.

During cross examination, Meeker's 1927 testimony was brought up, and he recalled working with Judge Griffin, George Barnhard from DC, and Mr Nickerson, who drew up the map of sites within the tribal boundaries. After mentioning that many people became mixed together at Muckleshoot, he discussed seasonal and localized activities, including drying salmon and clams "where they didn't have vegetables." He noted the importance of camas, of a white button root called *snook*, and of sunflower [balsam] roots. *Snook* were hard, like native wild onions, and found on the same prairies as balsam.

After a confused exchange about the native name of the upriver people on the Carbon River, which one lawyer misheard as "salal berries," Jerry rose to the occasion by saying "That's the only sugar the Indians had, was the berry, they dried them."

During Redirect, Jerry reviewed the use of mountain goats, elk, and deer. When asked for camas locations, he listed "American River and all over the prairie, Connell's Prairie, Steilacoom Prairie, Puyallup Prairie, and Olympia Prairie."

The great irony, of course, is that Jerry well knew the importance of plants in the Lushootseed economy, both for eating and trading, but he never had the opportunity to summarize what he knew because he was always being questioned about places like Minter that were far from these extensive prairies and meadows. Once these entered the discussion, Jerry could and did amplify the record, elaborating on the importance of regular burning to renew them.[346]

With age, his health failed. In 1952, Jerry's right leg was amputated, but he remained mobile by wheelchair. That August, he worked with Ella Clark,[347] who published a collection of native Northwest stories that has been a mainstay of the region, though she sanitized these versions. Jerry told her briefly about the five sisters at Orting who were changed into Cascade peaks, and about Starchild. Her bibliography indicates she had access to stories taken down by T. T. Waterman and then in the keeping of Arthur Ballard.

---

344 George Minter gave potatoes to natives when they visited their ancient haunts, further indicating soil productivity at the point.

345 Since Jim Meeker died in the early 1900s, he would have been buried in a coffin, suggesting his grave is indeed in the cemetery at Minter. He is not in the TPL Puyallup cemetery list.

346 Jerry added war stories to these notebooks because he was probably goaded by Arthur Ballard's 1952 (Duwamish Docket 109: 49) remark that, on the stand, Jerry ignored slaving and petty raids in favor of "too sweeping" views that "all was sweetness and light."

347 Ella Clark, *Indian Legends of the Pacific Northwest* 1953: 26, 28, 143, 218.

Preparing, from March 1953 to May 1954, for his expert land claims testimony, Herbert C. Taylor interviewed 40 elders in southern Puget Sound, including, for Puyallup, Jerry Meeker and Frank Wrolson.[348] Only Taylor adds to the record that Jerry Meeker was part Duwamish and did not recognize dialect differences in Southern Lushootseed.[349] Later in the court proceedings, William Kitsap, an important Shaker Church leader, was asked to comment on Jerry Meeker's testimony, and he replied "It is all true."[350]

On the witness stand, Taylor noted "to a considerable extent the ethnology of this area, particularly the Puyallup area, reflects the views and ideals of Jerry Meeker … He is a very good informant, but necessarily because he is intelligent, because he is willing to spend the time as an ethnological informant, and because he is quite available in Tacoma, there has become a tendency to rely very heavily upon him.... Marian Smith used him as her primary informant. She used him to standardize the dialectical differences."[351]

His major contribution, moreover, fills these three notebooks, safe in archives but underutilized until the scribe was identified and the information edited and printed for posterity.

---

348 Herbert C Taylor, Anthropological Investigation of the Medicine Creek Tribes Relative to Tribal Identity and Aboriginal Possession of Lands Docket 234, Defendants Exhibit 129, Coast Salish and Western Washington Indians II, 1974: 461.

349 Herb Taylor, RG 279, Docket 206, Box 1902, Volume I: 217.

350 William Kitsap, RG 279, Docket 132, Box 1274, Folder 6: 143.

351 Herb Taylor, RG 279, Docket 206, Box 1902, Volume I: 394.

11 WEALTH INTO WEEPING

The public identity of the Minter community, according to Jerry, changed a handful of times during the perilous 1800s, shifting its defining "spirit power" in the aftermath of local traumas. From earliest times, Minter had been the prosperous and protected locale of pedigreed elite families, famously sponsoring a training academy for noble children to be initiated into the Growlers guild. Its sheltered location, inside Carr Inlet behind a long sand spit, made it strategic for such dramatic events, both outside and inside a huge longhouse staffed by "professors."[352] But its young students attracted slave raiders, especially Taitnapams, until one boy gained a remarkable power, characteristic of high ranking shamans, that he then embodied in a special canoe that killed instantly ("electrocuted") those who saw it, especially in daylight. However, night slaving did continue, as did diseases, to take a toll on Minter, which came back from the brink by means of unusual ~ atypical marriages.

Nowhere else among Lushootseeds do we have as much evidence for the dynamic unfolding of a community's survival by shifting the identity, character, and sources of and for its defining spiritual support.[353] Minter is particularly significant because it establishes a baseline for understanding the Whulshootseed or Southern adaptation, which was early, urban, and much more accommodating to strong European influences from the fur traders at Ft Nisqually and later the Americans at Olympia, the state capitol. The Indian Shaker Church became its distinctive expression for living as native people in the modern world, balancing Catholic / Protestant, urban / rural, and logger / farmer tensions.

Eventually, reeling from these disasters, especially after the brutal and horrific 1782 smallpox pandemic, local men, led by the man named Broken Tooth, took inspiration from features of their terrain and local water conditions to become "swells" able to gorge on vast quantities of food at competitive eat-all feasts. Specializing in competitive eating or engorging by 1840 earned them huge returns in gifts and wagers as they accepted challenges from other communities who assumed, wrongly, they were vulnerable. Using the wealth they won, they redeemed many of their enslaved kin, and thereby sustained their long reputation as high class.

Genesis: Mythic Charters

The elite status of Minter relied on the possession of Wealth or Bounty spirit power, as is indicated by two instances that Jerry localized at Minter, subtly extolling underlying qualities of its members, even those supposed to be poor and unreliable <A20, A92>. Both reaffirm the later character of Minter as chompion eaters.

---

352 Exposed at the southern tip of the Key Peninsula, Longbranch had many archaeological sites around its large bay but these were seasonal and exposed. As noted, Jerry's report about the academy based in a huge longhouse is confirmed independently by Lucy Gerand.

353 Keith Carlson (2007b, 2007c) discusses other survival strategies, particularly migration and intermarriage, among the Salish peoples now along the Fraser River.

Woes

Within the regional network, like other Lushootseed communities, Minter traced its origins, specifically those of its leaders, to the Starchild epic.[354] According to Jerry's own version, chiefly lines descend from the "twin" brothers who became Sun and Moon. When Moon got home, people gathered in council to remake the world. They first asked Moon to travel across the sky to light the day, but he was much too hot, so the twins switched. Made bright and handsome instead of twisted up, Diaper Boy became Sun to shine during the day with Moon at night.

Once the new world was remade from the ashes made by setting the old one ablaze, humans appeared and were assigned to specific locales, where they thrived on local specialties but suffered from occasional hard times and sudden raids. Usually, a marriage or pact forged between local spirits and humans provided a community charter, like the bond between Killerwhales (Orcas) and Gig Harborers, but nothing was specified for Minters beyond the chiefly bonds to Wealth and Horned Snake powers.

Riches

In Jerry's comments on other versions of the Starchild epic, he pointed out the Moon story is *tiyuləbax̣ad* "rare, rich, treasured, abundant" because it involves the all-important dicta that comes from the Stars and enables elite families to control the minds and actions of others.

His story Spirit of Wealth is another version of the bloated boys, where Jerry told Thelma about a wealthy community distressed by these two "lazy" boys, who secretly quested to gain the spirit named *Tioɬbəx̱*, who provided *yabədib* "riches" power. Jerry specified these events "took place long before the flood, when Indians were almost animals – before the Transformer came."

Accordingly, two boys lived in one of the poor, small houses near Minter with their grandmother, who was noble and kept apologizing for their being lazy and dirty, apparently sleeping all day. Actually, they were up all night fasting and praying to receive spirit power, and thus were exhausted and grimy by day, until they triumphed. Strongly disciplined, their stomachs bloated with powerful songs until these were released. ("When they became men they got so powerful, they couldn't hold themselves back. Their stomachs … bloat[ed] when power wanted to come out + they called every body to hear them sing out the power" <A20>}. During the singing, they instructed "certain persons to go to certain places," one full of stunned ducks and another of slain deer. Together, these boys provided abundant food for important events and occasions that helped make Minter prosperous and famous.

The leader at Minter for the mid-1800s was Damasq (*tšiaɬitsa's*), herself of Minter noble family. As appropriate, her power was that called yiɬbix̌ʷ ~ "woman's riches" <A103> and featured a dancing staff that self-pounded against the roof of the house while being held by *xʷabulgʷadxʷ* [her son Humelgood] as she sang. Suspended from the pole was a paunch or stomach. Jerry Meeker's skeptical Uncle Charlie *wilq̓ʷ*, who regarded many rituals as "bunk," once "doubted [the] power of *tšiaɬitsa*'s pole to dance" so they gave the pole to him. His hands immediately stuck fast as it dragged him around the house and then took him outside. In similar

---

[354] As noted, Jerry strangely divided Star Husband from Star Child, Thelma Adamson, *Folktales of the Coast Salish* 1934: 351-361.

accounts of this "proof of spiritual powers," a doubting young man is dragged into the water and drowned, but, at Minter, Charlie was merely taught a lesson in respect for prestige, religion, and the immortals. By being spared, Charlie also confirmed his own family's high rank, with the resources and abilities to keep themselves safe.

Slaving Raids

In both advent and wake of Euro-Russian explorations came epidemic diseases, disruptions, attacks, and slaving that became memorialized as locally poxed place names. After Minter suffered all of these in waves, they were able to re-empower as "gorgers."

With growing competition fueling the trade of furs in return for manufactured good, of slaves for horses, and of labor for money, certain families became predatory raiders, especially after the Hudson Bay Company (HBC) set up forts on land in the 1820s. Minter, with its large, secluded, and desirable "student" population became a prime target.

Given the unsettled times, several slave raids weakened Minter, as Arthur Ballard learned. In his testimony for the land claim, given when he was 75 years old, he listed Puyallup villages (with a V- prefix), while Warren Snyder marked these locations on a map for the court.[355] Toward the end of the list are places across the Tacoma Narrows.

> #V-12 Gig Harbor "they were a distinct group. They had a special myth relating to the blackfish ... They were transformed from the blackfish, and they had a sort of ceremony they called "feeding their mother," the blackfish.[356]
>
> "the next bay is called Carr Inlet, and sometimes it is called Henderson Bay. Now, at the tip of Henderson Bay is what is called Burley Lagoon, and the Indian name is Tulelkthli. I think it means "the trip [tip] of the throat" ….[357]
>
> #V-14 "… and then I had on Minter Bay, on the west side of Carr Inlet, there was a village, and if you want the Indian name, it is Skhotthlib. It is derived from an Indian word meaning "the biters." There is a myth in connection with that name. The people of that village were persecuted by the Klickitats, – that is the upper Cowlitz People [Taitnapam] used to come down and murder them, and a boy by some magic power created something to cause their deaths when they attacked that village, and he saved his village. … I think it was [from] Alice Cross. … she was a Duwamish Indian

---

355 Arthur Ballard, RG 279, Docket 203, Box 1897, Folder 4: 57. At Ballard's death, his family withdrew his major book, *Listen My Nephew ~ Myth, Tradition, and History on Southern Puget Sound*, while it was in press in Portland.

356 Arthur Ballard, RG 279, Docket 203, Box 1897, Folder 4: 80, 81. Some of these animal spirit patrons ("totems") of towns and places are represented by the overall shape of the carved planks used in the soul redeeming rite, See Jay Miller, *Shamanic Odyssey*, 1988. Others are associated with epics, such as a Thunderbird with Lake Tapps and this Killerwhale family (pod) at Gig Harbor.

357 Arthur Ballard, RG 279, Docket 203, Box 1897, Folder 4: 80, 81, 82.

> married to a man who was born in this place, Jimmy Homalgood [headwoman's son] was his name, and of course she learned all these myths from her husband, because she was a member of that group after her marriage. Her doctor [daughter] is now living, however…. That is the village that Jerry Meeker claimed as his birthplace."[358]

Jerry mentioned at least three major raids on Minter, by Taitnapam, Nanaimo, and Haida.[359] The earliest was by these Sahaptin Upper Cowlitz,[360] probably overland from the south, followed by the repopulation of Minters by intermarrying "cousins" and the protection of the horned-snake canoe. Since their next attack came in daylight, these raiders were "electrocuted" at the sight of the vessel. Later came the attack from Nanaimo, by water, and the transformation into gorgers in its aftermath. Lastly was the more recent attack by a few Haida, with Sally's forewarning phrased within a stock memorate that is also told using names famously attached to other locales.[361]

At Henderson Bay, a woman went to get water, saw a face reflected on the smooth surface, and became wary. (Sometimes, a Plains feather headdress showed above the face, indicating clearly that these enemies were horse-trading Taitnapam.) To test her suspicions, she made a sound like flatulence and the face smiled. Acting normally, she returned home and gave warning of imminent attack, but only her own sisters listened and fled with their families to survive. Afterward, these cousins, the 12 children of these three sisters, intermarried to resettle Minter. [A more dramatic variant (above) repopulates Minter via the marriage of a set of twins.]

---

[358] Arthur Ballard, RG 279, Docket 203, Box 1897, Folder 4: 82, 83. "Klickitats" [Taitnapams] were regional slavers into the 1840s, selling children at Columbia River emporia, presumably for horses, See Robert Boyd, *The Coming of the Spirit of Pestilence* 1999: 258.

[359] Haida live on Haida Gwaii ~ Queen Charlotte Islands, off the northern coast of British Columbia, where enormous trees enabled them to carve huge canoes. Paddling south, large crews and families began to frequent southern waters and Puget Sound after Victoria, BC, was founded in 1843. Its diverse, thriving native encampment was burned out in 1862 during a smallpox epidemic. Displaced and diseased, natives fled Victoria and spread the devastation along the entire coast.

[360] In the mix of traumatic epidemic deaths, desire for horses, and community disruptions, the Cowlitz River sheltered a tribe speaking three distinct languages: \ Salish Tsamosan Lower Cowlitz, Sahaptin Taitnapam Upper Cowlitz, and Athapaskan Swaal Upland Cowlitz. Leaders also spoke Chinook Wawa trade jargon, and other languages, including European ones once the fur trade began.

[361] The recurrent placement of Jerry's mother Sally in these various accounts from different decades makes sense within a common Northwest Coast pattern. It was not Sally herself who was long lived, but rather her name (*də'at*), perpetuated through many generations living at Minter but further confused by its similarity to the English demonstrative "that"). Therefore what Jerry probably said was that *də'at* defended her people and forewarned of impending attack, but the scribe, having only Sally herself as referent, failed, like so many others, to grasp heroic attributes which attach to a renowned name over the centuries. In brief, the Minter's version focuses on sisters and a boy to save the day.

In time, a boy questing for a spirit successfully met a supernatural horned serpent, the greatest of shamanic powers, whose gaze produced instant death.[362] The boy survived the encounter and, empowered, made a canoe in its image which he kept hidden. Overconfident Taitnapam slavers from the Cowlitz River attacked in daylight so the boy was able to expose the canoe and instantly kill all these enemies. While he lived, Minter was protected by his fearsome canoe.

In other versions of this tale, protection was provided by a special weapon, such as a sheathed club, that had to be kept concealed because exposing it caused immediate death to the foe. Such warriors, from other more exposed villages, also helped to protect the huge training hall of elite children. Afterwards, slaving raids continued, but Minters no longer maintained a training academy, and eventually learned to protect themselves as chompions, waging and winning eating contests around the south Sound.

Jerry mentioned only briefly how Minters once staged a counter-raid, carried out by 20-30 men, by inviting men from another village to join them <A102>. While floating in canoes in front of the enemy's beach, warriors sang [to taunt] just before a brazen mass attack.[363] Before Jerry's time, Puyallup and Snohomish were bitter enemies (as shown by Dr Simon's fate), but intermarriages brought them closer, meeting together peacefully every 2-3 years. Of note, Jerry said that women *did* go along on these raids and even had special meanness powers {"like tiger, wild cat, bear"} that helped goad and inspire their warriors <A46>.

According to George Gibbs[364], "Dr [William] Tolmie informs me that the course of the slave trade has always been from south to north; the only exception in his knowledge being that the Kowlitz Indians, formerly a very strong tribe, used to make forays on the Sound and carry their prisoners to the Columbia river." These Upper Cowlitz Taitnapam traded in livestock and slaves, though most slaves, as noted, were usually captured from small tribes in California and Oregon. Slaving routes were well enough known that families intent of ransoming any of their freshly captured members went to known rendezvous points or middlemen located along the slavers return route to negotiate payment and release.

In the 1840s, when Sally was a girl, Minter had turned from physical to spiritual protections. In lieu of Warrior power, Minter's stout bodies and chewed-up terrain enabled them to specialize as chompions, renowned eaters who engorged themselves in the service of rival hospitality.

---

[362] This great power, variously described as a snake or reptile, sometimes said to be like an alligator, with retractable horns, was much feared because it killed instantly as the victim twisted up in great agony. It is another indication of Minter's association with the highest elite.

[363] The addition of these war incidents to the record was probably a reaction to Arthur Ballard's 1952 testimony in court (Duwamish Docket 109: 49) where, when asked to comment on Jerry's statements, said it was too sweeping: "all was sweetness and light among the Indians on the Coast, and that was not the case," ignoring the long petty disagreements endemic to any long-settled region. In these notebooks, Jerry supplies apt examples.

[364] George Gibbs, J. – Indian Affairs 39, Report of Mr George Gibbs to Captain Mc'Clellan, On The Indian Tribes of The Territory of Washington 1855: 189.

Another infamous raid on Minter involved attackers from {"Vancouver Island (from near Nanaimo) at night. After much fighting – they drove them away. Jerry's mother had gone after water a long way from village. She saw saw [sic, doubled] a number of faces in spring from top of bluff. When she returned she told about the Strange faces. Then they knew to be ready for the raid. She saved many by doing this. One or 2 were taken from Minter as slaves." Regrouping <A96>, "Minter brought the people stolen back. They were from well to do family (thinks related to Jerry's mother) doesn't remember names. But whole village contributed to money etc. to get them back" <A94-95>}.

After this raid, {"they felt so bad"} the main house at Minter was moved from the south to north side of lagoon.[365] The headwoman, as noted, kept her ceremonial objects (self-pounding pole, and regalia) in the abandoned house[366] because it was {"where her ancestors were"}. Presumably, before this, she had used the huge hollow stump for keeping her dancing poles. {"(thumping roof of house with long pole, approx[imately] 6 ft. [tall, called] təstəd … a stomach was tied to the pole in the middle, about 1 ft. long, made of wood ɸ* or Θ*. with deerhooves inside to rattle"}.[367] The stump was eventually used to store all of the dried salmon Minters continued to preserve there during Jerry's teenage years.

With the founding of Victoria in 1843, as noted, many northern tribes such as Haidas[368] camped in the region and attempted to capture locals to enslave for trade or to take far away to their home.

> Once when camping at Arletta, some QM [Quarter Master] harbor Indians beat some Haida raiders – a few of which escaped overland to Arletta and when they could not understand him (Haida) + they knew him to be one of the raiders + they stoned him to death. ½ dozen [warriors ?] Led by a Gig H[arbor] ind[ian] that happened to be with them at the time.
>
> John Swan (uncle) gig harbor, willatchet
>
> Jim sq^{w}aq^{w}uyub "brother" stilcum [Steilacoom]
>
> James Coates (Yuko•ts) "brother" mother's stalalt [?] wollotchet
>
> Tsidat'alq "brother" stilcum
>
> "Jack" ? (from Gig Harbor) was leader<A 117-118>

---

365 Marian Wesley Smith, Microfilm Roll 3 (Reel A1738), British Columbia Archives, MSS 2689: Box 6, Folder 9 (Houses 26); Royal Anthropological Archives, MSS 2794, Houses p26.

366 Unlike north Pacific towns, where clan regalia and crests were ~ are kept in a special room at the back of the house, behind an elaborate screen opposite the front door, Salish usually kept powerful objects hidden in the forest, inside hollow cedar trees or in caves, until brought into the house for display and use at a public event. This seclusion also protected them from house fires, raids, and misuse.

367 Melville Jacobs Collection, UW-MSCUA, Sound Recordings, Box 120, Folder 34.

368 Indeed, Haida was, at this time, often used as a generic term for natives from the North (British Columbia, Alaska) so these raiders might well have belonged to another nation.

In typical diplomatic fashion, local hostilities seem to have been resolved by the marriage of Tyee Dick, eldest son of Cowlitz head chief Scanewa, to a Nisqually woman related to Leschi with many Lushootseed relatives. Jerry also associated him with Minter. He is buried in the Puyallup cemetery, where his tombstone reads Richard Sinnaywah, 1814-1904 (Tyee Dick).

Growler Academy

Minter was once famed for its group training and initiation of rich children. This guild was a collective ritual, unlike the individualized training and initiation of "Siyowin dancers" during the winter ceremonial season. As public displays of prestige, Growler initiations were held in good weather.

Elite youngsters – both boys and girls, when they were about fourteen, especially if acting like "know-it-alls" – were initiated into the Growlers by their families "paying" huge sums of money and goods to its members.[369] This obligation kept them humble because they had to listen and learn from respected older people. Each had a family claim to Wealth power, as well as renowned names and prestige as a prerequisite for being inducted. After their initiation, they also became especially susceptible to acquiring these family-owned spirit powers in highly potent forms, assuring luck and strength. This emphasis on wealth, prominence, and prestige distinguished the academy from the more multiplex sources of spirit patrons inspiring winter dance initiates.

Growlers, sometimes called a secret society by academics,[370] formed an intertribal organization (guild) of privilege which existed solely to initiate new members from wealthy families, usually during the first days of a large potlatch. When a cohort of youngsters reached the appropriate age, an initiation was held. Members, as a way of reminding or intimidating others as to their high status, held meetings during the winter to dramatize their powers. The role of Minter was to recruit, prepare, and instruct children for membership.

In the south Sound, the academy predominated, though natives in recent times have confused it with the better known and more public shamanic Redeeming Rite, which retrieved a vitality (mind, soul, or spirit) snatched away by ghosts and taken to the land of the dead.[371] Their memberships were mutually exclusive because anyone except shamans could join the guild, but only shamans took part in the Redeeming to restore lost vitalities. Both could, however, bring back a baby soul from the land of the dead and place it into a barren woman – well past child bearing – who then gave birth to a normal child.[372]

---

369 In terms of such insistence on high rank, it is worth repeating that the Marriage dance of the 1830s Prophet, which wed one set of Jerry's grandparents, was stopped by the Klallam because it mixed ranks and classes, See Wayne Suttles, The Plateau Prophet Dance among the Coast Salish, *Coast Salish Essays* 1987: 167.

370. Another native name of this guild has the sense of being on guard, watchful, fearsome, and protective. The best translation is 'vigilantes', but it has wrong connotations in English.

371 Marian Smith, *The Puyallup-Nisqually* 1940: 92-99. In the best known instance, however, the result was the well-known dwarf Moses Seattle, grandson of this famous chief.

372 Smith, *The Puyallup-Nisqually* 1940: 94.

The guild's patron spirit was available only by public initiation into membership and was variously described as a huge black man or a baby covered with blood, who lived in the air and traveled north with ducks, represented by carved wooden rattles. For some groups, it also had aspects of the wolf.[373] Indeed, a name of this spirit, identical with the usual term for the guild, made reference to "growling," often as a reciprocal phrase meaning "growling at each other."

The best general account refers to neighboring Twana,[374] and the most detailed to Klallam.[375] Wealthy Twana placed the abode of this spirit patron at the mouth of the Skokomish River so it is likely that Minters also located their own patron nearby, probably underwater. Tribes who participated in this guild were the Songish, Lummi, Klallam, Swinomish, Twana, Puyallup, Nisqually, and Suquamish. Members belonged to the overlapping continuum of septs (kithreds) which serve(d) to interlink "tribal" communities and languages along the entire North Pacific coast (Chapter 5).

At Suquamish, according to Wilson George,[376] this guild was known as the Dog Eaters. Meetings were held in the dead of winter solely to initiate new members, who acted "crazy" or "frenzied" when they came under the influence of its patron. If they encountered a dog, they seized it and tore it to pieces like a pack of carnivores (wolves). Then they ate it (or gave the impression that they did). Each community adhered to its own minor distinctions, while sharing in overall characteristics of this ritual display.

Lasting over three to eight days, each rite began with a dance by all the members in a carefully cleaned and readied house, but the hosting community did not provide specialist initiators. Rather, each locale brought its own master to oversee the direct transfer of their patron spirit into the bodies of its own new initiates. Power clearly was based in, inspired by, and derived from specific place.

Every dramatic initiation proceeded in seven stages, each intended to progressively gain control of this collective spirit patron: summoning display, "shooting" (benumbing intrusion), conjuring, reviving, bathing, possession (with blood pouring from the mouth), and a final gifting (give away) to guests and payments to initiator members.

---

373. Indeed, the most direct source for this guild was the Klukwali Wolf Ritual of the Nuchahnulth (Nootkan) tribes of the West Coast of Vancouver Island and others of the Washington coast. In distribution, the guild is a southern extreme of the dancing orders of the Kwakiutlan (Kwakwaka'wakw and Heiltsuk) peoples of the middle coast, centered at Bella Bella, See Philip Drucker, Kwakiutl Dancing Societies, *Anthropological Records* 6 (6): 201-230, 1940; Pamela Amoss, *Coast Salish Spirit Dancing* 1978: 72.

Within the regional prestige network, Lushootseeds held their own with the dramatic Redeeming Canoe Rite while also participating in the expanding membership of the much more international Growlers.

374 Elmendorf, The Cultural Setting of the Twana Secret Society, *American Anthropologist* 50: 625-633.

375. Elmendorf, *Twana Narratives* (1993: 59) described hand gestures used by initiates to suggest their spirit powers.

376 Wilson George, Secret Society Guild, Suquamish Traditions, *Evergreen Ethnographies*, 20015: 212-13; JONA 33 (1) 1999, Jay Miller, ed.

During the first night, duck-like wooden rattles flew around the house from one group to another as proof of the guild's powers, while masters indicated their superior abilities by vomiting up blood. Some members wore carved masks to represent their powers, and some were so frenzied that they had to be restrained by ropes tied around the waist and grasped by handlers. Others acted fierce, brandishing knives, spears, axes, and clubs.

Initiates fell down after being "shot" by their town's patron's power, and the lifeless body secluded so the parents could bathe their child after he or she revived. A novice then returned to the house for a public session enabling him or her to master, control, and use this power.

By Ri(gh)te of Prestige

Lucy Gurand's bare mention of theater and Jerry's of instruction evoke the dramatic impact of the Growlers (Klallam xūnxanīte) throughout the region. Minter, with its open spit and high bluff viewing area on the south, as well as sloped terrain on the north, was ideal for staging these ceremonies.

At an initiation, a flotilla of canoes arrived in front of a huge host house, singing special songs.[377] Youths to be initiated were secluded in homes until Growlers kicked in those doors and searched for them in a frenzy, while brandishing weapons, bleeding from the mouth, and tossing everything around. As each initiate was found, he or she went limp as though dead and was carried to a curtained off section of the hosting house. When all those already initiated had been gathered together, the Growlers stood outside the blanket enclosure and sang a song, bobbing slightly at the knees, to calm their shared spirit. Members wore seven eagle feathers sticking up from a headband, two at the front and sides, with one in the back. Many songs were vocables said to be in foreign languages, befitting an other-worldly mystique of this guild.

Initiates might be secluded for as long as a week, eating sparingly of any food that was brought covertly to them. Members, with black-painted faces, would gather periodically outside the enclosure to sing and dance, some wearing masks. Women members sometimes danced sideways in a circle, waving outstretched arms up and down, around a man in the center who danced back and forth. More often these women kept one arm bent at the shoulder and the other outstretched, changing arms with the tempo, and men danced with both arms straight out from the body, slashing up and down.[378] At other times, a watchman stood outside the enclosure, using songs and his duck rattle to cover any noises that the "deceased" initiates might make.

On the fourth night, initiates were taken outside to a secluded area, often a forested bluff, patrolled by Growlers, to practice their return from the dead and to dance. They were also told the origins of the guild, and pledged to secrecy under pain of death. Brave initiates cut their own tongue or inside cheek, smearing some of their blood on the mouths of the more timid.

Finally, on the next to last day, each inert initiate was carried out of the host house, lifted into the air three times, and revived. Naked boys and girls wearing tiny aprons to be minimally modest were each hurried off by two young men, grasping either arm, to be bathed, clothed in

---

377 Robert Collier of Jamestown here describes his own initiation at Washington Harbor, Erna Gunther, Klallam Ethnography, UWPA 1 (5): 281-288 1927.

378 These arm gestures can be seen in contemporary Hamatsa dances, a living expression of these guilds.

their appropriate regalia, including a buckskin (later red flannel) tunic smeared with ochre, and given a token, made by a family member, to show their particular aspect of the shared patron power. When all was ready, separate lines of boys or girls paraded back to the front of the hosting house.

Just outside, each initiate gained two "handlers," one on either side, who rushed the initiate into the house and lowered him or her onto a large mat set on the ground. Lying prone, each began to groan and growl. An older leader danced beside each of the initiates, transferring power from the elder into each one, who then ran off until constrained. An initiate then stopped growling, and calmed down. Eventually, all the tamed initiates were taken home by their parents.

The next day, parents and family gave money and lavish gifts to the Growler members, validating their own wealth and the high rank of their child. New initiates could not wash their faces for a month, and each had an ironwood probe tied to their wrists to poke other children who mocked or teased them.

Incongruously, while slaves could never be initiated after capture, those who had been members when free were allowed to join in local initiations. Otherwise, anyone knowing its secret but judged to be unworthy was covertly killed, as were members who scoffed or joked in public, though Sally Meeker's brother was a notable exception who was saved by the status of his family.

Supposedly, the guild was founded to cover the embarrassment of a noble who misjudged the chewing of a duck bone and bled from the mouth. This, of course, sounds like a diversionary explanation to throw off further inquiry from a deeper meaning and significance, as with the Nootka canoe, whose wolf head prow was said to merely be handles to lift and carry the vessel. A clue that Growlers indeed have a more profound meaning is the repeated phrase "the heavens rest on the xūnxanīte."

12 SWELLING CHOMPIONS

Though native Minters were rarely mentioned by other researchers, as the following discussion shows, those who did so were among the best and most involved in native Puget Sound, though only Jerry and Marian Smith seem to have grasped the horrific changes that Minters suffered. In eventually becoming gorgers, they shifted their identity from being trainers and magical warriors in the early 1800s to safer engagement as champion gorgers from about 1840 until Minter disbanded after arsons. Indeed, it was gorging that "turned the tide" for them. While Minters shared the Winter Dance, Growlers, and Redeeming Odyssey with other Lushootseeds, what most recently and famously distinguished them was their empowered eating as Chompions.

Secluded, dispersed, and weakened, Minters received a challenge from Gig Harbors intended to prey on their vulnerability, but the old man named 8h <B11> rose to the threat, "turned the tide," and triumphed. {"One old man from small house had a Spirit to eat & never got full. Jerry never saw him <A94> … After the slave raid from Nanaimo, Chief at Gig H. [Harbor] heard that everybody at Minter was taken but one old woman. Most hid in the woods. … One or two were taken from Minter as slaves…. Gig H chief invited old man (the eater), thought he would kill him by feeding him to [too] much. The old man almost ate him out of house & home. Finally sent him home with many gifts, canoes & lots of food" <A95>}.

This leader at Gig Harbor was named Skʷini, who, knowing the feeble condition of Minter, challenged Broken Tooth to an eat-all, intending to enslave them or force dependency. Since both belonged to the Puyallup drainage and speech community, Skʷini's intended outcome was probably the kind of tributary status that Wayne Suttles[379] has described for other towns in the region. The lesser town lost any claims to nobility and had to perform menial services, such as getting firewood when it was bitter cold and much needed. But instead Broken Tooth triumphed and reversed their fortunes, so {"Minter people again grew rich and influential"}.[380]

Broken Tooth, of note, moved up from the leadership of a secondary house into the primary one after he defeated both Gig Harbor and Mission Creek. Using the many gifts that he earned, from both side bets and his own triumphs, those captured by the slavers were redeemed and brought back to Minter. He also trained youngsters to acquire this ability and thereby protect the community. The large, hundred-fifty-foot training house would have added this empowered ability to its curriculum, along with the existing spectrum for training and initiations.

Those at Minter, in becoming the sx̣əƛ̓əbabš "biters" ~ sx̣əƛ̓alikʷabš "chompions," seem to have shifted their previous aggressive identity to safer engagement as champion gorgers about 1840, though there were occasional traumas. In more recent times, it was not communal expressions of spiritual ability but rather the carpentry and other skills of Gizmo which added to their local renown.

Their identity as "biters" implies something that pinches together or squeezes between jaws. By implication, supported by features of the locale – creeks biting into bluffs, tidal swaths,

---

379 Wayne Suttles, Coast Salish Intervillage Ties, *Coast Salish Essays* 1987, Chapter 9: 152-198.

380 Marian Smith, *The Puyallup-Nisqually* 1940: 75.

steady outpourings at Hupp Springs, the stomach attached to the power pole of Damasq, and the huge hollow stump – indicate their strong gustatory orientation, enforcing their status as chompions. Minters were also regarded as "swells," though moderated by the cautionary tale of bloated boys to indicate the dangers of retaining instead of sharing any bounty. The huge stump, used first to store Damasq's sacra and later bundles of dried salmon, is also implicated since "hollow stump" was one of the stronger spirits conferring gorging ability.

One tale, recorded by Arthur Ballard from Joe Young (Puyallup),[381] makes this clear, probably after Broken Tooth had transformed Minter into gorgers. What is known of Joe Young's life is discussed below.

THE BIG EATERS OF MINTER BAY

Two men got in a fast traveling canoe and went to visit at Long Branch an old man who came from tlia'tlEd (?) to see how much they could eat.

They arrived. The old man welcomed them. He was rather hungry but thought best to cook them a dinner. He cooked bet', i.e. dried roots, fish, etc., a canoe full of it.[382] *Dinner was ready at middle of forenoon. The eaters sat down, one man on each side of the canoe. One man was facing east looking at the water. The other man, looking west, talked and said "We have plenty of time to eat; how is the tide?" "It looks as if it were standing still now." Half the bet' was gone. "How is the tide?" "It is beginning to rise now." They got full with the tide and conquered the old man.*

Ballard included this story in his first published folklore collection, and he undoubtedly knew more details than he included here, based on a lifetime of experience in the South Sound.

Longbranch, the site of the contest, is on Filucy Bay near the tip of the Key Peninsula, across from McNeil Island, below Carr Inlet. After Minter, it has the largest number of local archaeological sites. It is at the southern point of the same continuous eastern shoreline as Minter, explaining how the two men got there reasonably quickly in a swift canoe. It is also a place, as noted, with a "mind of its own" because it refused to change when the Transformer came through this area.

A helpful footnote adds "The people at Minter Bay were known as tux sxotLibabc, Eaters ([or] according to [James] Goudy, an informant, Biters)."

The next Ballard story, War Bonnet, about a mother with a son and daughter escaping from an attack after seeing the head of an enemy warrior reflected in the water, again told by Joe Young, was set at Burton on Vashon Island. Its Note 15 mentions

> "A similar story ... of the *sxo'tLibabc*, at the head of Carr's Inlet, by John Xot, a Puyallup. The word is derived from sxotaliks, chewing, biting. ... these people fought

---

[381] Arthur Ballard, Some Tales of the Southern Puget Sound Salish 1927: 59.

[382] sbit̓ is the generic word for soup (*LD* 40). tlia'tlEd was probably at Burley, see TT Waterman place name # 139. Ballard thought it meant "tip of the throat."

till all were killed but one woman, who kept herself in hiding. She gave birth to a boy and a girl who became parents of the race."

Other notes identify Joe Young (wil̓ək'ədib) as Puyallup with Snoqualmi, Snohomish, and Yakama ancestry, "born [1863] at Fort Nisqually of an Indian mother and a German father. He is well informed. He attended school for a short time." Yet two years later, Ballard noted that his "father was a white man, probably Scotch, employed by the Hudson's Bay Company. With the exception of three years on Green River, most of the informant's early life was spent on or near saltwater." Cited within parentheses, James Goudy, born 1865, was Skagit with some Snohomish and Puyallup ancestry.[383] Thus, both men were familiar with the waterways around Minter, if not also related there.

Supporting 1927 footnotes from Joe Young, Jim Goudy, and John Xot explain that the root of this tribal name, sx̣o'tl̓ibabš, is said to mean "to eat, bite," while the form sx̣o'tl̓alikʷabš (with the insertion of *–alik–*) indicates a repetitive activity done with finesse. Overall, the ramifications of this crucial account are that there is something about the slow, steady progress of the water, if not the tides, at Minter that gave its human residents, infused with this same ability, skill as champion eaters adept at gorging themselves at public feasts. More than just timing their eating with the rising tide, these men were identifying with it and drawing upon its ability to fill up a huge area. By watching the west sun to measure time and east tide for flooding space, these eaters paced themselves. Augmenting power seems also to have been supplied by their huge local stump.

Eating Up Hood Canal

While the Ballard "big eaters" text provides a basic understanding of historic Minter, two of the notebooks <A94, B11> detail an eat-all contest between Broken Tooth and the Skokomish Twana at Mission Creek along Hood Canal where he finished off an entire nine-foot canoe filled with fish stew (salmon mulligan). This was after he bested the leader at Gig Harbor, as noted. In consequence, Broken Tooth became the prime leader at Minter, and his fame spread throughout the region. He had literally taken his town from impending extinction to renewed success, and other towns and leaders throughout the area duly noted how his triumph restored the entire community. It marked him as a true leader, especially since he also, in turn, hosted eat-alls at Minter.

To the west of Minter is Hood Canal, home of the Twana, whose largest community of nine villages on the Skokomish River survived better to become the site of the modern reservation, bearing their name. Surrounding Minter were fellow Lushootseeds, including the home villages of the Sahewamish near Shelton, of the Squaxin near Allyn, and, to the east, the Puyallup and Nisqually living along these same rivers. As "biters" the Minters competed with these communities, with their triumph among the Twana especially well reported.

---

[383] Arthur Ballard, Some Tales of the Southern Puget Sound Salish 1927: 59; Arthur Ballard, Mythology of Southern Puget Sound, 1929: 40. A list of revisions (16 May 1949) in the Erna Gunther papers at the Burke Museum indicate Goudy, a Skagit-Snohomish, was born about 1860 not 1865.

In his masterful ethnography of the Twana, William Elmendorf provides cultural background on the eat-all or competitive feasts.[384] Ordinarily, twice a day, people ate with their fingers, or a spoon, from common dishes, using a water container as a finger bowl to wash up after the meal, with shredded inner cedar bark as napkins to dry the hands. Each food was eaten separately, in successive courses. All food was taken in moderation because overindulgence was offensive to spirit powers. Thus, ironically, even a spirit that enabled engorging had to be acquired by fasting and thirsting.

The exception to this general rule, of course, was the eat-all among friendly foreigners. Twana took on Satsop Chehalis and Lushootseeds, such as "one small community on Carr Inlet, considered a 'branch' of the Puyallup, the čusxʷóƛ̓ab (PSd sxʷóƛ̓babš)[385] or Shwotlemamish." These eating challenges took two types. One was a "surprise visit" (sx̣a'k̓ak̓) after sending a messenger a day or two ahead with a warning of their impending arrival. In the second type, sduxʷ'ó'txʷ, "breaking into the house ... guests arrived unannounced and danced into their selected host's house, singing of their intention of 'eating him up'." The host and his villagers laughingly announced that they would provide all the food the visitors could possibly eat.

In both types, along the way, the eaters would test their collective power by drinking up small streams or ponds. When they entered the home of their host, they were served immediately with huge quantities of food, some quickly contributed by neighbors. Everyone ate all they could, with the chompions calling on their q̓ʷax̣q spirit power to consume even more. This kind of lay or career power conferred abilities of a ceremonial and dramatic nature, such as the levitation and animation of special artifacts, such as flying birds or running planks. Among these, the eat-all was less obvious but more impressive. When everyone was finished, the host sang a song from his wealth power (s'iyalt) and gave everyone small gifts that were never graded by social rank as was done at a potlatch.

After all the guests left, the host community packed up in preparation for a return visit within a few days or weeks so these guests could act as hosts. All told, these contests enhanced community solidarity, the host's honor and prestige, public festivity, and continued familiarity among near neighbors of different speech communities.

Twana Eat-Alls

Further proving the worth of Al Smith's notes from Jerry, in the parallel Twana account, their own champion eater, named sda'yəltxʷ, directed his supporters to a small lake between Allyn and the tip of Hood Canal.[386] Along the way, as a group, they tested their powers by "wishing" [magically shooting] an eagle to death and taking its body into one of their canoes. Once they beached at the trailhead, they sent a boy ahead to Minter as messenger to announce their imminent arrival.

---

[384] William Elmendorf, *The Structure of Twana Culture* 1960: 138-141, 292, 490.

[385] (PSd) abbreviates Puget Sound Salish, another name for Lushootseed.

[386] William Elmendorf, *Twana Narratives* 1993: 13-20, # 5. Elmendorf dated it to about 1840, which further indicates that it was the defining intertribal event that recast Minters as chompions. Since Al Smith also worked with a Twana elder the same summer he worked with Jerry Meeker, he may have been the link between these parallel accounts.

Meanwhile, they relaxed on the beach, plucking eagle feathers and passing them out to everyone. Then they walked up the hill to a little lake, where the eater sang and danced. He asked everyone to kneel down and sip from the lake until its water level dropped down the width of two hand spans and four fingers. Then an old woman sang, accompanied by everyone present. Afterwards, they walked along the trail around North Bay on to Minter, arriving that evening.

Two local headmen, named waɬačalq and hʷixʷƛ̓dis [Broken Tooth], met them, and they danced into the house of the first one, singing and waving eagle feathers.[387] After four circuits, they sat down. Their host served clams, seal, porpoise, but no salmon since Minters {"had no river"}.[388] The Skokomish sang and danced to bless this food, before they ate and ate, tossing each empty kettle into the middle of the floor. This gesture meant they wanted more, so additional food was cooked and served four or five times. Then, as they went on to the home of Broken Tooth, the second leader, their first host waɬačalq invited them to stop by on their way back. They did the same in the other house until, after several servings, they {"ate him up"}.

They sent a messenger on to another village, probably Burley or Glencove, where the headman was bəsxʷay'iqʷaᴅ. The visitors danced into his house, moving counterclockwise, before they sat and ate flounders, seals, and wild carrots, which they especially liked, tossing the emptied maplewood platters into the middle of the floor to ask for more carrots.

These Twana were invited to stay for two days until Steilacoom inlaws came with gifts of camas, acorns, and salmon. They ate the acorns mashed raw because they were so sweet.[389] They ate up all that the Steilacooms brought to give to their own son-in-law, this leader who had married their daughter. In return, he and the Twana gave dentalia [tusk shells] to these visiting inlaws. A Skokomish man acted as speaker, passing out strings of dentalia to each inlaw by name as a sign of thanks and respect.[390]

The next morning, as everyone departed, the Twana were sent off with the remaining acorns. They again stopped at the home of waɬačalq, where a woman was sick and a chief among the visitors with Lizard power agreed to cure her. Her power had left [deserted] her and

---

387 These are clearly versions of the names of the first husband of the headwoman and of Broken Tooth.

388 Glencoe was their primary (Fall?) fishery so Minter and Huge Creeks may not have had the right timing or quality of fish runs and thereby Minter could be said to have 'no river'. It may well be, on the other hand, that an aspect of this competition was to taunt or disparage what were actually key features of the host territory. Jerry does say his family went back to Minter to dry more fish each August, yet the creek is considerably smaller than any Northwest river.

389 Since most raw acorns are dangerously toxic, I initially assumed this referred to some other nut. Nathan Reynolds (email 15 Dec 2012), ecologist for the Cowlitz, indicated to me that Garry ~ Oregon white oak are native to Washington state, do not require leaching, are less toxic, and sweeten when roasted. Nisqually boiled then cached them in openwork baskets buried in lake mud, also sweeting taste (Herman Haeberlin and Erna Gunther, Indians of Puget Sound 1930: 22). Nathan added that this process also kept them from going rancid.

390 This is a classic example of the process described so clearly by Wayne Suttles whereby inlaws gave perishable food to each other in return for more permanent gifts that could be saved for later distribution at sponsored invitationals ~ "potlatch" locally called *sgʷigʷi*).

he had to send his own to find hers in order to "fix her up." It had gone to Mt Rainier because it was mad that she never went to pick berries in the mountains.[391]

He got it and put it back, but everyone had to sing all that night and the next day before that woman could again properly sing her own song. Then the other headman hʷixʷƛ̓dis [Broken Tooth] came in and challenged the Twana to prepare for his return visit by cleaning out a small canoe once they got home and filling it with salmon eggs to feed him. They agreed. That night wałačalq sang his Wealth power, while his wife passed out a few dentalia shells to each visitor and he personally gave each one a handful of wild carrots to snack on along the trail home. The patient's husband gave the Twana curer his valuable hunting dog as thanks.

The next morning they walked back along the trail, noting that the small lake had refilled. Once home, they began to gather salmon eggs. Soon after, the Minters landed. A nine foot canoe, heaped with cooked salmon eggs, was presented to the visitors, who sang to bless the food. Then they knelt and began to eat until the Minter headman and others held back so hʷixʷƛ̓dis himself could finish off everything, tossing away his own spoon to suck up the last eggs through his lips. When the canoe was empty, the Skokomish brought out servings of dried meat, salmon, berries, and dried clams for the visitors to eat still more.

A hunter came down from Vance Creek to offer the meat from two bears. Many neighbors were invited to join the gathering. Since the Minters had "never known war," these Skokomish staged a display of Warrior powers, including a Bear power song to cause wind and rain, Clam power to cause hives (skin irritations), and Wolf power to attack skillfully.[392] Everyone sang and danced the night away before the Minters went home in the morning with very full bellies.

Likely Dating

Disrupted and destabilized, the Sound suffered during the early 1800s as native leaders and communities vied for access to ships and forts to gain fur trade goods, while trafficking in native slaves to increase productivity. The earliest European written record, observations by the 1792 Vancouver expedition with namesake Peter Puget, confirms oral traditions.

A tentative chronology, based on these three notebooks and other documents, dates events and key people roughly by decades. Conflict marked historic times. The battle of allied Puget Sounders against Cowichans is usually dated about 1825.[393] The Upper Cowlitz Taitnapam attack was a decade (30s) later, and that of the Haida was even later (after 1843) since

---

391 Neglect of resources was once a great worry since unpicked berries felt unwanted, as did uneaten salmon, and might take revenge on humans.

392 Such a reference to not having seen war is confusing. It might extol their remote location, or, more subtly, refer to their defeat and decimation in slave raids. More realistically, Minter did have the academy, "zapping" canoe, and other protections that kept it out of active warfare. While other shore towns had a famous warrior or champion to protect it, Minter had supernatural protections like the canoe for a time, before becoming a target of slaving raids.

393 William Tolmie, the HBC factor, dated to 1825 the battle between Cowichans and 200 allied canoes led by Kitsap (1790-1845) and others, Edmond Meany Papers 85-8.

Sally (də'at), Jerry's mother, gave early warning after seeing faces in a pool of water.[394] After her eldest living son, John, she lost several children before remarrying and giving birth to Jerry in 1862 when she was in her 20s.

Before and after Lt Peter Puget surveyed in 1792, diseases took a terrible toll, jeopardizing the ancient chiefly line whose last representative was the headwoman Damasq [tšia'łits'a]. She would have been born about 1820, outliving her own children and dying about 58 years old in 1878. If Broken Tooth, the heroic chompion, was born in 1800, leading a lesser house in 1830, he assumed prime leadership, based on his gorging successes, after the massive slave raid about 1840 just before Lt Wilkes used the 'eaters' name in 1841.

If Dr Simon, the headwoman's slave, were born about 1835, captured about 1840, sold to Minter about 1845 (at 10), gained a doctoring power about 1848 (at 13), and earned money for his native masters until 1852, he would have been last sold (and then freed) at 17 years of age. At the end of 1866, when he was 30, given his fancy purchases listed in the Ft. Nisqually ledger, he probably hosted a feast or give-away that may have marked his marriage to Lucy. A census of 1888-89 lists Dr Simon as 45 and Lucy as 40, when Jim and Sally Meeker were both 50.[395] Both Jim and Sally would have been born in the early 1840s. Sally moved into the Puyallup valley about 1850 <C3>, married into native Steilacoom before the 1855 treaties, then marrying Jim early in the 1860s, with Jerry born healthy in 1862. Their other children did not survive.

In his touching obituary, Ezra Meeker said Jim (*Sky-ock*) was a ten-year-old orphan when he joined Ezra's household in the autumn of 1855. Jim and Sally married four times without having been divorced or separated. "They were first married under the prevailing Indian custom, and lived as man and wife for several years. When it became quite the fashion for the Indians to adopt the ways of the whites, and be like the "Bostons" (whites [Americans]), as it was termed, Jim and his wife were again married by a justice of the peace, and lived happily together, until, finally becoming devout Presbyterians, concluded they must be married for the third time (1878 by Rev Mann). Finally drifting into the Catholic church they were led to believe that all their marriages were void, and consequently celebrated their fourth honeymoon."

Jim Meeker died 27 June 1890 and was buried by Catholic rites on June 29 in the Puyallup cemetery. Jim and Sally "picked the first box of hops by the box that was ever picked in the state." This replaced pricing in terms of the labor of an entire day with a rate of $1/box, with 5 boxes a day the norm for this Meeker family. Starting their own farm, Jim eventually employed 5 white men, and died with an estate worth $20,000.[396]

During the early 1800s, as noted, Jerry and Lucy Gurand agreed that the Minter big house near the sandspit was over 100 feet long and 50 feet wide, to provide a training facility for elite children. Since the house ran east and west, the front beach was open and used for public events

---

394 Jerry probably had his mother's heroism in mind when he named the streets through his Brown's Point development, whose many "native names" include Hyada Blvd NE, along with Tok a Lou Ave NE, Ton a Won Da Ave NE, La Hal Da Ave NE, Klapache Ave NE, Wana Wana Pl NE, Mona Wana Pl NE, Hi Ab La Pl NE, Le Lou Wa Pl NE EE, from Marine View to East Side Drive NE.

395 Edwin Eells Papers, Box 3, Folder 10B, #11; Folder 12A #412, 413, 523, Washington State Historical Society.

396 Ezra Meeker, Indian Jim Was True, *The Daily Ledger*, 30 June 1890: 3.

like ceremonial abductions, initiations, and dances, while "intimidated" commoners floated offshore in their canoes or sat up on the high bluff. Protecting the community then were specialized defenders ("warrior champions"), though this career did not survive the epidemics. Instead, Minter survival was told in terms of the names of outstanding individuals who rose in rank to assume leadership and find a way to give the community a new identity. In addition, the notebooks provide invaluable data, by name, on the highest rank (a headwoman at that) and lowest class (the slave Simon) in Whulshootseed society.

In all, Minter's corporate identity began with the founding of chiefly lines by Moon and Sun, the sons of Stars. Possessing dicta and skills, they grew wealthy, bolstered by spirit powers as professors and fighters. With the diffusion of the Growlers guild, it set up a training academy in a huge cedar plank longhouse, with staging areas for public initiations on the beach in front of it or farther out on the spit.

Preceding European arrivals were devastating epidemics, especially the 1782 smallpox, killing many people before Captain George Vancouver assigned the mapping of the Sound to its namesake Peter Puget in 1792. The fur trade encouraged increased slaving in the 1830s, and Minter suffered badly, but survived with the help of an "electrocuting" horned-snake-prow canoe. At population nadirs, close kin married and their remarkably healthy children, proving special powers, reestablished the community. After a massive raid about 1840, Minter, under Broken Tooth, reconstituted itself by means of Chompion power, and so entered the ethnographic record.

Minter leaders attended the Medicine Creek treaty council in 1854, and Jim and Sally married a few years later. Less publicized was the torching of Minter by logging families in 1874, and then their refuge at Glencove until 1886. These events provide background for understanding the successful real estate career of Jerry Meeker, a Minter native son who managed to benefit from the loss of native lands to American settlers and urban sprawl as a wealthy high-profile native elder, real estate tycoon, and Tacoma booster.

13 (UN)SOUND HISTORY

Northern Puget Sound, though it had a series of minor reforming prophets, has largely remained closer to its ancient food sources and ancestral traditions. Those in the South Sound, however, have been forced in other directions, often accommodating to European pressures during rivalry between the Spanish, French, and English. The South Sound has had a long written history involving famous names, both globally and locally, but the arson and early homesteading of Minter has not yet been included.

Instead of hearty pioneer families clearing the forest and "taming the land" of romantic national lore, the truth was often unscrupulous intruders putting the torch to communities of sturdy cedarplank longhouses and productive gardens in extensive clearings to avoid toil and benefit from protecting soldiers and police. These dispossessors were often already neighbors, workers, and sometimes inlaws with ethnocentric arrogance.

Though the Spanish left behind artifacts and diseases, their records relate to the outer coast. British came to stay, after the George Vancouver expedition sailed around the world. In May of 1792, he charged Lt Peter Puget (1765-1822) to map what became his own namesake Sound, moving counterclockwise (starting to starboard on the western shore) with only a single confrontation along the route.

Puget's only hostile if harmless encounter involved "disorderly behavior" near a native community some distance up "the first arm leading to the westward within the narrows" in Carr Inlet, probably in Glencove near Minter, though most writers have suggested Minter itself. Vancouver later wrote, "In their persons they were apparently more stout than any other Indians we have hitherto seen on the coast. Two of the three in the canoe had lost the Right Eye & were much pitted with the Small Pox," probably from the 1782 pandemic. At a small bay, sailors were deploying a beach seine to catch fresh salmon for lunch when six canoes arrived and threatened hostilities. The seine was put away, officers had a leisurely lunch, and the crew left, followed by natives in their canoes who, away from shore, traded their garments of "Bear Raccoon Rabbit Deer" (but no sea otter) for trade goods. The sailors had earlier traded for native bows at the head of the inlet. Thus, Minters enter written history, stout, challenging, and trading.

The outpost of British Empire in the Northwest became the Hudson Bay Company's (HBC) Fort Vancouver, founded on the lower Columbia River in 1824 to replace Forts Astoria (1811) and George (1813). From there, expeditions departed to find other favorable locations for establishing trading post forts, such as those at Ft Langley in 1827 and at Ft Nisqually in 1833.[397] In 1837, HBC expanded as the Puget Sound Agricultural Company to include ranching and farming at Nisqually and Cowlitz Prairies for sale and trade within a region stretching from Alaska and California to Hawaii. Nisqually was also port to the early steamship *Beaver*, which traded furs and supplies along the entire coast claimed as British territory. Eventually, HBC moved its operations from the north bank of the Columbia to that of the Fraser, as well as founding Victoria on Vancouver Island in 1843, taking early documents and records along with them.

[397] Morag Maclachlan, ed, *The Fort Langley Journals*, 1827-30, 1998; Cecilia Svinth Carpenter, Fort Nisqually 1986.

During the last two months of 1824, John Work (or Wark, 1792-1861) kept a journal for forty Hudson Bay Company men, including Iroquois, French, and Hawaiians, who trekked from the Columbia to the Fraser River through a series of miserable portages. He described hiring a couple as guides from the native village of Steilacoom. The husband was Snohomish and the wife, who was the more helpful, spoke Chinuk, the regional trade jargon.

Later, one of Work's daughters married Dr William Fraser Tolmie, whose children preserved this journal in Victoria (BC), and another wed Edward Higgins, the last HBC employee who eventually bought Fort Nisqually, became an American, and retired to Tacoma. Dr Tolmie, long based at Fort Nisqually, maintained a keen academic interest in local natives, and willingly shared his knowledge with many. Of note, he ransomed Dr Simon, the Snohomish Slave, from the Minter headwoman, and employed him as a herder.[398]

Hoping to hold off the American onslaught, the HBC resettled former employees from the Red River (now Winnipeg) onto leased farms at Muck (now Roy), Spanaway, and Steilacoom, but these Metis quickly moved on to the Willamette Valley, where they could own their lands. Instead, Joseph Heath (1805-1849), a disgraced remittance man, rented one of these farms, hired many native workers, and kept a journal of local activities until he died.

In 1841 (April 30-August 4), the US Exploring Expedition (1838-42, under command of Lieutenant Charles Wilkes (1798-1877)[399] sailing with six ships around the globe to proclaim US might) was in Puget Sound, anchored off Ft Nisqually to again map the region. Among the few native names they placed on their map was that of "Sa-hote-lum" at Minter in Carr Inlet, clearly an attempt at the new tribal name that proclaimed their recent fame as native chompions. Presumably they had learned it from men of the Hudson Bay Company (HBC), one of whom, Pierre Legard, homesteaded at the southern tip of the Key Peninsula at Filucy Bay. Wilkes named adjoining inlets, split by Minter's Key Peninsula, after staff Lieutenants Augustus Case and Overton Carr, who, respectively, loathed and liked their captain, who ran a tight ship.[400]

---

398 British subjects could not legally own slaves after 1834, and in 1837 the HBC was to end slavery in vicinity of its posts. See Leland Donald, *Aboriginal Slavery on the Northwest Coast of North America* 1997: 240-3.

399 Wilkes had been raised in privilege in New York City, and one aunt was convert Elizabeth Seton, canonized as the first American saint in 1974. Among his crew were artists and "scientifics," including Horatio Hale, philologist [linguist] later famous for his work among Canadian Iroquois, and Lt George F Emmons, father of George T, Northwest ethnographer and artifact dealer. Wilkes came to later fame in the "Trent Affair" during the Civil War.

400 Herman Viola and Carolyn Margolis, *Magnificent Voyagers*, The US Exploring Expedition, 1838-1842, 1985; Murray Morgan, *Puget's Sound* 1979.

Concerted inroads by American settler began in 1845,[401] when the Bush-Simmons party left New Market (Missouri) for Oregon, but veered north into the south Sound (North Oregon) to protect George Bush from harsh anti-Negro (mulatto, black) laws. His visibly-evident multiracial ancestry (as freeborn Pennsylvanian) put him at odds with Oregon laws intended to ban the racial hostilities that eventually led to the US Civil War. Kind and generous to all who came to his thriving homestead at Centralia, Bush only became a state citizen by a special legislative act that nevertheless denied him the vote. Their colony founded New Market (Tumwater, 1845), grudging aided by British traders at Ft. Nisqually, and fostered Olympia (the state capitol), Steilacoom (1850, which featured a Catholic girl's school), and Alki (1852), birthplace of the city of Seattle.[402]

Steilacoom was founded by Lafayette Balch, after he was deliberately priced out of Olympia, with a prefabricated house brought by ship from Maine. He soon generously gave some of his homestead "land for building to the Masonic Lodge, the county, the school district, and the Methodist Church." John Butler Chapman founded the rival Steilacoom City until a decree by the first territorial legislature joined the two towns at Union Avenue. After Balch dropped dead on a San Francisco street at the age of 37 on 25 November 1862,[403] native homes and camps were driven off the town beach even as native labor remained vital to the development of this town. Town leaders, however, built a floathouse for Jerry Meeker's half-brother John and his wife Annie so they could readily move out of harm's way.

George Gibbs (1815-1873), lawyer and linguist, lived at Steilacoom for a decade, after he came west for the California Gold Rush, worked at Astoria, and served as secretary at treaty negotiations and signings. Keenly interested in native languages, he collected many vocabularies, as well as assembled the first dictionary of (southern, Nisqually) Lushootseed from his cook. He gathered reliable ethnographic information from tribes in Washington State, and drew maps of major rivers to record native place names. Returning to New York, he was

---

[401] US claims were represented by Albert Gallatin (1761-1849) – Swiss-born banker, US diplomat, friend of Thomas Jefferson, and comparative Americanist linguist – who negotiated the 1818 accord that set the US boundary at north latitude 49 to the Rockies, and allowed joint US and British occupation of "Oregon" between the Spanish (N 42°) and Russian (N 54°) claims. In 1827, while Minister to Great Britain, he renewed that convention, which held until the US gave a year's notice of abrogation on 28 April 1846, leading to a treaty that set the US border at N 49° to the Strait of Georgia, then down the middle of the channel. Such a line was too vague, leading to the famous "Pig War" on San Juan Island until Kaiser Wilhelm I of Germany set the boundary though Haro (not Rosario) Strait in 1872.

This treaty encouraged Sally, Jerry's mother, to move (marry) from Minter to Steilacoom, indicating that some natives were well aware that international decisions could add new options. While she was probably betrothed into the Steilacoom chiefly family, she also could take advantage of more local job choices for girls and women. Sustained labor was a hallmark of noble status.

[402] Months earlier single males homesteaded nearby but they are ignored in official histories of Seattle in favor of the families in the now-famous Denny party.

[403] Balch's sometime partner was Dr Joseph B Webber, tippling physician briefly in charge of the natives confined on Fox Island during the Treaty War, See Green, Chambers Collection Guide 1972: 29, #224, #233. Pierce County Auditor ledgers during 1863 record many sales from the Webber preemption claim 3¾ miles south of Steilacoom.

involved for the US in settling of accounts with the HBC, especially for Fort Nisqually. Over recent decades, in the series of federal trials to affirm treaty rights to fish, shellfish, and hunting, Gibb's notes in DC archives have been crucial for the success of these native causes because they specifically date to the time the treaties were signed in 1855.

With the end of the Oregon Compromise and the American takeover of the land between the Columbia and Fraser Rivers, Isaac Stevens was made Washington territorial governor, Indian Agent, and railroad route finder. During Christmas of 1854 (at Medicine Creek, derived from the Lushootseed *x^wdab* = for "shaman, doctor"), he forced the first of a series of treaties on local tribes (including Puyallup and Nisqually) to cede lands to the US, some of it already homesteaded in anticipation of such legal transfers. Shortly after, in response to his high-handed (and drunken ?) ways, the Treaty War broke out.[404] Hostile Nisqually were led by Leschi, who had relatives at Minter. Muckleshoots and others attacked Seattle, delaying its growth for years.

An early settler on Ketron Island near Steilacoom was Ezra Meeker (1830-1928), who eventually founded the town of Puyallup, made and lost a fortune in hops, and, most importantly, befriended the Jerry Meeker family, who took his family name as their own. In the aftermath of the Treaty War, when Governor Isaac Stevens made an example of Leschi, the Nisqually war leader dissatisfied with their reservation's small size and lack of horse pasture, Ezra and another juror prevented conviction at the first trial at Steilacoom when Leschi was defended by Clanrick Crosby (Bing's grandfather). For the second trial at Olympia, jurors were pre-selected to "railroad" this native patriot to the gallows. In 2004, a special legal panel composed of state judges exonerated Leschi.[405]

Thus, Puget Sound, as it had been during the fur trade era, was multiethnic and multiracial, within certain bounds and social ranks. Fur traders and clerks married into local families, producing Metis offspring, who were educated in both worlds to take up positions in the company. In addition, French Canadians, themselves often Metis, added another ethnic and Catholic element. During the 1855-57 Treaty War, their loyalty was much questioned by state officials, especially Governor Stevens.

The region figures in an early US "best seller" *Canoe and Saddle* (originally *Klallam and Klickitat*), a clever, rollicking book,[406] though hugely unkind to native peoples,[407] by Theodore Winthrop describing his eleven-day (21-31 August 1853) rush from Port Townsend to Fort Nisqually in a canoe, then overland by horse to the Dalles of the Columbia River to meet up with companions for a trek to Salt Lake City and on to the East. Then 25 and a Yale graduate,

404 Native friends now call it the First Treaty War, referring to subsequent cases fought in federal court.

405 Similarly, stories passed down in the family of Leschi's brother Queimuth have been returned to print, See George Sanders, Honne, The Spirit of the Chehalis 2012.

406 Philip Ritz, who founded Ritzville, visiting founders Morton McCarver and Jacob Carr, read this book and urged that the new city be platted as Tacoma [takoba] instead of the intended Commencement City.

407 Buying a huge salmon from fishers on the "Puyallop," he noted "yet if to this most brilliant of fish his hour of destiny had come, how much better than feeding foul Indians it was to belong to me, who would treat his proportions with respect, feel the exquisiteness of his coloring, grill him delicately, and eat him daintily!" When the fish was cooked and served, however, two of the three diners were natives.

Winthrop was 33 when he became the first Union officer killed in the Civil War. The remarkably accurate information on the native languages of the region interspersed with accounts of derring-do must have come from William Tolmie.

After reading the 1804-06 Journals of Lewis and Clark's, Thomas McCutcheon Chambers (1795-1876) decided in 1845 to leave Missouri with his wife, two daughters, and five sons, two of them married.[408] In 1847 they homesteaded at the mouth of what had been Steilacoom River, but soon became namesake Chambers Creek. There, they ran a grist mill in 1850, saw mill in 1852, and flour mill in 1855. While in Portland, as noted, Chambers encouraged the Denny party to settle what became Seattle.

A poignant local story indicating growing tensions over US national issues, health conditions, and Indian~White relations features the artistry of self-taught Jimmy (1857-1888) Pickett, Bellingham-born son of George (1825-1875), who led the famous Confederate charge at Gettysburg, and a "Haidah" woman, Morning Mist. Jimmy was named James Tilton Pickett for a fellow Southerner who was first surveyor general, first head of the University Board of Regents, and, famously, had his slave, Charles Mitchell, escape to safety in Victoria in1860 because anyone became free upon reaching British soil. When George went East, he left Jimmy behind with a south Sound family, who encouraged his art, though he died while still a young man, writing and illustrating for regional newspapers, and is buried in Portland.[409]

Missionaries had their own agendas. Unlike priests such as Fr Casimir Chirouse, engaged in Lushootseed liturgical translations, the missionaries in the south Sound were concerned with self help. The sons of early missionary Rev Cushing Eells were particularly active. Edwin was Indian Agent at Tacoma and Rev Myron Eels (1843-1907) lived among the Skokomish on Hood Canal. Under US policy, after the Civil War, Puget Sound northern reservations were assigned to Catholics and southern ones to Protestants, though ancient beliefs and rituals continued covertly until a more public Native religious freedom was "granted" in the 1970s.[410]

Judge James Wickersham (1857 - 1939)[411] began his legal career in Tacoma, became involved in the legal battles to dismantle the Puyallup Reservation, amassed a large library and artifact gallery, legally incorporated the 1910 Indian Shaker Church, and spent his later years as an Alaska judge and politician. At his death, his body was brought back for burial in Tacoma.

The key institution of cultural revival in the south Sound was and is the Indian Shaker Church, based in the revelation of John Slocum after he died and revived on 20 October 1882, when his wife Mary Thompson Slocum received the healing trembling ("the shake") that distinguishes this faith.[412] Together, the Slocums revealed the Word of the Christian God to

---

408 Andrew Jackson Chambers, *Recollections* 1975.

409 Robie Reid, How One Slave Became Free, An Episode of the Old Days in Victoria, BCHQ 6 (4): 251-56 1942.

410 Jay Miller, *Lushootseed Culture and the Shamanic Odyssey*: An Anchored Radiance 1999.

411 Evangeline Atwood , *Frontier Politics* 1979.

412 Robert Ruby and John A. Brown, *John Slocum and the Indian Shaker Church* 1996: 45.

Natives, benefiting from legal protections within Washington State.[413] Today it is spread from British Columbia to Montana to northern California.

Its tenets strictly identify it as an Indian religion inspired by the Christian God and Jesus Christ, as well as another supernatural figure they address as the Spirit, who is compatible both with the Holy Ghost and the aboriginal immortals who act as guardian spirits. The Shaker Church represents a blending of ancient and Christian beliefs that provides native peoples with their own form of religion recognizable as such by outsiders. It became the salvation of poor and traumatized peoples much maligned by their grasping neighbors and expanding corporations in control of railroads, timber, and resource extraction. Today, Shakers undertake the redeeming of souls and other healing once provided by the Spədak rite.

The consummate local amateur ethnographer was Arthur Ballard (1876-1962). His father Levi had trained as an MD in Ohio, but rarely practiced. Founding Auburn near the Muckleshoot Reservation, the living sons of the first marriage were Irving (with a goldmine in the Cascades) and William Rankin (who developed the Ballard neighborhood of Seattle), and of the second were Charles and Arthur. As a child, Arthur learned to speak Whulshootseed and took a keen interest in native culture. After his 1899 college degree in Classics, he worked as a public servant and official of the family gold mines. The Ballards served as the linchpin between native and settler families, both old and new. The older brothers were witnesses to land sales around Minter, while Arthur introduced generations of Boasian students to native elders, including Marian Smith to Jerry Meeker.

University of Washington, owning timber lands near Minter,[414] became a local hub for scholarship and research, often closely tied to Berkeley and New York. In 1910, John Peabody Harrington came north from California to teach summer classes there. In 1915, Thomas Talbot Waterman joined the faculty after he finished a degree at Columbia University under Boas and soon enjoyed working beside Arthur Ballard. His own contribution was a lengthy study of local place names at the twilight of the speech community. Boas sent his would-be heir, Herman Haeberlin (1890-1918) to Tulalip in 1916 and 1917, but he soon succumbed to diabetes.[415] In the 1920s, Melville Jacobs and Erna Gunther (at both the UW museum and college) began life-long careers at Seattle, encouraging locals such as Verne Ray, Viola Garfield, William Elmendorf, and Wayne Suttles. They hosted Boasians such as Thelma Adamson, working at Chehalis and Nooksack, and Marian Smith, at Puyallup and Nisqually. They also developed ties

---

413 Darleen Fitzpatrick, The 'Shake': The Indian Shaker Curing Ritual among the Yakima 1968: 7-8.

414 In September 1952, the newly-formed Seattle Young Archaeologist's Society negotiated with landowner Thomas Meyer to begin their careers "with a keen interest" in a shell midden on the point(e) of Minter Bay. Before they could put shovels into the ground, however, a new concrete bulkhead destroyed the site. Recent hires, Douglas and Carolyn Osborne brought from New Mexico their own experiences teaching teenaged boys and girls proper scientific techniques, but, again, the University of Washington missed out at Minter. See Charles Luttrell, Archaeology for Young Diggers: Douglas and Carolyn Osborne, the Seattle Young Archaeologists' Society, and the Washington Archaeological Society. *Archaeology in Washington* 2006: 12, 6.

415 Jay Miller, ed., Regaining Dr Herman Haeberlin: Early Anthropology and Museology in Puget Sound, 1916-1917, 2004; On Line 2007 @ osu.edu.

with Jerry Meeker and other community leaders. In 1935, Ethel Aginsky, doing fieldwork with the Hawk family, researched a grammar of the Puyallup dialect.

After World War II, the GI Bill encouraged graduate work by men and women who had never planned to attend college. The State (now Burke) Museum had cars and boats to loan for research projects. Separate archaeological surveys of southern Puget Sound were conducted by Ethel Carlson, by Florence Howard, and, most significantly, by John and Marcia Winterhouse (just after they were married).[416] Their map on graph paper marked archaeological sites all over the south Sound, but the densest concentration (7 locations) was on Minter Bay, though Wollochet (5) and Filucy (10, scattered) Bays were also heavily occupied. In 1973-74, Dale McGinnis, who grew up locally but seemed unaware of recent ties to the historical and ethnographic record of the Puyallups, excavated at Minter and received three radiocarbon dates of 1200 +/- 270 years.

Engaging local histories were provided by Andrew Jackson Chambers, Laura Belle Downey-Bartlett (intimately involved at Minter and Glencove), photographer Edward Curtis, Floyd Hall Oles (who seined with Minters), Betsey Johnson Cammon, Hazel Heckman, and, especially, Murray Morgan. Gary Fuller Reese, before his abrupt departure, amassed a crucial archive and data base at the Tacoma Public Library. Native writers include Henry Sicade, of a prosperous Puyallup family, and Cecelia Svinth Carpenter, a Nisqually. Local novelists, such as Archie Binns and Stewart Holbrook, added boyhood memories of native events to their books.

Missing from these histories, however, are claims in these notebooks and documents in county and federal archives that expose arsons of the 1870s and 1880s. Riches were made in the booming logging industry, especially for the California construction market, by logging off old growth forests and then abandoning the land for unpaid taxes. Later homesteaders, well known to history, bought and resettled these lands. Behind the scenes, tragically, native homes at Minter and Glencove were burned. The first before the Act of 3 March 1875 with homesteading by Calvin G Burkett (1820-1894), Isaac Hawk (1836-1905), and Nehemiah G Bartlett (1841-1874).[417] The second before the Indian Homestead Act of 4 July 1884, when Glencove was filed

---

416 John Winterhouse, A Report on an Archaeological Survey of Lower Puget Sound 1948.

417 His widow was Laura Belle Downey Bartlett (1851-1932), who was dedicated to the preservation of Chinuk Wawa Jargon, the local trade pidgin, and published a songbook translating many popular songs into Wawa. She composed a musical drama (opera) on native themes, "Wah-Mah-Whah-Lah," staged in Portland and Tacoma, and served as "interpreter in debates between older Quinault Indians and visiting congressman on the issue of public lands." Her other works included a Chinook Jargon dictionary, *Student's History of the Northwest and State of Washington*, a cookbook for Klondike gold seekers and draft entries for *Who's Who of the Washington Pioneer Empire Builders*.

After keeping boarders and teaching music, as specified in her homestead claim at Burnt Point near Glencove, she served as president of the Oregon State Mining Association (1910) and of a mining and milling company run by business women, as well as director of the International Studio of Music in Portland. She was first president of the Business Women's Club of Oregon and of the Pierce County Pioneer Association (1903), as well as a member of the Oregon State Women's Press Club and the Washington State Republican party. See A Remarkable Woman, *Town on the Sound*, Joan Curtis, Alice Watson, Bette Bradley 1988: 118-21, 189.

on by William Rains. All these men were Masons.[418] In 1882, the George Minter family came from Nebraska to start the official record, providing the current name for our point of concern.

In all, official history, especially in terms of the transfer of native lands to alien settlers, has skirted the truth and ignored the abundance of details that do not reflect well on many of the pioneer families whose descendants still occupy prominent roles in this region of south Puget Sound.

< §11 Surplus WWI Wooden Ships Burned for Scrap Metal on Minter Spit >

[418] Masons bonded WASPs at this time. Even Rev Myron Eels is buried in the Union Pioneer Cemetery owned by a Masonic lodge. See Rodika Tollefson, Historians record nearly forgotten WA cemeteries, *Kitsap Sun*, 1 August 2009.

14 FAILURES, FIRES, FORGETTING

The Unsettling

At Minter, their native world spread out from spirits and species on both sides, above, and beneath Carr Inlet, portages west into Case Inlet or east to Gig Harbor and Puget Sound, and routes directly across to Steilacoom (Chambers Creek) and to the sprawling City of Tacoma beyond the Narrows. American settlement later spread from the logging out ~ off of the Northeast, moving west in stages. Of note, as farmers later fled the Dakotas for Seattle in the 1930s, following along northern land routes, the sea had earlier linked the Northeast and Northwest by "sailing around the horn." This maritime connection along the northern tier relied on shipping skills such as those of Captain William Renton, an early lumber baron from Maine whose name became attached to his mill and town just south of Seattle.

Indeed, natives on both coasts quickly benefited from improved marine technology. Canadian Mikmaq's adapted to sloops of the 1600s as Washington Salishans took to canvas (instead of woven mat) sails in the 1800s. They added oar locks to canoes before they later cut off and squared sterns to install outboard motors in the early 1900s. Natives were never passive to the changes in their lives, often putting new technology to their own uses while trying to avoid bureaucratic, zealous, and legal impositions. One apt example was the use of shiny alarm clock parts to make fishing lures, a good illustration of the local value of fishing over the constraints of measured time.

For Carr Inlet, moreover, we have names and biographies for many of the crucial people who motivated the major changes and stresses in the lives of these native peoples.

Hot Properties

The history of coastal Washington, as elsewhere, is essentially one of Europeans increasingly outnumbering and overwhelming the indigenous population, who had always been careful to maintain balanced ratios among all resources and species, their own included, so as not to overstress their shared environment. Species relied on each other and numbers were kept proportional to the landscape, avoiding damage to their shared habitat. Only natural disasters like "wild" fires, earthquakes, tsunamis, and volcanic eruptions, which natives often blamed on their own careless transgressions ("faults"), were of a scale whose remedy was the earth's taking over its ("her") own recovery.

This landscape was park-like because it was regularly tended with **fire** and good eco-sense. New ashes-fed berry patches gave easy access to plump pickings. Weirs along rivers and traps set in forest runways always allowed some escapement, both for the sake of the migrating species and for other people living upstream. Throughout, natural products were used to make ecologically sound houses, vessels, tools, and containers. Resources were nominally owned by local leaders, active managers planning for best harvest and use – as judged on the basis of rank, residence, or requests from those in need. Always, these foods were to be shared, not hoarded nor guarded, or spirits would be mightily offended. Still, proprieties and courtesies needed to be respected, as Peter Puget's crew did not do at Glencove when they boldly put a net in the water.

Visiting explorers needed fresh food and water, as they mapped and charted the Sound's twists and turns for later use by profiteers of their own and other nations. Staking claims, commerce, and settlement were long-range goals, though survival was just then their most immediate concern. As evidence from the earliest Spanish visits we have only the scars of smallpox, especially the 1782 pandemic, and less obvious defects. From George Vancouver, we have written accounts of the 1792 menacing actions of the native men from Burley, Minter, and Glencove as Peter Puget set a net for a fresh lunch. The objection was probably not that the net was deployed, since these were clearly crow-eating aliens in need of food, but that neither permission, plea, gifts, nor prayers had been offered in acknowledgement of the care that Minters, then on the defensive after suffering plagues, had been routinely offering their vital local resources.

John Work's 1824 Hudson's Bay trek along the Sound and its shores at least had the courtesy and forethought to hire native guides. Even if they were not locals from Steilacoom itself, they (really a wife) could scope out situations along the way and evoke safe conduct. In time, the intellectual curiosity and sustained record keeping of William Tolmie, trained as an MD, and James Douglas, who began as a clerk, provided substantial archival glimpses of the changing, growing, if not mutating, relations among natives and newcomers, specifically at Minter.[419]

Two international treaties put the squeeze on locals. Sally herself (Jerry's mother) seems to have drifted from Minter in the aftermath of the 1846 Treaty of Washington ~ Oregon that asserted American primary claims over those of the British throughout Oregon Territory. Reports from the east, often spread by Metis Iroquois, did not bode well for occupation by pioneers from the states (US). Sparse British traders had been good neighbors, but overcrowding Americans were sure to threaten. At the very end of 1854 and through 1855, US claims were legally launched by a series of Indian treaties, the first at Medicine Creek, signed by men that included Tyee Dick of Minter, with allied Puyallup, Nisqually, Squaxin, and others. This place was also near the McAllister homestead, where husband James paid the ultimate toll during the Treaty War and was buried near Minter homesteaders in the Masonic Cemetery in Olympia.

Traders had come as just that. Their concern was on-going cordial commerce, allowing free access to all regions, rather than altering the landscape or policing the native populations. Increased desire was more potent than force for encouraging sales. Necessary hooks, axes, pails, needles, cloth, and threads strongly motivated good conduct. A shadowy threat of cannons and firearms – like traditional sorcery, maladicta, and gloating at another's grief – further enforced good behavior among natives. Joseph Heath[420] and others did some farming, but it had less useful impact on the total landscape than the annual burning over or the massive deer ~ duck

[419] A constant source of amazement in my Puget Sound research is the continuing if faded echo of a once dramatic custom. A case in point at Minter is the bagpiping in fine Celtic tradition by Andrew, the son of Denis, the former Minter hatchery manager. In semi-feudal style, managers of the HBC across the Sound at Fort Nisqually were piped into public events over a century before.

[420] Joseph Heath, *Memoirs of Nisqually* 1979.

drives by natives with nets. Except for fire-maintained prairie clearings, of course, everything remained forested.

These trees lured the loggers, like William Renton, Pope and Talbot, or the many small gyppos who wanted to clear land for a homestead, feeding family with potatoes grown in an open clearing and with clams from the beach.[421] Early logging relied on floating barges called wanagans serving as sawmill, kitchen, or bunkhouse. These were moved along shorelines with easy access to timber. Loggers put in long hours while any daylight remained, returning in the dark only to eat and sleep.

On logged-over land, the resulting stump ranches nurtured a family while ground was further cleared for more extensive use as open plowed fields. Such was the start for the Binn family of four boys, including Archie, who wrote about it.[422] For some families with money but few children, much of this clearing was actually done by Indien men, such as Jim Meeker and others, paid in clothing, food, and rarely cash by homesteaders. At the same time, native women were washing clothes, cleaning houses, cooking meals, and digging clams for income. Indispensable baskets, bowls, spoons, and canoes were sold by natives to local "whites" of whatever national origins.

Stump ranch loggers claimed Minter Point(e) (or most of it). Already homesteading and logging nearby, Calvin Burkett would have seen these natives come and go (commute) with the seasons, using their summer house and storage stump. Minter was their home, both ancestral and personal, even as taxes, wages, and outside commitments scattered them during the year and, indeed, made their last decades there so sporadically seasonal. Of maximum importance, however, wherever they were living, Minter remained the storehouse and emotional ~ spiritual support that "fed" them in all manner of satisfying ways.

Finally, after great personal trials and displacement by land-hungry settlers, the Minter plank houses were torched, just as legal (supposedly) ex-native homesteading on the public domain loomed in 1875. Fortunately, no one was there to object or die because it was probably done in March when harsh weather kept people inside and elsewhere. With the help of older children, Burkett built a milled lumber house over these ashen remains and had only to "prove up." Word must have reached the headwoman Damasq and others almost immediately because Minter Point is such an exposed location. Ever resilient and resourceful, these Minters built a new home at Glencove, where native families were unmolested for another decade until William Rains filed a claim, as another more-specifically pro-Indian Homestead Act came into play.

Throughout the Northwest, settler origins determined racial and commercial attitudes. Those successful on the coast were largely Down-Easters from Maine, such as William Renton willing to hire anyone from anywhere who worked hard. The ancestors of Bing Crosby were also from Maine, though their oppressed Irish origins probably had more to do with his grandfather's defense of Leschi at his first trumped-up trial. While the latitudes of Maine and Washington were the same, not everything else was.[423]

---

[421] The local joke was that pioneers ate so many clams, their stomachs rose and fell with the tides. Among natives this was a source for empowerment instead of humor.

[422] Archie Binns, see all.

[423] Stewart Holbrook, Green Commonwealth 1945: 83.

Along the inland Sound, successful pioneers were from the Midwest, such as the Dennys of Seattle and all-important Ezra Meeker, who provided constant advice, employment, and encouragement to the native Meekers and their allies.

More problematic were the missionaries such as the Eells family, though Cushing's sons divided up the political (Edwin) and the religious (Myron) realms. Catholic priests were foreign born, and more sympathetic to and of natives, who enjoyed the rich church pageantry. Matthew Mann, though born in Germany, espoused highly American goals, which he instilled in Jerry Meeker and Peter Stanup. His enthusiasm for the early Shaker Church contributed to his voluntary leaving, after a brief official expulsion, the Presbyterians in favor of Christian Science.

Most unsettling of all (in present terms) were those from the Southern states or with secessionist sympathies, such as George Pickett or James Tilton, who relied heavily on the clout of DC federal sponsorship. That Tilton's own slave Charlie Mitchell escaped five years after natives had to manumit their own, and that Tilton himself later died in the South could not have boded well for local natives. Arthur Denny's election victory over Tilton to be an early territorial delegate benefited natives in many ways.

Lastly, with the turn of the century, native languages were accurately committed to paper, along with memories, tales, and all-embracing kin terms. A record of *evidence* could now be archived that more truthfully reflected native perspectives than some outsider's warped notions of an alien "other." Through publications, letters, documents, and anthropological tradition, we know that the lynchpin for this local scholarly community was Arthur Ballard, raised to be sympathetic by his family and native nanny. Through Ballard, academics such as John Peabody Harrington, TT Waterman, Erna Gunther, Melville Jacobs, Marian Smith, and, significantly, Alfred John Smith were introduced to key native elders, ready to leave an account of their richly textured pasts. Even the archaeological survey by the Winterhouses relied on input from Ballard. While many academics were leery of Jerry Meeker for selling out his reservation and seeming grandstanding, these notebooks reveal him to be a skilled, articulate, and informed elder, as does his earlier work with Marian Smith.

If we had a similarly detailed record for the homesteaders, it should be possible to reconstruct a similar community of interests among the Burketts, Bartletts, Knapps, Rains, and others. In particular, Horace Knapp appears in a variety of contexts that suggest he had an intriguing role. This small community, knowing that the close ties between the white and native Meekers would surely pass on word of the impending 1875 law (allowing native homesteading at a "public" place like Minter), probably tacitly collaborated on the torchings and claims that kept that from happening. Certainly, their common Masonic tie only increases present-day suspicion. The role of the elder Ballard brothers in Horace's sale of Minter Point to Burkett's first wife shows that these different social networks sometimes intersected.

The most perplexing and shadowy figure in this mix is Isaac Hawk, who seems to have gotten along with virtually everyone, native and other, male and female, leaving a trail of descendants that seems to have been ethnically varied. He clearly had more money and connections than Knapp, and so was more heavily involved in local enterprises. His paper trail, however, is suspiciously sketchy. Unlike Burkett, Hawk's grave in the Masonic cemetery is well marked with a large tombstone, surrounded by his children.

With great irony, as repeatedly noted throughout this work, many of the confirming documents are both preserved and obscured in their repositories. In particular, at the University of Washington, the hasty departure of Erna Gunther from the state museum, its move to a new building, and her own donation of records to the separate library archives disconnected her materials, complicating my attempts to identify and understand the contents of these three notebooks provided by Jerry Meeker to Alfred Smith. Knowing the native source by name but not the academic one has kept these notebooks from professional use for half a century (calling it academic bias seems far too mild). My own lifetime of scholarship, cross-referencing, and personal contacts finally allowed them to be rationally restored to provide truthful background to American history.

Charred History

Fire is the overlooked strength of the Native Americas, in both its tame and wild varieties. Used with care, it served natives for cooking and warmth, nourished new berry patches, and hollowed out canoe logs, as well as providing a night lure for fish, ducks, and other dazzled foods. It fueled torches and it burned upon packed earth or sand piled in the bottom of canoes. During spring and fall, when the wind was right and rain was due, berry patches, meadows, prairies, and other terrain were set ablaze to encourage new growth. In its unleashed wild forms (caused by lightning, human carelessness,[424] or willful hostility), fire burned out human settlements – destroying all in its path, blackening the skies for days, and smearing local soils.

With fire, natives manicured their lands for thousands of years, until settlers from faraway lands used it to burn them out of their ancient homes. Its effects were profound because the best land, already long occupied and sustained when Europeans arrived, now "legally" belongs to their heirs. That this transfer occurred so quickly, or so it seems, has more to do with fast acting germs (than with speeding bullets) and roaring fires that destroyed a vulnerable native population. Only the thick carbon residue in the ground hints at the huge level of destruction.

Throughout the native Americas, fire was used for cremation and cleansing.[425] Burning could mark a new beginning, a fresh start. Flames also provided a passage between worlds and dimensions, as Lushootseeds continue to "burn for the dead" by placing favorite foods on special fires after a funeral and at memorials. In this regard, the arson of the houses served to reunite them with their deceased residents, thus providing an ironic continuity across dimensions even as it removed physical evidence of the ownership from the land.

Minter on Carr Inlet was once its own world, but that special universe continues only in written notes, scattered memories, and now inside these covers. Its truth can still be seen on the ground, but time has taken a terrible toll. Throughout, **fire** has been a constant presence, for good and bad. It warmed homes and cooked food, but it also destroyed these same houses. It burned whatever it was set upon, whether maliciously, as at Minter and Glencove, or

---

[424] A famous instance is the second bonfire – to celebrate July 4th, 1853, set inside a huge stump on a hill above Willapa Bay – which got out of control and "set fire to the forest, which continued to burn for several months, till the winter rains finally extinguished it," James Swan, *The Northwest Coast* 1857: 134.

[425] Jay Miller, Ashes Ethereal: Cremation in the Americas 2001. Recall too that Starchild and his brother remade the world by first burning up the old one before they became Sun and Moon.

beneficially, as when the Arledge homestead on Filucy Bay a few years ago became a practice burn for local volunteer firefighters.

Massive forest fires in 1847 and 1902 were devastating, caused by acts of nature and careless logging. The earliest settlers complained that smoke often darkened summer skies for weeks as lightning-caused forest fires burned out of control until Fall rains put them out.

In 1927, natives of Puget Sound went to court, unsuccessfully at first, for some kind of restitution for their lost lands, timbers, houses, and foods.[426] Witnesses testified to routinely burning over of the landscape in October and March to keep down underbrush and to prevent huge forest fires. They also detail the hostile burning of native homes by settlers, who wanted land already cleared. A few poignant examples of the many consequences of the 1875 and 1884 federal acts include Mary Jerry Dominick, a 60-year-old Muckleshoot, who said,

> Answer. The white settlers informed my father that we must move from his home and that he must buy and pay for some piece of land somewhere else.
>
> Question. What did the white people do with the house that you and your father lived in?
>
> Answer. They destroyed the building as they did other Indian buildings.
>
> Question. Did the white people destroy any of the homes of your relatives?
>
> Answer. Yes; because they wanted the Indians to move away from their homes.
>
> Question. Which ones of her relatives did they destroy the homes of?
>
> Answer. The white settlers destroyed every Indian building there was along the river.[427]

Sam Tecumseh, a 72-year-old Duwamish driven to Tulalip reported

> Answer. When the white settlers came, then they took possession of their [natives'] cleared lands and also destroyed the house, some of the houses, they set fire to it.[428]

Major Hamilton, 71, a Duwamish leader living at Muckleshoot, said through an interpreter

> Answer. He says when the settlers came, they drove us away and then they destroyed the houses and even set fires to get us away from these villages.[429]

---

426 Another round of court hearings for Indian Land Claims was more successful in the 1950s, with payment checks made out in the 1970s.

427 Duwamish and Others (Court of Claims of the United States # F-275) 1933: 170. Ironically, in time, these settlers would also remove the major waterway in this region, the White River, by redirecting its flow from the Duwamish into the Puyallup.

428 Duwamish and Others (Court of Claims of the United States # F-275) 1933: 685.

429 Duwamish and Others (Court of Claims of the United States # F-275) 1933: 695.

Another major witness in these proceedings was none other than Jerry Meeker, then 65.

Thus, for 86 years, the charred history of the region has been in the court record, but not in the popular one. What settlers did was not illegal after the treaty was signed and approved, though natives, like other people, were entitled to personal damages, though no one was ever directly compensated. Of note, the other treaties after the first at Medicine Creek were not affirmed by Congress for years because of the confrontations of the Treaty War of the 1850s.

When smallpox hit lowland Lushootseeds in the 1700s, upland peoples were spared to be able to move downstream, where they suffered the 1830s epidemic that killed off 80% of these natives.[430] Officials of the US and others argued for medical fumigation to justify the burning of unhealthy dirt-floored cedar plank longhouses (such as the enormous Oleman House of Chief Seattle). These flames also obliterated tangible proof of native legal claims.

In the north Sound, a native man searching for pox survivors on Jarman Prairie and at Friday Creek along the Samish River found only a baby niece alive. He burned down both towns, adding the clothes he was wearing to the flames, and took the baby to his home at the head of Edison Slough, where they stayed in quarantine as he built, fumigated, and then burned down a series of shelters until he was sure both had escaped contagion.[431] After decades of such epidemics, natives had finally developed effective strategies to survive them.

When the outlet of Lake Washington originally came through what is now the city of Renton, conflict developed over the use of the Black River. In 1854, a sawmill was built at a prime fishery. The next year, natives burned it down to reclaim the fishery. When coal mining began nearby, the whole landscape was polluted, and natives were made most unwelcome. In 1869, thirty settlers asked the BIA to remove all natives still on the Black and Cedar Rivers, but the earliest pioneers, such as the Dennys, came to their defense. Eventually, time and self-interest led many of these natives to seek refuge as individual Duwamish owning their own private homesteads or by enrolling at local reservations, where they now live among Suquamish, Muckleshoots, Snoqualmies, and others. Some blended into general society.

While it was always a strong theoretical possibility, after diligent search, I could find only one instance, and that justified, of a named native who burned out an illegal homesteader. Again, it was in the context of desirable land in what became the wealthy waterfront community at La Conner, Washington. This singular documented turnabout occurred at the northern end of the Swinomish reservation. What is notable is the care and caution used by these natives against a homesteader who was in direct and persistent violation of federal and trust laws intended to protect this reservation for the continuing use of these allied tribes, as guaranteed in the 1855 treaty at Mukilteo (~ Point Elliot).

On 6 July 1953, at Swinomish, George Dan told anthropology graduate student Sally Snyder that Charlie Ayesee (pronounced eye-see, also written Isee) had trouble with a white man who kept moving onto his family allotment on the reservation. These were prime agricultural

[430] Such fill-in by uplanders has been termed Morey's Law by Henry Dobyns, *Their Number Become Thinned* 1983: 306.

[431] Martin Sampson, *Indians of Skagit County* 1972: 25.

lands on the sharp bend of the Skagit River delta known as the Flats.[432] Since this was reservation land in federal trust, Swinomish Indians had undisputed title, though some neighbors apparently thought it was "too good" for Indiens. This man built a house on the flats, though he had been driven off by Ayesee twice previously.[433] Frustrated, Ayesee gathered together his supporters, went there, tied the man up, took all of his possessions, groceries, and guns out of the cabin, and then burned it down. After the building was blazing, they untied the man and returned his guns. He immediately filed against Ayesee in court. That the forces of "white justice" could be imposed so quickly against a native supposedly under federal protection says reams about the racial fairness of local law.

In a few days, a boat came from Bellingham with police, who handcuffed Ayesee, and put him in a tiny jail cell where he could only crouch, not stand or lie down, in the dark. He only saw light when his food was served. At a hearing, Charlie Ayesee won in Bellingham court, but the man filed in higher (federal?) court in Port Townsend. Ayesee was taken there for trial, but again won because it was his allotted reservation land. His goal, however, was to fight for rights to the nearby islands and Deception Pass, but he "lost out" because, Dan said, "white soldiers claimed them." Today, an Air Force base and other military instillations still occupy these nearby islands.[434]

While **fire** is an ever-present danger, circumstances determine whether or not there is criminal intent or the malice of arson. The Coeur d'Alene of Idaho tell the story of Agatha (locally pronounced Ajat), a devout Catholic elder who had helped build their old mission at Cataldo and provided funds for the large church at DeSmet. As she became the last living builder, she often said she intended to take this church with her to Heaven. The day after she died in 1939, the church burned to the ground. Parishioners assumed that this burning was a mark of her special favor and devotion.[435]

When greed is involved, however, fire was definitely misused. While it was becoming federal trust land as the Quileute Reservation, the town of La Push was burned down in 1889 while everyone was off picking hops in the Puyallup Valley. That arsonist, the local school teacher, was never punished and indeed founded a famous pioneer family. Near the Canadian border, Nooksack villages were burned while residents were away. The local paper was amazingly matter-of-fact in quoting elder Sindick Jimmy, "White settlers were moving in, crowding and burning the Native Americans out."[436] We learn only these bare facts. The details of the torching of Minter and Glencove, therefore, serve as instances of a larger aspect of the American Frontier.

---

[432] Charlie Wilbur, a wealthy Swinomish who testified about Jerry Meeker's Chinuk Wawa abilities had built up a productive farm on the Flats that eventually was foreclosed on and lost to a local banker, whose family retains it.

[433] He was able to keep returning, according to the present native owner of this property, because this site was beside the Slough along the dike still draining this rich farmland. It is a small peninsula, so the interloper must have thought it was detachable from the reservation once he rowed across and built on it.

[434] UW – SC [MSCUA], Sally Snyder notes, Melville Jacobs Collection, 109-3-112. One of these islands was finally returned to joint use with the Swinomish in July 2010.

[435] Thomas Connolly, SJ, A Coeur D'Alene Indian Story 1990: 80.

[436] *Lynden Tribune*, 19 February 1975.

< §12 Burning Down the Port Gamble S'Klallam Town at Point Julia >

On 27 October 1940, the old S'Klallam village at Point Julia on the flats across from Port Gamble was burned because new federal houses had been built for tribal members on the bluff above. The loss and move was especially hard on the elderly, who wept openly. True to its times, the newspaper noted "Indians are supposed to be an inscrutable and unemotional people, stoical by training and inclination [but this] got a kicking around … At 4:30 p.m. a score of younger Indians, at the behest of the government, put the torch to twenty ancient homes and outer buildings which, since the early 1850's, have comprised the community of Little Boston."[437]

Puzzling Out Place

In thought, word, and deed, therefore, "Place is a puzzle."[438] As occupied and claimed space, localized cooperation or competition has to be sorted out according to varying agendas arrayed over the longest time period in as many voices as possible. External and internal influences should be identified, as well as the impact of the global forces.

Ideally, "Place is security, space is freedom: we are attached to the one and long for the other [and] it is by thoughtful reflection that the elusive moments of the past draw near to us in present reality and gain a measure of permanence … place is an archive of fond memories and splendid achievements that inspire [and inform] the present; place is permanent and hence reassuring to man, who sees frailty in himself and chance and flux everywhere."[439]

Each human has a uniquely personal sense of the very same spot because "places, like voices, are local and multiple. For each inhabitant, a place has a unique reality, one in which

[437] Seattle Post-Intelligencer, Sunday, 27 October 1940, p15.

[438] William Lang, From Where We Are Standing: The Sense Of Place and Environmental History, *Northwest Lands, Northwest Peoples. Readings in Environmental History* 1999: 97.

[439] Yi-Fu Tuan, *Space and Place. The Perspective of Experience* 1977: 3, 148, 154.

meaning is shared with other people and places. The links in these claims of experienced places are forged of culture and history."[440]

Identifying four dimensions of multilocality, Margaret Rodman[441] lists: 1) seeking to understand the construction of places from multiple viewpoints, 2) undertaking comparative or contingent analysis of place, 3) studying reflexive relationships with places, either as familiar or strange, and 4) grasping the sense in which polysemic meanings of physical landscape are shaped and expressed for different users. The result presents "the idea that a single place may be experienced quite differently" by varied humans constructing and contesting it over time.

Minter resettlement cost no lives. By contrast, some places and times are toxic, as seen in print and image of Black River Falls, Jackson County, Wisconsin. By pairing glass negatives by photographer Charles Van Schaick with selections from the *Badger State Banner* newspaper edited by Frank Cooper and his son George, *Wisconsin Death Trip* haunts the reader.[442] Insanity, suicide, depression, infant death, and family breakdown abound within its pages, as they did when first chronicled in 1890-1910.

Some places experience pain. At Minter, arsonists and natives probably knew each other and must have interacted. At least one probably had a native wife or consort, as well as children. Arson seems to have been timed for when the villagers were away harvesting the fruits of nature. Otherwise, the only open hostilities were reported battles during native slave raids.

One of the homesteaders, whose grave remains unmarked to this day, shares space with a famous first casualty of the 1855 Treaty War in the Olympia Masonic Cemetery, but timing was more important than aiming guns for claiming land. Settlers wanted both land and native labor to achieve their goals. Relations, guided by native leaders, remained cautiously good.

The horrific ethnic violence so prevalent in California, where some of these grasping loggers spent time during the Civil War, did not come north with 49ers. They did bring racist attitudes and the term "rancheree," from Californio Spanish, to refer to a native settlement. The violence in confined space like Round Valley was lethal, beginning with genocide of the native Yuki, including enslavement of their young women, and ending with local land barons turning guns on each other.[443]

Elsewhere, a brutal incident is writ large, such as *Massacre at Camp Grant* which ponders the strategies of forgetting or commemorating the 1871 massacre of over one hundred Apaches by the town fathers of Tucson and, especially, their native allies among Tohono O'odham and Hispanics. The massacre became

---

440 Margaret Rodman, Empowering Place: Multilocality and Multivocality, *American Anthropologist* 94 (3): 643 1992.

441 Margaret Rodman, Empowering Place 1992: 646-647.

442 Michael Lesy, *Wisconsin Death Trip* 1973.

443 Lynwood Carranco and Estle Beard, *Genocide and Vendetta: The Round Valley Wars of Northern California* 1981.

> "a kind of phantom history, a story at once strangely present and absent, palpable yet illusive, haunting places yet never fully inhabiting them, at the periphery of conversations yet just beyond them."[444]

> "Thus instead of thinking about historical accounts as an heirloom, an object, … history [is] a form of remembrance, a kind of *trace* [with] two related meanings – that which is left behind, a vestige; and that route which is followed, a path. Remembrances result directly from preceding events and thus present historicity; they also are avenues that lead us to the past, a process that involves social engagement. Traces are *representations* and therefore require interpretation, making the question one of translation, of decoding and unraveling the twisted cultural, historical, and political skeins of narratives.[445]

> While many scholars focus on "violence as a cultural practice and … how violence is remembered, misremembered, and forgotten, surprisingly few explicitly discuss how re-tracing past events is a means of engaging in justice [though] reparation is best argued on the grounds of past injustices that continue to the present day rather than claims of original occupancy."[446]

> "… the "past" is essentially a cultural strategy that people use to filter their present experiences … with victims and perpetrators who do not make their world but rather are made by it … History is a form of power … to promote nationalist ferment, justify appropriations of land, and advance agendas of war."[447]

Later, in 1887, prosperous Apache survivors, like those at Minter, were driven off their homesteaded land.[448] In Arizona as in Washington, natives had few defenses to protect themselves, their lands, and their abiding places.

For the Northwest, the most recent, most expensive, and most disheartening puzzle of place involved the ancestral S'Klallam village of Tse-whit-zen at Port Angeles on the Olympic Peninsula. The Washington Department of Transportation (Wash-DOT), intent on digging a pool for the building and floating of pontoons, disturbed hundreds of burials of the Lower Elwha Klallam, whose reservation remains nearby. Tribal members were hired at good wages to exhume their ancestors and haptically[449] experience their tools and traces, renewing interest and knowledge in their culture and history, however grim.

---

444 Chip Colwell-Chanthaphonh, *Massacre at Camp Grant: Forgetting and Remembering Apache History* 2007: 5.

445 *Massacre at Camp Grant* 2007: 46.

446 *Massacre at Camp Grant* 2007: 105-6.

447 *Massacre at Camp Grant* 2007: 6, 101.

448 Massacre at Camp Grant 2007: 74.

449 In this case, meaning "by means of a visceral sense of touch, hands-on experience."

> "Filling the tidelands and starving the beaches of sediment trapped behind the dams on the Elwha completed the destruction of the Klallam people's food supply. Like the salmon, the Klallam people were confined to a smaller and smaller homeland and a restricted food web.... Period newspaper clippings recount residents being burned out of so-called squatter's shacks on the Ediz Hook, right as the first fall rains began.... Some 150 years of disease, dispossession, industrial development, and forced assimilation took their toll. Within the tribe, a cultural gap opened, as tribal members left to find work and elders decided not to pass their culture on. They didn't want more children to suffer as they had. So deliberately dug, it's a cultural gap that this town, this state, and this tribe soon fell into together."[450]

Tse-whit-zen was a major village that morphed into the large town of Port Angeles, after settlers overwhelmed native populations, sometimes with a prod from arson. At Minter, later sparse settler replacement was a comedown from what the native community had been.

In all, then, Minter tells the story of a place, once famous among native communities for its elite members and training academy, that fell into "ghost" settler ownership briefly enough for them to cut down and float away its valuable forests. Its space, place, and voices – some of them wails, others alluring siren calls – speak of alarm, warning, tragedy, and delayed justice. Missing entirely from official history is the full truth of this place and its defining events.

Bite Into ~ Not Off

Flaring disputes at Minter have faded, except under the auspices of lawyers protecting waterfront property. The older, richer history of the locale has been lost. Now, 66 years after Jerry Meeker summarized its community dynamics, this digest of them restores a significant facet of Whulshootseed efforts to survive in the shadow of Tacoma and urbanizing Puget Sound.

In the native view, everything is connected, interwoven together as an interrelated whole. As a tiny but profound example of a cross-cultural chasm, consider the Lushootseed conceptions of diving and of biting. For native people both of these acts are religious activities, once performed by fasting teenagers.

To plunge into the water, aiming for great depths, a person had to be physically and spiritually purified and in quest of dangerous powers "who" were known to be living deep at the bottom of a lake, river, or inlet. Those truly committed, coached by elite trainers, would tightly grasp a boulder during the dive to sink even farther down.

In the stories Jerry told to Thelma Adamson, Bluejay insisted on competing in the diving context, against the natural endowments of Mink or Kingfisher, and only won because he cheated with a concealed weapon. His negative example showed how, in mythic times, spirit powers gave benefit to the later abilities of each species, as these were appropriately earned.

---

[450] Lynda Mapes, *Breaking Ground*: The Lower Elwa Klallam Tribe and the Unearthing of Tse-whit-zen Village 2009: xxi.

Biting, while necessary for the healthy intake of food, also provided natives with a metaphor for gaining knowledge and power. In English, "bite" (and the milder form "nip") means "to sever, to wound, to remove by teeth, a mouthful of food (morsel), to impress (get a bite on), to grip by friction (bite of an anchor), to restrain (bite the tongue or lip), to champ (gnaw impatiently), to gnash, or to end (bite the dust)." Synonyms include "to sting, slice with an edged weapon (ax bite), corrode (etch), cause sharp pain (bite in the side), or freeze (frost bite)."

In Lushootseed, however, "bite" is a means of connecting. In lieu of the English meaning "sever," the native sense of biting "links into." The basic form is x̣əƛ̓ = bite, with extensions of x̣əƛ̓gʷas = to come together, and of x̣ix̣əƛ̓ustəgʷəl̓ = to converse, literally to nibble each other's faces. As such, bite is distinct from the word for sting (t̓əbxʷil), signifying a painful and unwanted connection between pest and human.[451]

Probably the most dramatic Northwest Coast expression of this biting as linking, wildly misunderstood by outsiders, particularly academics for decades, is the Hamatsa or "cannibal" secret guild made up of elite members of Kwakwaka'wakw (Kwakiutl) communities on the central coast of British Columbia. Called the "consumers" in my study of Tsimshian, the sense of the name is that you are what you eat and if you eat human flesh you will become more human.[452] Spreading north and south along the coast from Heiltsuk (Bella Bella), the expression of this organization at Minter was the academy of Growlers (also called Black Tahmanawas), denounced as bunk by Jerry's uncle wilq̓, but dramatically conveyed by the bleeding mouths and frenzied behavior of members, often the children of wealthy parents, at intertribal initiations and displays.[453]

To be known as Biters, therefore, was not simply a description, but an implication of spiritual force with greater than human abilities. For such a tucked-away place, Minters promised, threatened, and *traced* mighty influences throughout the Sound.

Just and Truthful Memories

Finally, "Truth" ends up as a matter of pluralities, in perspectives, inclusiveness, and chronologies brought to bear on the carbonized residue at Minter. No one person, race, or authority can claim it. History at Minter did not begin in 1792, 1874, or 1882, but thousands of years before when people spread from the lower Puyallup River across to Gig Harbor and Burley, then overland (or through the Narrows) into Carr Inlet, where the advantages of Henderson Bay became all too apparent in terms of view, shrimp, fish, oysters, deer, berries, and plants. While many of these place names are of recent vintage, the places themselves are not. Sympathy for today's readers requires the English names used here, but such consideration, in turn, requires that the past be cherished equally with the present. Lushootseed and other Salishan

---

451 *LD*: 263, 292.

452 This "phagohierarchy" is described in Peggy Reeves Sanday, *Divine Hunger ~ Cannibalism as a Cultural System* 1986.

453 Jay Miller, *Tsimshian Culture* 1997: 118; *Lushootseed Culture and the Shamanic Odyssey* 1999: 101; Drawings by James Swan of a rite in progress at Port Townsend appear in George Miles, *James Swan, Cha-Tic of the Northwest Coast* 2003: 60-61.

languages replaced others much older about two thousand years ago, so Minter descendants who themselves now speak English are, at least, in their third major language shift. Pride and prestige made the natural shift to speaking Lushootseed advantageous, not pain, shame, and repression as English was forced to be learned in boarding school, store, and woods. Knowing that all these cultures existed separately and together allows similar differences to exist in the here and now.

Hints in the oldest fieldnotes of Herman Haeberlin imply that every river drainage was a world unto itself where the manner of making fire, taking fish, and relating to the landscape was specific to that water and air flow.[454] Instead, a sameness has taken over because in simplicity is survival. While fours have been used throughout this book to capture a native sense of order, the pattern number was four only for those Lushootseeds north of Seattle. To the south, including Minter, it was five, as Jerry well knew and used in his epics, but that bit of truth has now faded in the common interests of conformity because 4 has become the sacred number for most Native Americans.

Minter survived a series of disasters that included epidemics, aboriginal attacks, and slaving raids, though its elite members were quickly redeemed from their captors. Then came the crushing blows from foreign invaders, demands from a money economy, treaty stipulations, and finally the torchings that destroyed homes at Minter and later at Glencove. Tacoma, with the able assistance of Jerry Meeker and Peter Stanup, dismantled the Puyallup Reservation for thirty years, while tribal bickering and gunfire took a later toll. Yet Jerry committed to paper a vivid account of his mother's chompion ancestors, and other records, archived far and wide, confirm it.

Work remains ongoing, by myself and, now, thankfully, others. Like the page turning that led to this moment, Minter and its people continue to unfold in the blazing light that follows this searing exposure of their greatness in the past and resilience more recently.[455]

They are not alone any more. What happened at Minter, happened many other times and places, but without the detailed record that Jerry Meeker provided in these notebooks. That the best evidence remains buried in court records says reams about the state of "history," "violence," and "justice" for native peoples of the Americas and the world.

---

[454] Herman Haeberlin, Notebooks 1916-17; Herman Haeberlin and Erna Gunther, Indians of Puget Sound 1930: 24.

[455] Lastly, a 12-5-29 list of village sites assembled by Arthur Ballard and Erna Gunther for the archaeological sites survey by Claude Schaeffer along the Puyallup River, includes "# 30 stL'tL'Abatxw 'Clallam Home' at Glencove. Home of the Clallam before the flood." Klallam are Straits Salishan speakers from the northern Sound; how or why they were associated with Case Inlet "before the Flood" boggles (UW – SC [MSCUA] Gunther Box 2, Folder 10). Two possibilities are that Klallam call themselves "fierce people" and the confrontation with Lt Puget at this cove in 1792 may have earned locals the same name, leading to this later confusion, or, more likely, the name commemorates the ancient killing there of Klallam warriors intent on enslaving, an honor that cost their lives.

15 MINTER IN AND OUT OF MEMORY

This place, a point(e) of land, now called Minter, faces east with a spectacular view of Mount Rainier on rare sunny days. Set among expensive waterfront houses, a state fish hatchery upstream on Minter Creek is its best known local landmark, though a namesake oyster business has widely spread the name throughout regional groceries. Otherwise, on the ground, Minter is now inconspicuous. For native peoples in Puget Sound, however, it was the home base of a community once famous for its pedigree, elite school, and dynastic intermarriages.

But that memory has been lost from the place, forgotten and perhaps erased entirely except for three neglected fieldwork notebooks in Special Collections at the University of Washington. Early research for this book has now served to refile them correctly after they had been awkwardly labeled under the name of a famous white pioneer, Ezra Meeker. Moreover, the notebook's scribe, Alfred Smith, did not identify himself and had to be found by other means.

Ironically, the source of this knowledge of the past, the voice (Greek chorus, siren, or banshee wail) for this place as an ancient homeland and cultural center, is Jerry Meeker, a Puyallup elder and Tacoma land tycoon, whose beach front home is still occupied by the last of his family line. His business success, according to his own Presbyterian lights, is not without criticism in the native community. Yet his cultural memory is very long and his mother's home village can now be appreciated within a wider context of official history.

Under the guise of homesteading a supposed unoccupied space, as with other unreported native villages, the houses, large and small, at Minter were arsoned by men who then made "legal" claim, logged off the well-tended old growth, and departed. Taxes unpaid, the land returned to public trust and was then homesteaded by other families known to history as it pioneers and who are still prominent in the region. This second wave is remembered, the early arsonists less so, and the native Minters not at all. It is these resettlers who pioneered history, not those indigenous and "prehistoric." Yet their native kin still fish in these waters by treaty right, as has been recently confirmed and upheld in US federal court.

Native Minters truly belonged to this land, place, and space, benefiting from all of its foods, resources, community, and spiritual help. But this land had many native voices, ranging from residents to visitors, graduates to bumpkins, nobles to slaves, and friends to enemies. For nobles, honored names were fixed in this locale, passed on through far-flung generations which traced the name's origins and associations back to this community's pedigrees. They all belonged to Minter forever.

Spiritual endowments came from the land. Minter seems to have transformed its communal identification over time, from trainer to warrior to gorger. These abilities came from the land and its characteristic features, as will be seen. They defended Minter from attack, provided goods to ransom captives, and bolstered it during Eat-all competitions.

Like other watersheds, community cohesion, loyalties, bonds, and affiliations expanded in terms of (a) hearth mates eating together at the fires within one household, (b) residents of all neighboring houses, (c) birthright locals – those born there as distinct from inlaws, visitors, and foreigners, (d) seasonal locales, camps, resorts, (e) wider community networks, (f) tributary waterways, and (g) the entire drainage of a river basin.

Throughout the Americas, tribes have special relationships with their lands, usually a spiritual connection derived from a pact, especially a marriage, with that place, often in the guise of a prevalent species. Some are plausible, as with human-like Bears, and others, such as an Oyster, are more perplexing until it is understood that each species has a human form underneath its outer pelt, which is worn like an outer cloak. Any specific bond at Minter is not reported, though their neighbors at Gig Harbor left food offerings for ancestral orcas (Killerwhales). Minter leaders, moreover, had personal bonds with the most powerful of spirits in the region – rich, famous, and deadly. Because their Chompions became "swells," the possibility remains that the Tide itself became the ancestral spirit of Minter, conferring its ability to swell up and eat into the landscape upon special members of the community who know how to seek it out.

A tentative chronology, based on these three notebooks and other documents, begins with smallpox devastation about 1782 and the survey by Lt Peter Puget in 1792. Many diseases took a terrible toll, jeopardizing the ancient chiefly line whose last representative was the headwoman Damasq [tšia'łits'a]. She would have been born about 1820, outliving her own children and dying about 58 years old in 1878. At population nadirs, close kin married and their remarkably healthy children, proving special powers, reestablished the community. After a massive slaving raid about 1840, Minter, under Broken Tooth, reconstituted itself by means of Chompion power, and so entered the ethnographic record. If Broken Tooth, the heroic eat-all chompion, was born in 1800, leading a lesser house in 1830, he assumed prime leadership, based on his gorging successes, after the massive slave raid about 1840 just before Lt Wilkes learned the 'eaters' name in 1841 from HBC.

Competition and conflicts escalated. The battle of allied Puget Sounders against Cowichans is usually dated about 1825. The Upper Cowlitz Taitnapam attack was a decade (1830s) later, and that of the Haida was even later (after 1843) since Sally (də'at), Jerry's mother, gave early warning after seeing faces reflected in a pool of water.

Minter leaders attended the Medicine Creek treaty council in 1854, and Jim and Sally married a few years later. From her first marriage at Steilacoom, her eldest son John survived to marry Annie. Sally then lost several children before remarrying to Jim Meeker and giving birth to Jerry in 1862 when she was in her 20s. Less publicized was the torching of Minter by logging families in 1874, and then their refuge at Glencove until 1886. The first took place just before the Homestead Act of 3 March 1875, implicating claimants Calvin G Burkett (1820-1894), Isaac Hawk (1836-1905), and Nehemiah G Bartlett (1841-1874). The second was before the Indian Homestead Act of 4 July 1884, when Glencove was filed on by William Rains. All these men were Masons and buried in their cemeteries. In 1882, the George Minter family came from Nebraska to start the official record, providing the current name for our point of concern.

The key institution of cultural revival in the south Sound was and is the Indian 9 Church, based in the revelation of John Slocum after he died and revived on 20 October 1882, as his wife Mary Thompson Slocum received the healing trembling ("the shake") that distinguishes this faith. Together, the Slocums revealed the Word of the Christian God to Natives, benefiting from legal protections within Washington State.

Ten natives figure prominently in these notebooks. These are 1) Damasq, my name for the headwoman (tšiałits'a); 2) her son Lashibya; 3) Broken Tooth, the champion eater; 4)

Simon, the slave and shaman; 5) Tyee George and his brother 6) Gizmo (kay'wey); 7) Moses, with threatening Snake power; 8) Jim Hummelgood, a cousin; and 9) Jim and 10) Sally, Jerry Meeker's parents. To fill out a dozen, 11) Lucy Gurand, an elder twenty years his senior, provides support for 12) Jerry Meeker's own information given to Alfred Smith, the scribe.

These people and events provide background for understanding the successful real estate career of Jerry Meeker, a Minter native son who managed to benefit from the loss of native lands to American settlers and urban sprawl as a wealthy high-profile native elder, real estate tycoon, and Tacoma booster.

In all, these notebooks appeal for many scholarly reasons: assessing their reliability, discovering the name and dates of the scribe, exploring the complex (auto)biography of the Puyallup elder and real estate tycoon interviewed, preparing materials for future tribal use, solving the mystery of their misattribution by archives, restoring the erased history of earliest homesteaders as loggers and arsonists, fleshing out the local archaeological record with its ethnohistorical context, testing these data against previously published ethnographic models, and expanding our knowledge of traditional southern Lushootseeds in Puget Sound. Above all, the challenge of these notes is to set the record straight for one vibrant community at a specific place over several centuries during which it recreated itself after a series of traumas, setbacks, and triumphs. With a woman leader, shaman slave, and academy for elite families, it has much to contribute to our better understanding of local and global issues.

Appendix A ~

Lushootseed as a Spoken Coast Salish Language

For Lushootseed Sounds, the rule is one sound = one letter. Glottalized (marked ‘) means the gate in the back of the throat is closed tight and the sound is explosive. Labialized (marked ^{W}) means the lips are rounded to produce a breathy quality. “Same” means it sounds much like that English sound.

a	same, like father
b	same, replaces m of other Salish languages
c	ts like cats
c̓	glottalized ts
č	c wedge, ch like church, chair
č̓	glottalized ch
d	same, replaces n of other Salish languages
d^z	ds like rods
ə	schwa, like a in sofa, u in but
g	same, like get, go
g^w	labialized g
h	same, like hit
i	ee like seed
j	dj, sqajet (Skagit)
k	same, k like kin
k̓	glottalized k
k^w	labialized k, qu like queen, quick
$k̓^w$	glottalized and labialized k
l	same, like look
l̓	glottalized l
m	now replaced by b, rare use in archaic, baby, and Ravenese words,
n	now replaced by d, rare use in archaic, baby, and Ravenese words
n̓	glottalized n
o	same, written as u in Lushootseed alphabet
p	same, p like post
p̓	glottalized p
q	like k but with back of the tongue raised against the back roof of the mouth
q̓	glottalized q
q^w	labialized q
$q̓^w$	glottalized and labialized q
s	same
š	sh like sure, shore, shut
t	same
t̓	glottalized t
u	same, sometimes o, Lushootseed speakers regarded both sounds as the same
w	same
w̓	glottalized w
x̌	same as x̣
x̣	ch like German ich, Scottish loch, said deep in the throat
x^w	labialized, wh like where
$x̣^w$	glottalized and labialized
y	same, like yell, you
y̓	glottalized y
ʔ ‘	glottal stop, throat gate closed, like pause in uh’oh
ɬ	barred l, said out of the sides of the mouth with the tip of the tongue behind the upper front teeth
ƛ̓	glottalized barred lambda, tl like night-light, said deep in the throat with tongue flattened against the front roof of the mouth

Coast Salish Languages

Lushootseed (Puget Salish) has northern and southern dialect chains. Those of the north (dx^{w}ləšutsid) were Skagit (including the Sauk-Suiattle), Swinomish, and Snohomish (including the Skykomish). South of Whidbey Island, Southern Lushootseed (Whulsutseed (t)x^{w}əlšutsid) includes the Snoqualmi in the foothills behind Seattle; the Duwamish (including Muckleshoot) along that same river, as well as the bays and lakes around Seattle; the Puyallup around Tacoma (including Minter), the Nisqually below the Narrows; the Sahewamish (Squaxin) on islands and inlets at the very south; and the Suquamish along the Kitsap Peninsula on the west side of the Sound.

Important dialect distinctions are separate names for salmon species, respective accents on the first or second vowel of the basic root of a word, and the use of 4 as the pattern number in the north and of 5 in the south, shared with the Columbia River Chinooks and upriver Plateau tribes. Within Salishan, Lushootseed is characterized by an ancient reworking of the two sets of transitive person markers, regularization of the suffix system, and an elaboration of prefixes.

Lushootseed, as written by linguists, has separate letters for each of its 46 sounds. The first attempts to write down this language, as elsewhere, were by missionaries, particularly a learned French Oblate (Fr Eugene Casimir Chirouse) long based at Tulalip. The complexity of its sounds derives from using different parts of the mouth to produce four different pronunciations of the same basic sound. Routinely, these are the back of the throat (as k, q, x = German ich), the nose (nasals), the lips (labials), and doubling up of throat and lips.

Such fourway sets include a sound that it is plain (said much like ordinary English), glottalized (said in back along with a raspy pop of air released from the voice box ~ glottis in the throat), and labialized (said in front through rounded or pursed lips). These are indicated by an ordinary letter, a letter under a stroke (glottal t'), a letter beside a raised W (labial -^{W}), or by both the apostrophe and the raised W (t'^{W}). Schematically, K is said unadorned like kin, K' is "harsh, explosive" back sounding [Cf geek], K^{w} is said in front like Queen, and K^{w}' combines both:

↗ k̓ ↘

k   k̓^{w}

↘ k^{w} ↗

Other fronted sounds that are probably unfamiliar include ł (known as barred L), a sound used in Welsh and a letter (for a different sound = W) in Polish, said by pushing air around the tip of the tongue while it is pressed against the roof of the mouth -- something like the middle sound in Catholic or athlete, and Ž (a glottalized barred lambda) said with a click at the back of the throat while tapping the tip of the tongue against the back of the front upper teeth.

Lushootseed functions with many more consonants and fewer vowels than English because many of the sounds produced at the back or sides of the mouth continue to force air through the lips and so can take the place of the more open, free flowing sounds known as vowels.

In rank-conscious communities, densely inhabited for centuries, special words had to be invented during certain conditions, such as a taboo on a word resembling the name of the deceased during mourning,[456] so neighboring communities usually did not share the same word for something. The status of a family was indicated by the extent and intensity with which others

[456] William Elmendorf, Word Tabu and Change Rates: Tests of a Hypothesis 1970b: 74-85.

observed their word taboo. In the case of the highest ranks, they could insist on substituting a new word for something as common as the name for "ax" and have it become permanent.

Lushootseed belongs to the Salishan Language Family, which aboriginally spread from the Pacific shore into western Montana and Canada. It was a localized original of the Northwest, with no obvious links with the dozen or so major linguistic stocks (Algic, Iroquoian, Uto-Aztecan, for example) across the continent.

The Salishan Family has 23 interlinked languages, separated by the Cascade Mountains, divided into Coast (16 members) and Interior (7 members) divisions. Coast Salishan branches, from the north, are Nuxalk (Bella Coola), Central, Tsamosan, and Tillamook. Central Coast Salishan includes Comox, Sechelt, Pentlatch (extinct), Squamish, Nooksak, Halkomelem (including Chilliwack, Musqueam, Cowichan), Straits (including intergrading Sooke, Saanich, Songhees, Lummi, Samish, Semiahmoo, and, more apart, Klallam), Twana, and Lushootseed. Tsamosan, once called Olympic, includes Cowlitz, Upper (including Satsop) and Lower Chehalis, and Quinault.

Interior Salishan consists, from the north, of St'at'imcets (Lillooet), of Nlakapamuxcin (Thompson) and of Sexwepemxcin (Shuswap), and of Mid-Columbia dialect chains with "upriver" Methow-Okanogan-Nespelem-Sanpoil-Colvile-Lakes and "downriver" Chelan-Entiat-Wenatchi-Columbian, of Kalispel-Spokan-Selish (Flathead), and of Coeur d'Alene.

Over a century ago, the shift from nasals (M > B, N > D) by Lushootseeds, Twana, Chimakum, and southern Nootkans (Makah and Ditidat, still called Nitinat in English) may have been a counter-response to territorial aggression by nasal-using Straits Salish speakers such as Lummi, Klallam, and Samish (Duwaha, Nuwaha, dxa?ha). Thus, any snowcapped mountain is now called *taq^{w}oba*, which is the source for what the settlers applied as *takoma* (Tacoma) to Mt. Rainier and a nearby city.

The Lushootseed dialect spoken at Minter, with a few distinctions of its own as noted by Arthur Ballard, was Whulsutseed ~ Southern Lushootseed, and most closely related to Puyallup.

Throughout this region, for simple exchanges, a pidgin called Chinuk Wawa [Chinook Jargon] was used.

Appendix B ~

Chinuk Wawa on Trial

During every federal court case involving treaty rights in the Northwest, each judge asks after the native understanding of the treaty-making process. Invariably, testimony turns to the limitations of the local trade pidgin, Chinuk Wawa (Jargon), the lingua franca used to barter and trade, as well as to "translate" the treaty proceedings at the time. Intended only for easy, quick transactions of goods and flesh, this jargon could be used in more sophisticated ways, as when Franz Boas undertook preliminary folklore and ethnography along the coast. In matters of law and court, however, where lives hang in the balance, it has been deadly.

While each court relies on its own witnesses and testimony, as an example to all, consider the efforts of Jerry Meeker (V-2) to render Article Six of the Stevens treaties into jargon and the efforts of other prosperous natives (X-2), such as Charles Wilbur and Peter James (Duwamish and Others, 1933, 689, 713), to back translate it. The mark ˇ indicates insertions ˇ into the written text.

Exhibit V-2 Filed 3 Oct 1927

okoka highas tyee alka ya ka wawa, kopa okaka elyehee spose kopa closh, kapa mika tilecum closha. pae alka plotche, yake mash ˇkopaˇ misika highas elyehee, spose ˇyakaˇ tumtum, peo alka mash highwee chickman. pee alten misika milthita ˇkopaˇ closh tilkcum.

pee alten misika milthitas kopa closh elyehee, kopa quinsum.

delate kauka okoka tilekcum kopa omaha spose okoka delate.
pee alten okoka highas tyee, plotch hiyan chickman kopa misika ekitess

Exhibit X-2

you big boss after while your talk to this people to them. To your friends good. After while gave my [OK ??] to you your big land. What you think, after while gave big things and after to all my close relation

And after while you be all in good land for all times

it is time those friends at Omaha it is time, after while this big boss will gave lots money to you. Things

The targeted text is from the 26 Dec 1854 Treaty with the Nisqualli, Puyallup, etc at She-nah-nam or Medicine Creek:

ARTICLE 6 The President may hereafter, when in his opinion the interests of the Territory may require, and the welfare of the said Indians be promoted, remove them from either or all of said reservations to such other suitable places or places within said Territory as he may deem fit, on remunerating them for their improvements and the expenses of their removal, or may consolidate them with other friendly tribes or bands. And he may further, at his discretion, cause the whole or a portion of the lands herby reserved, or of such other land as may be selected in lieu thereof, to be surveyed into lots, and assign the same to such individuals or families as are willing to avail themselves of the privilege, and to locate on the same as a permanent home, on the same terms and subject to the same regulations as are provided in the sixth article of the treaty with the Omahas, so far as the same may be applicable. Any substantial improvements heretofore made by any Indian, and which he shall be compelled to abandon in consequence of this treaty, shall be valued under the direction of the President, and payment be made accordingly therefore.

Finally, in the telling exchange between Arthur E Griffin for Claimant and George T. Stormont for Defendant, Jerry Meeker had the last word about his own effort (Duwamish and Others, 1933, 681).

"You would not guarantee that the Indians would understand it, would you, Mr Meeker.
A. Oh, No, No."

Appendix C ~ Rev Matthew Mann

Mann was ordained by Presbyterians in 1873, serving first in Astoria (Oregon) before, in 1876, becoming superintendent of instruction at the Puyallup Reservation. His report for 1878 appears at the end of this appendix. Trouble brewed when Mann opposed Agent Edwin Eells, brother of Congregationalist missionary Rev Myron Eells, by supporting native efforts to sell a right-of-way across the reservation to the Northern Pacific Railroad. He, as well, encouraged the founding of the Indian Shaker Church by a few former native church elders. Edwin Chalcraft, himself an Eells ally, recounts a version of this conflict in *Assimilation's Agent* (2004).

Understandably, Mann was replaced as missionary, accused by the Presbytery of "unethical conduct toward a fellow minister" and convicted, though quickly absolved by public opinion. Leaving the Presbyterians, in 1901 Mann became a Christian Scientist. He died in Tacoma, where he had lived for 75 years, on 28 December 1945. A week later, *The Tacoma News Tribune* printed his death notice on 2 January 1946, and the *Seattle Times* on 13 January 1946, misreporting that he would have been 104 [!] on 1 February.

On-line census records indicate that Matthew G. Mann was born in Wurtemberg (1 February 1842), and died in Tacoma (28 December 1945) at the age of 99 [!]. He was married three times; to Minnie, born in Oregon during the 1850s, to May F., who was listed on 1 April 1892 as 50 years old, and to Emilie (Emily, Amelia), in Germany during World War I. Three daughters appear in census records: Leona, Jane Gertrude, and Lotta.

On the 1880 federal census, he is listed as 36 [likely 38] years old and a reservation teacher. His wife Minnie is 26, with a German father and a Scots mother. Daughters are Leona at 3, and another at one month. Living in their household were CP Cole (ship carpenter, 26, Wales), RL Gray (building contractor, 23, Scot) and John McKenisey (ship carpenter, 36). In the census of 1883, he was 41, Minnie was 25, Leona was 5, Jane Gertrude was 3, and Lotta was 1. In 1885 he is listed as single; and, on 27 June 1887, was naturalized in the Tacoma 2nd judicial district.

In 1900, at the age of 54 after 40 [likely 52] years in the US, he was at Lewiston (Idaho) serving Nez Perces, and married to Minnie May F., aged 58, born June 1841 in Maine. The next year he changed religions. On 5 May 1907, he sailed for Hamburg, arriving on 19 May. In 1907-9, he was in Berlin, then in England in 1909. He returned to Germany just before WW I, remaining there until sailing back to the US on 12 October 1919 on the *Saxonia* at the age of 77, with his new wife Emily, aged 54. In 1920, he and Amelia served Christian Scientists in Los Angeles Assembly District 64. Some time later, they returned to Tacoma for their last years. Amelia died 3 April 1944 at the age of 79, a year before Matthew.

~ C ~

Report of M.G. Mann, teacher of Puyallup Reservation[457]

PUYALLUP INDIAN RESERVATION, WASH.,
August 10, 1878

Sir: The industrial boarding school has been maintained on this reservation since July 1, 1877, at which about 30 scholars were in attendance. It is but justice to them to say that they learn well, and that they have made commendable progress in writing, reading, and arithmetic, and they have demonstrated the fact that Indian children have capacities very little inferior to white children. The great drawback to their more rapid advancement, and, indeed, to that of the whole Indian race, in their addictedness to their native language. The teacher {!} has lately made such rules and inaugurated such measures as will tend to entirely exclude their language in social intercourse. The school and the church have been the centers of civilization, progress, and light, radiating throughout, and extending to the most distant and darkest corners of the reservation.

The Indians have made advancement along the line this year. They are materially more prosperous than they have ever been before in horses, cattle raised and bought, in lands cleared and cultivated, and their efforts during the past year give proof that they intend to derive their subsistence chiefly from the produce of the soil.

Of their own accord they have done away with all manner of gambling, and they have condemned and abolished the practice of making *tamanamous* or incantations and other heathen rites heretofore used in cases of sickness. They now entirely depend upon the limited supply of medicines dispensed to them from the dispensary at the school.

At this time while the country is troubled and startled on account of the atrocities committed by hostile Indians east of the Cascade Range of mountains, our Indians are plying their peaceful vocations, or rather are making war on their forests, clearing their lands and cutting their hay.

The Puyallup tribe is decidedly on the increase, due to immigrations from affiliated tribes and to the increased number of births in excess of deaths during the past year.

The Indians care very little now for their tribal relation, and are independent of each other, each family living by themselves upon their allotments of 40 acres, which they all cultivate to some extent.

A *bone-fide* title to their lands cultivated by them as their homesteads, and they themselves citizenized, would at once transform them from being aliens and from the danger of being enemies into sure friends of our government.

I have the honor to be, sir, respectfully, your obedient servant, MG Mann, *teacher*.

M.G. MANN
Teacher

457 Report of the Secretary of the Interior, being part of the Message and Documents communicated to the Two Houses of Congress at the beginning of the Second Session of the 49th Congress 1886, Vol I: 135.

Appendix D ~

Homesteading

Because homesteading laws once raised and then dashed the hopes of native Minters to claim their home base, a brief survey of this bewildering and arcane situation is in order.

In his masterful summary of public lands law, Paul W Gates[458] listed six aims of this policy as producing revenue through sales, facilitating growth, rewarding war veterans, building educational, charity (technically "eleemosynary"), or penal institutions, and improvements such as swamp drainage and irrigation, imposing conservation, and, now, encouraging multi-purpose uses.

General Land Office (GLO)

Surveys, based on the township and range of 36 sections, changed the landforms of the United States from 1785 onward. [459] Land entries and appropriate filings had to be made through the General Land Office (GLO), as legislated by congressional acts. To dispense the lands in thirty states acquired by treaty with native leaders, who were sometimes imposed or invented by US officials, the GLO was founded by Congress in 1812 to manage the 1.8 billion acres of public domain west of the Appalachians, and, in particular, to provide for its legal transfer from "public" to "private" hands. New lands were divided on the basis of a north-south principal meridian line (for townships) and an east-west base line (for ranges) to create the township grid. For the vast Oregon Territory, the Willamette Meridian is set along the axis of the north-flowing Willamette River near Portland, and the base line is along a stretch of the west-flowing Columbia River.[460] This meridian runs beside Glencove, edging northward along the east side of the Key Peninsula and Port Townsend.[461]

---

458 Paul W Gates, *History of Public Land Law Development* 1968, 765. Indeed, this business spawned an array of speculators, agents, landlookers (for loophole properties), timber cruisers, dealers in land warrants, scrip, and tax titles, loan sharks, and, of course, lawyers. Petty in-fighting became vicious to locate county seats, capitols, land offices, state universities (as with UW), agricultural and normal (teaching) schools, and asylums for the blind, poor, insane, or criminal.

459 The most notable exception attempting to replace this gridwork was a 1878 proposal by Major John Wesley Powell, head of the Bureau of American Ethnology and US Geological Survey, to allot land by water drainages in arid regions, such as the Great Basin of Nevada and Utah, See Wallace Stegner, *Beyond the Hundredth Meridian, John Wesley Powell and the Second Opening of the West* 1992, 211.

460 Fred Yonce, The Public Land Surveys in Washington, PNQ 64 (4): 129-141, October 1972, based on his UW dissertation, Public Land Disposal in Washington (1969), shows Guide Meridians called Columbia, Ruby, Moses, San Poil, Joseph, Kettle River, and Colville, most of which impacted the Colville Reservation.

461 This intersection is high in the hills of west Portland and is called the Willamette Stone -- an original wooden stake set on 1 June 1851, a stone shaft set on 5 July 1885 and stolen in 1987, and a stainless steel "monumentation" (a surveyor's term) placed in July 1988, according to a brochure "Celebrate BLM's 50th Anniversary, 1946-1996," which emphasizes that final

Each township is divided into 36 sections, each 1 mile X 1 mile (640 acres), numbered continuously as an S. Running literally back and forth, these six switchbacks, each of six squares, are numbered from the right, then left.

6-1
7-12
18-13
19-24
30-25
31-36

Certain sections were set aside by law to support special needs, most often for schools at sections 16 and 36. Laws allowed one, then two, then four sections of each township to be dedicated for special purposes, usually schools but also agricultural colleges, roads, canals, railroads, dredging rivers, and irrigation dams and reservoirs.[462] Their sale or revenues supported these purposes.

However, "From colonial times land sharks proved equal or superior to any act of crown, province, state, or federal government".[463] Free land for homesteading had been championed first by George Henry Evans, then guided through Congress by Galusha Aaron Grow of Pennsylvania,[464] who saw his chance when he became Speaker of the War Congress of 1861 after the delegates from the South seceded. Lincoln quickly signed the bill into law. Evans had asked Robert Dale Owen of Indiana to introduce a free Oregon land law in Congress, but it failed. In 1873, an amendment added another 160 acres (for 320) to compensate for conditions in the West. For several decades, abuses increased until, before he was assassinated, William McKinley appointed as his Secretary of the Interior Ethan Allen Hitchcock, grandson of the namesake Vermont patriot, to clean up homesteading frauds. Backed by Teddy Roosevelt, who had been Vice President, Hitchcock moved into action, resulting in the amazing 1906 confessions of Steven A. Douglas Puter, king of Oregon land fraud.[465]

The earliest Washington pioneers settled in over the objections of the British, represented by the Hudson Bay Company (HBC), already in peaceful occupation of the region. Fort Vancouver was their trading headquarters, relying on native desire for manufactured clothes, tools, and gadgets to acquire local furs and foods. After the agreement for joint occupation of 1826 - 1846, Americans, avowedly determined to out-breed and out-populate the local British

---

surveys are intended to be unchangeable law rather than any effort to revise knowledge, as is the goal of science. Since the earth is round, township squares are not a perfect fit except in law courts.

462 Paul W Gates, History of Public Land Law Development 1968: 766.

463 Galusha, at six foot two and 200 pounds, was formidable; EA Hitchcock made a fortune from the first plate glass works, Stewart Holbrook, *Dreamers of the American Dream* 1957: 147, 159.

464 Stewart Holbrook, *Dreamers of the American Dream* 1957: 114, 150, 151.

465 At the end of the Archie Binns 1947 novel, *You Rolling River, Life on the Columbia* – 1880, 1971: 270-273), newly-rich George Black describes a variety of land claim scams to Willard Pearson, his childhood friend-cum-stunned-law-student.

minority, formed a government of Oregon Territory, which was divided by the Columbia River into Oregon South and North (eventually to become Washington).

Colonies at New Market (Tumwater, 1845), up inlet from modern Olympia (the state capitol), Steilacoom (1850), and Alki (1852), across from Seattle, were among the first American impositions.[466] Squatters such as George Bush, denied a haven in Oregon because of alleged African ancestry, founded large homesteads that were beacons of support to all subsequent settlers. Sawmills followed immediately (killing salmon runs with dams), with land entries concentrated along shorelines to provide easy access to timber, the most valuable local resource.

As anticipated, based on prior frontier experience, a man, who was resident in the territory before the 1850 law that allowed homesteading was passed, could then freely take 320 acres for himself, and his wife could take another 320 acres, to claim a full section. Those who came after 1850 could only take half or 160 acres. Within 3 months of settlement, or after the first survey confirmed prior off-the-grid occupation, notification was filed at a land office (Vancouver, Olympia, Walla Walla, Spokane Falls, later Seattle). Before the end of another nine months, proof had to be filed of a year's residence and cultivation, supported by the affidavits of two "disinterested" but honorable witnesses.

At the end of four years, proof had to be made again for the Surveyor General to issue the claimant a certificate for this land, which then had to be sent on to the commissioner of the General Land Office in DC, who finally issued the all-important patent for the land. All records passed through the local land office as a double-check on consistency, and to assure a duplicate.

Printed 8" tall and 3" wide along the middle of a 14" sheet of paper, a sample blank patent, top to bottom, labels lines and spaces for Final Certification No., Homestead Application No., Land Office at [stamped > Olympia, W.T.], blank for date ending 188_, Section , Town , Range , a double line, long space, then Approved , 188_ Clerk , Division , Patented 188_, Recorded, Volume , page.

Since only the Washington territorial surveyor general could issue the final certificate as based on the government survey, and he deliberately only approved the work of his own men, these surveyors charged excessive fees. After enough settlers sent protests to DC, however, this first surveyor general was fired and his racket ended, though errors in these surveys remained to plague future transactions.[467]

---

466 Months earlier single males homesteaded nearby but they have been ignored in official histories of Seattle in favor of the families in the Denny party.

467 Charlotte Shackleford, Donation Land Claims, *Building A State* 1940: XVI, 403-452. She insists on this local surveyor racket, but Donaldson's UW dissertation mentions only a few outsider surveyors as dishonest. Newspaper clippings (*Tacoma News Tribune*, WSHS) enabled me to sort out the impressive daughters of John Shackleford, Pierce County Superior Court Judge. His brother Lewis was a force in the Alaska Republican Party, often in conflict with Judge Wickersham (Chapter 10). Charlotte was a teacher who died at 89 on 9 December 1990; Elizabeth, who wrote a 1918 history of the Puyallup Reservation, articled with her father, joined the bar in 1922, became a Justice of the Peace, Pierce County District Court Judge (1954-67), practiced law until she was 85 in 1981, and died at 94 on 6 September 1989; Martha seems to have been an MD in Chicasha, Oklahoma. Their uncle John [??] Shackleford was a lawyer in Duluth who retired to Seattle, where he was killed at 65 by a car while he hobbled across a street eating a cupcake.

If complete, these homestead records include a filer's affidavit stating the length of time s/he had been on and cultivating the claim, marital status, birth date and place or intent of US naturalization, and other details thought applicable, such as educational skills and the names of children and heirs. Since land could only be claimed by citizens, foreigners had to declare their intention to naturalize. Of note, the naturalization of a father extended to his entire family automatically.

Some claims include bewilderingly different identifying numbers, variously for certification, notification, final patent, along with possible surveyor numberings starting with 37 and above (for those somehow beyond the 36 sections in every township, as at the very early town of Claquato).

In time, general (pre-emption) homesteading was allowed, with fewer restrictions on its "proving up" because this land was actually paid for, often purchased at the nominal fee of $1.25/acre. Any owner expected to double this value (or more) at subsequent sales or in legal transactions such as exchanges.

Later, other laws were enacted to further the sale of these public lands, including that of 1875 allowing native peoples to homestead on the public domain as long as there were no other claimants. It was anticipation of that law (I am convinced) that led to the arson of the native houses at Minter Creek.

Of over 40 applicable acts, land entries usually relied on legislative citations such as Cash (1820), Preemption (1830-40s), Donation (1850), Mineral (1860-70s), Timber Culture (1873), Desert Land (1877), and several Military Bounty land warrants (1840-50s) for service in foreign and "Indian" wars. Land entries, from the beginning, were intended to provide revenue to the US government (as Gallatin intended). Contrary to popular opinion, "free land" was not available for proving up until the Homestead Act of 1862 provided each homesteader a quarter section (80 acres), though the Civil War then engaged the men who would later file.[468]

When the local land office was satisfied that conditions of a particular act had been met by residence, payment, or surrender of a bounty land warrant, it issued a final certificate that was then forwarded to the GLO in DC, which then issued, if all of the paperwork were satisfactory, the final patent to the entryman [sic, or woman]. All of this paperwork was sorted in DC depending on whether it was by military bounty, or by general land claim -- before or after July 1908.

Military bounties rewarded enlistment and service in various wars and "Indian actions," including forced removals. These cases are filed by year of authorizing congressional act, number of acres granted, and warrant number. Before July 1908, general entries were filed by state, land office, enabling act, and final certificate number. A Seven State Index has simplified locating names for Alabama, Alaska, Arizona, Florida, Louisiana, Nevada, and Utah. After July 1908, cases were filed by serial number patent, regardless of other political considerations.

Tract books for thirteen states designated as "Eastern" by the BLM-ESO are archived in Springfield, Virginia; while those for the seventeen "Western" states are archived in DC. Nothing original came west, only copies. Survey notes and plats are dispersed between NARA and BLM offices. Cadastral surveys (from the Greek "by line") were done on foot along boundary lines, but the quality of these notes depends on the skills and dedication of the walker.

---

[468] Thomas Donaldson, *The Public Domain*, Its History with Statistics 1884; Paul W. Gates, History of Public Land Law Development 1968; Paul W. Gates, The Jeffersonian Dream ~ Studies in the History of American Land Policy and Development 1996.

Those for Washington State, for example, are kept in Boise, though available on microfilms of dubious (uneven) legibility.

Most entries claimed only subdivisions within a section, known as aliquot parts (from the Latin "how many others"), with a 20 acre aliquot fairly standard. During much of the 1800-1900s, the GLO worked to put itself out of business.

Because the income from the sale of public lands was originally pledged to retire the Revolutionary War debt, the GLO started under the Treasury Department (as defined by Albert Gallatin), then transferred to the new Department of the Interior from 1849 to 1946, when this USGS and GLO merged into the BLM, which manages the remaining 270,000,000 acres of public lands. Inherited BLM land records are inventoried as MTP (Master Title Plats) and HI (Historical Indexes, replacing Tract Books).

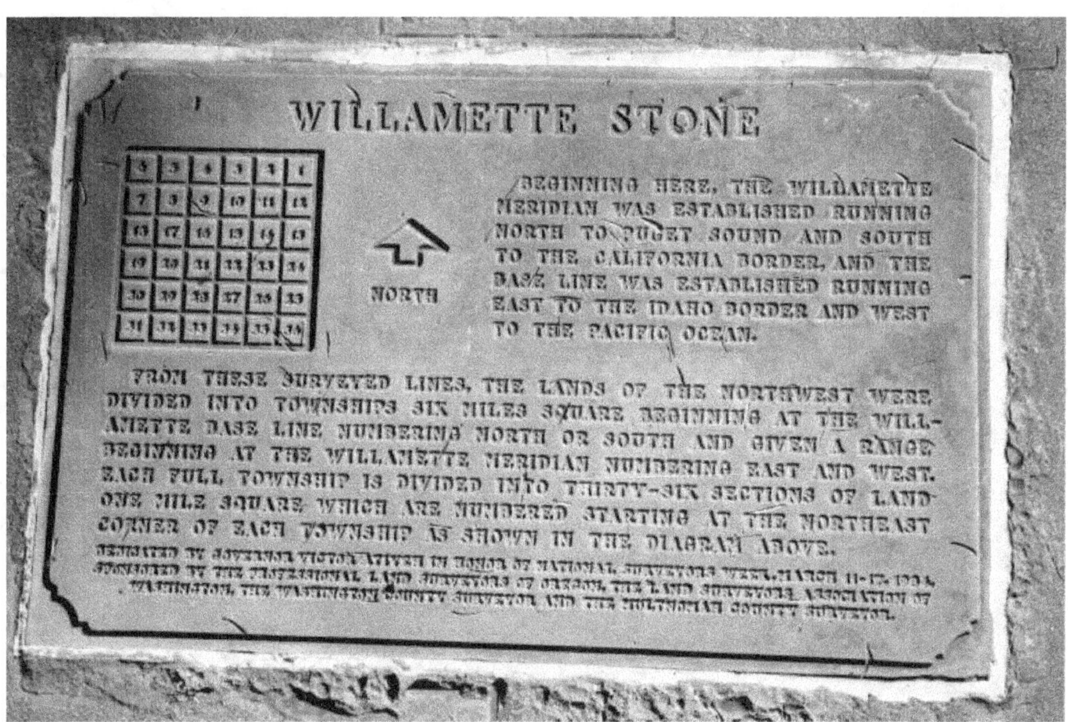

< §13 NW Survey Crux >

Appendix E ~

Lucy Slagham Gerand (1836-1929) was born at Quartermaster Harbor off Vashon Island, where her mother's father was leader and married a woman from Protection Island near Port Townsend. Her mother was from Black River, the former outlet of Lake Washington at modern Renton, and her father was from Victoria, BC.

In the 1860s, Lucy first married John Slagham and had five children, Mary Ann, Thomas, Henry, Grace, and a baby, but the first three died as teenagers and the survival of the others is in doubt. In 1874, John and Lucy were allotted 160 acres on Hylebos Creek, which they sold in 1896 for $30/acre the remaining 120.22 acres, moving back to Jensen Point at Burton on Vashon Island, where Lucy sold her knitting and clams. John died 12 September 1903, at the estimated age of 70.

The next year Lucy married Tom Gurand, whose mother was Cowlitz and father French Canadian. In 1906 they paid $50/acre for 10 acres on Mileta Creek on Maury Island across from Burton. Lucy died 7 January 1929, leaving a grandson named Joe Craig. She was buried in an unmarked grave at Vashon until the Puyallup Tribe put up a tombstone on 20 February 2008, giving her life dates as 1836-1929.

Appendix F ~

White River Dynamite Wars

Combat between farmers, engineers, and officials of King vs. Pierce County alternated the Stuck and White Rivers into either the Duwamish or Puyallup drainage. An explosion sent the White into the Stuck at the end of 1897 and armed guards kept it there. On 4 July 1899, however, the guard on duty went to a horse race, and dynamite returned the flow to the lower White. And so it continued until the 1906 flood, when the Army Corps of Engineers under Hiram Chittenden took charge. This dam, dubbed the "Great Wall of Auburn" was finished in 1913.

Major Chittenden is famous in Seattle because his name became attached to the Army Corps locks at Ballard that link the Sound with Lake Washington, lowering these inland waters about ten feet, obliterating the Black River, and redirecting the Cedar River outlet. While based in St Louis, near relevant archives, he wrote classic histories of the fur trade and Catholic missionary Fr de Smet.

In 1901, the state met concerns about depletion and extinction of the Green River fish stocks by building a hatchery on Soos Creek, displacing a native home and weir that belonged to Big John, the first Muckleshoot elder to educate Arthur Ballard in details of Lushootseed culture. Leslie Darwin, state fish commissioner at this time, was particularly racist toward non-Wasp fishers, especially natives exempt from the taxes that supported his programs.

Today, the main stem feeding the Duwamish is most obviously called the Green instead of the White because the White now flows into the bed of the Stuck River, and thereby into the Puyallup River feeding into Commencement Bay at Tacoma. The White River salmon runs, hence, have had to learn to find their home redds (spawning beds or nests) by bypassing Seattle and heading for Tacoma and its river outlet. Their precarious fate is discussed at the end of Chapter 7 because the Minter hatchery personnel have helped to save them, a bright spot amidst many sad events there.

Appendix G ~

Main Household

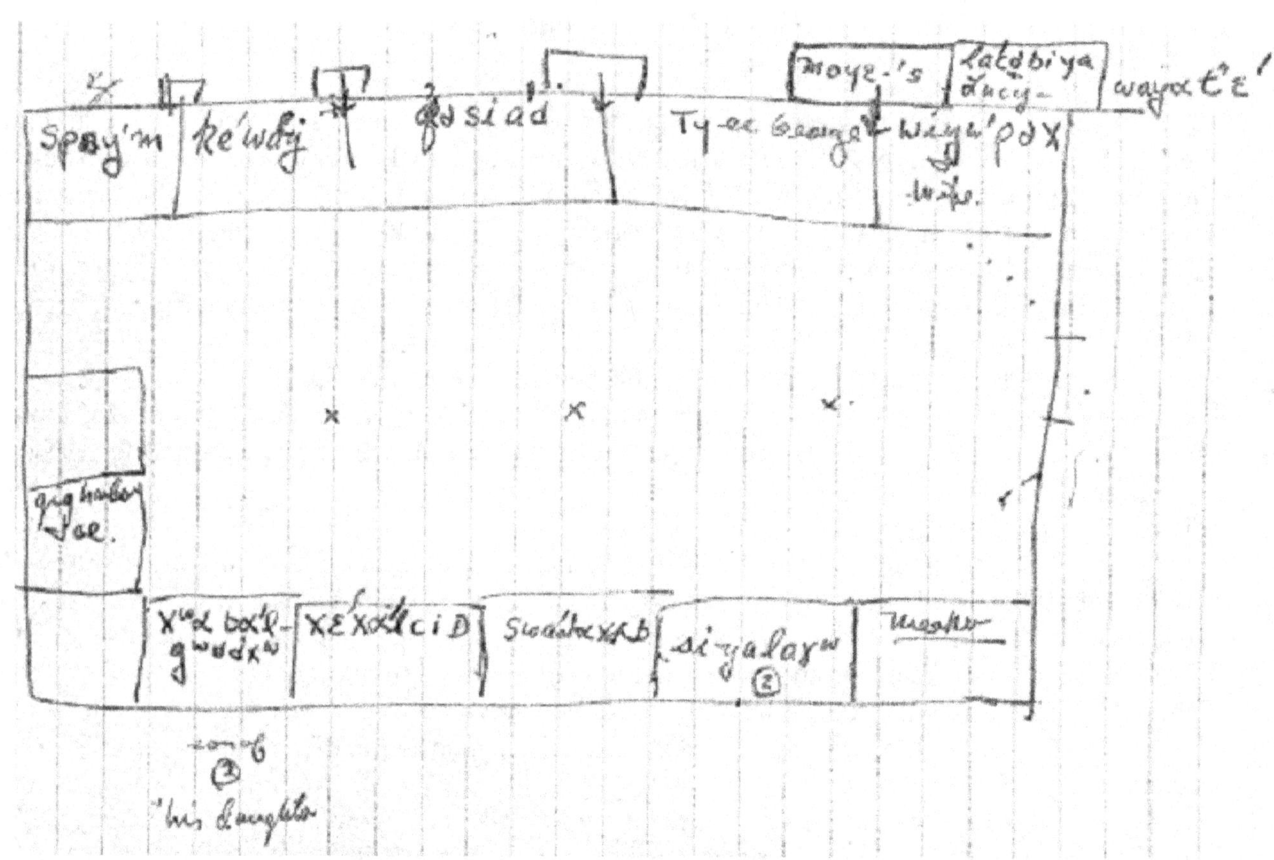

Kinship Codes

G = grand, great

mother =	M	F	= father
daughter =	D	B	= Brother
sister =	Z	S	= son
niece =	Nc	Np	= nephew
aunt =	A	U	= uncle

Main Household

R1
Spɛym

Δ=O¯¯ΔL7
Δ¯Δ¯¯O 2S 1D

R2
Kay'wəy

=Δ= trainer > R6

ΔA4Δ=O

R3
q̓əsiad

Δ=O¯O¯OL1

Δ¯Δ¯Δ¯O¯O 3S 2D George = tsa'əlab (Renton)

R4
Tyee George (suq[w]amš)

Δ=O

Δ¯Δ¯¯O¯O 2S 2D 3Np Mary = ? = sx̣ələpin (Sx)

Δ OLottie = ΔWilliam Bagley(Kl)

ΔJimCross = OBetsy(N) ΔR4

ΔCross

Δ¯Δ¯Δ 3S George, Silas, Jim?

R5
Moyɛ

Δ = OSally(Py) = O = ΔM1

Δ¯Δ¯Δ¯Δ¯¯O¯ O 4S 2D 3Ch
Andy = Laura (Ch)

R6
Lashibiya

O

Δ = OLucy = ΔJohn Slogen(Py)

O¯O 2D (Lucy Williams) + ch

L1
Meekers

ΔJim = OSally¯O¯O¯Δ¯Δ¯Δ OSally = ΔChambersCk
Δ¯Δ¯Δ¯¯O¯O 3S (twins) 2D ΔSteilacoom John a'ə

L2
Tsiyaləxʷ

Δ=O¯O¯Δ¯Δ¯Δ
Δ(L5)Jim ¯¯O = Williams = Charlie

L3
Sxʷadaxab

Δ = O
Δ = O
Δ¯Δ¯Δ¯Δ 4S a'ə

L4
Henry XɛxalciD

ΔHenry = OSarah(Py) Sally Cz
6ch (d-y) a'ə

Δ¯Δ¯Δ¯¯O¯O 3S 2D George = tsa'əlab(Renton)

L5
Jim Hummelgood

ΔL2= O
O¯Δ = OGig Harbor

L6

B1
Gig Harbor Joe kʷɛyadx̣ʷ

R1Δ = O¯Δ = O¯O¯OL1 Δ¯Δ¯Δ = OR5 Otsəltsi
Δ¯Δ¯O¯O 2S 1D a'ə`

B2
Headwoman ?

Slaves: Lummi (tᵘlubi) woman (8x8 feet hut);
Snohomish man called Simon, dakʷiłałʷ, or daxʷiłał (8x8 feet hut)

Residents

Inside the high-born house, moving counterclockwise, along one (R) side, lived

R1 Speym (spɛm) with his wife (sister of L7), 2 sons, 1 daughter, and 2 grandchildren whom he trained to fish and to hunt for bears and seals

R2 kay'wey (ke'way ~ kɛwɛ ~ Gizmo) and his wife; a half-brother of Tyee George [R4] so famous as a harpooner and canoe maker that his nickname means "mechanic," [gadget, gizmo, clever, "techie" (of today)]. With 5-6 helpers (or 2-3 slaves) he could finish a canoe in two months of steady work, but usually he did well to make two canoes per year <A24>. He also made all the fiber netting used by everyone at Minter. The father that he shared with George had been the trainer for teenagers at Minter <A99> until he retired and lašibiya took over

R3 q̓əsiad [Sloane ?], husband of Jerry's oldest aunt [MZ] Mary, with 5-6 children; He was high born from the White River of the Muckleshoot,[469] and later helped build the new house at Glencove. Mary had three boys and two girls. Her oldest son George Sloane (soʷwlab, sxʷolab) married tsa'əlab from Renton.

R4 Tyee George (swətša'bɫxt, sʷətša'bɫx̣t), with his wife, 2 sons, 2 daughters, and 3 Puyallup Nisqually nephews (George, Silas, Jim Cross), grandsons of Jimmy Cross and his Nisqually wife Betsy. Tyee George was a {Sukwamish} [Suquamish, via his mother], and his daughter Mary was named kʷatəlitsa. After her son died young, she married sx̣ələpin from skʷalskin [Squaxin] Island. Their daughter Lottie married William Bagley, a Klallam, and their children lived near Bremerton.

R5 Moyɛ's [Moses, wiyaypəx̣, wiyaɫpəx̣] and his wife and 3 children lived at the right hand corner beside the door, giving him prominence within the house. Moyɛ's had earlier been married to qʷəltɛbta (Sally), a Puyallup, but of their daughter and 4 boys, only Andy Moses lived, married Laura, a Chehalis, and they settled at Muckleshoot. Moyɛs's power was a snake, but he sometimes put it to "underhanded" use and became so suspected of sorcery that he "disappeared" on the tideflats near Tacoma <A26>. His widow married Gig Harbor Joe [M1]

R6 lašibiya, son of headwoman Damasq (tšia'ɫts'a) and her first husband walatšalq, with his wife Lucy and 2 daughters, nearest the door, until he briefly replaced his mother [M2 ?

---

[469] Apparently, kabay' was the leading man at the Muckleshoot (Inland Duwamish) winter village where {Slotter} [Slaughter now Auburn] sits at the former confluence of the White and Green Rivers. It was plated by Levi Ballard, father of Arthur Ballard, and named in memory of Lt William Slaughter slain in the Treaty War, then renamed, by popular demand, as Auburn in 1893, so its main hotel would no longer be known as the Slaughter House. Arthur devoted his life and funds to fully recording Southern Lushootseed stories, traditions, and kinship, but his magnum opus *Listen My Nephew* was suppressed by his children while it was in press in Portland at his death. Even without it, his articles are mainstays of research.

before dying about 1878]. Lucy [moved out and] married again to John [t̓salaxad] Slogen from Puyallup and had lots of children who all died unmarried. William Lucy [Lucy Williams, a daughter and Arthur Ballard source] was the main testimony against the treaty [wrongs ?].

R7 wayat̓έ added square with this name, little known, at the end of this side

Across, along the other (L) side, lived, starting nearest the door,

L1 Meekers – parents (Sally, Jim), two sons (John, Jerry), mother's 3 brothers (William, Charlie (walq̓), tšu'kbid)

L2 siyaləxʷ (tsialaxa, tsialxʷ's) married to Sally's sister [cousin?] tsiaɬtsə, with their children, including a son xʷəbalgʷədxʷ (anglicized as Jimmy Hummelgood, L5) who married Susie from Renton, and a daughter who married ? Williams, then Charlie ? to have many children and live at Muckleshoot {both ? in original}

L3 sʷadaxab with his wife, his own parents, and 4 boys

L4 xexalciᴅ (xεxal'cid, called Henry, cousin to Sally) with his Puyallup wife Sarah ___ {blank line in original} and 6 children who died young so there are no descendants

L5 xʷdəbalgʷədxʷ (Jim Hummelgood), son of L2 siyaləxʷ and tsiaɬitsə, who married a girl from Gig Harbor, reformed, but had no children

L6 a suspiciously empty corner, probably for the head woman (otherwise missing) or for guests

At the important location at the back (B) were

B1 Gig Harbor Joe (kʷεyadx̌ʷ), his wife (tsəltsi, Jerry's youngest aunt who died young), with 3 children, 2 boys and a girl, all of whom also died young. This couple was married by a Catholic priest across from Cushman hospital, when the groom gave out prestigious goat wool blankets <A115>. Both the headwoman and the wife of tsialx's [L2 ?] wove these for some years.[470] After tsəltsi died, he married her first cousin, the Puyallup widow of Moyε's, when they were both over sixty years old. His own sister married Speym [R1]

B2 The empty space opposite the door that was the most likely abode for the leading or chiefly family of this household. Left blank probably because of the rapid deaths of the headwoman and her son [R6] between 1876-78.[471]

---

470 Woven mountain goat wool blankets were high prestige currency in the potlatch system, as were lowland wooly dog hair weavings, both indicative of elite status of Minters, See Pamela Amoss, Hair of the Dog: Unraveling Pre-Contact Coast Salish Social Stratification, *American Indian Linguistics and Ethnography in Honor or Laurence Thompson* 1993: 10, 3-35.

471 I suspect this diagram shows the house about 1870, though the lack of the leader and her son suggests reference to about 1877, when the leader of this household was at Glencove.

Abbreviations Used

Agencies

BLM = Bureau of Land Management

GLO = General Land Office

HBC = Hudson's Bay Company

MSCUA = Manuscripts, Special Collections, and University Archives, UW

NARA = National Archives and Records Administrations

SC = Special Collections, UW, formerly MSCUA

TPL = Tacoma Public Library

UW = University of Washington, Seattle

WSHS = Washington State Historical Society, Tacoma

Graphics

~ = equivalent, same as, comparable

[ ] = Lushootseed ~ whulshootseed terms

( ) = inclusions, clarifications

< > = volume and page number from the three notebooks by Alfred John Smith from Jerry Meeker, 1948

LD = Lushootseed Dictionary, by Dawn Bates, Thom Hess, and Vi Hilbert, 1994.

BIBLIOGRAPHY

A Boston Tillicum [pseudonym], see James Wickersham 1892.

Abbott, Donald 1981 *The World Is As Sharp As A Knife*, An Anthology in Honour of Wilson Duff. Victoria: British Columbia Provincial Museum.

Adamson, Thelma 1934 *Folktales of the Coast Salish.* New York: Memoirs of the American Folklore Society 27.

Allen, Edwin 1976 Intergroup Ties And Exogamy Among Northern Coast Salish. NARN 10 (2): 163-69.

Amato, Joseph 2002 *Rethinking Home. A Case for Writing Local History.* Berkeley: University of California Press.

Ames, James 2000 E-mail of 27 October.

Ames, Kenneth, and Herbert Maschner 1999 *Peoples of the Northwest Coast.* Their Archaeology and Prehistory. London: Thames and Hudson.

Amoss, Pamela

1975 Catalogue of the Marian Smith Collection of Fieldnotes, Manuscripts, and Photographs in the Library of the Royal Anthropological Institute of Great Britain and Ireland.

1978 *Coast Salish Spirit Dancing*, The Survival of an Ancestral Religion. Seattle: University of Washington Press.

1981 Coast Salish Elders. *Other Ways of Growing Old*: 227-261. Pamela Amoss and Steven Harrell, eds. Stanford University Press.

1982 Resurrection, Healing, and "the Shake": The Story of John and Mary Slocum." *Charisma and Sacred Biography.* Michael Williams, ed. Journal of the American Academy of Religion, Thematic Studies XLVIII (3/4): 87-109.

1987 "The Fish God Gave Us": The First Salmon Ceremony Revived. *Arctic Anthropology* 24 (1): 56-66.

1990 The Indian Shaker Church. Handbook of North American Indians, *Northwest Coast*, Volume 7: 633-39. DC: Smithsonian Institution Press.

1993 Hair of the Dog: Unraveling Pre-Contact Coast Salish Social Stratification. *American Indian Linguistics and Ethnography in Honor of Laurence C Thompson.* Anthony Mattina and Timothy Montler, eds. Missoula: University of Montana, Occasional Papers in Linguistics 10: 3-35.

Anderson, Bern 1960 *The Life and Voyages of Captain George Vancouver.* Seattle: University of Washington Press.

Anderson, Bern, ed. 1939 The Vancouver Expedition: Peter Puget's Journal of the Exploration of the Puget Sound, May 7 – June 11, 1792. *Pacific Northwest Quarterly* 30 (2), April.

Angelbeck, Bill, and Eric Mclay 2011 The Battle at Maple Bay: The Dynamics of Coast Salish Political organization through Oral Histories. *Ethnohistory* 58 (3): 359-392. Summer.

Appleby, Andrew, and Keith Keown 1994 History of the White River Spring Chinook Broodstocking and Captive Rearing Efforts. Olympia: Washington Department of Fish and Wildlife.

Asher, Brad

1995 A Shaman-killing Case on Puget Sound, 1873-1874. American Law and Salish Culture. *Pacific Northwest Quarterly* 86 (1): 17-24, Winter 1994/95.

1999 *Beyond the Reservation*: ndians, Settlers, and the Law in Washington Territory, 1853-1889. Norman: University of Oklahoma Press.

Arledge, Raymond T. (Father Thaddeus) 1998 *Early Days of the Key Peninsula*. Vaughn, WA: Key Peninsula Historical Society.

Atwood, Evangeline 1979 *Frontier Politics*: Alaska's James Wickersham. Portland: Binford and Mort.

Avery, Michael, Martha Gray, and Linda Perez

1983 Chambers Bay, A Historical Perspective. Ft. Steilacoom Community College, Anthropology Department.

Avery, Michael, Fred Crisson, and Todd Tucker

1984 Archaeological Investigations of Chambers Bay 45PI50. Ft. Steilacoom Community College, Anthropology Department.

Bagley, Clarence

1905 Issac Hawk Obituary. Clarence B Bagley Scrapbook, volume 8, page 119. SC [MSCUA] Microfilm B 1784.

1905a In The Beginning, Early Days on Puget Sound. Everett: The Historical Society of Seattle and King County. Reprinted 1980.

1931 Chief Seattle and Angeline. *Washington Historical Quarterly* 22: 243-275.

Bagley, Clarence, ed.

1915 Journal of Occurrences at Nisqually House, 1833. *Washington Historical Quarterly* 6 (3): 179-197; (4): 264-278.

1916 Journal of Occurrences at Nisqually House. *Washington Historical Quarterly* 7 (1): 59-75; (2): 144-167.

Ballard, Arthur

1927 Some Tales of the Southern Puget Sound Salish. University of Washington Publications in Anthropology 2 (3): 57-81.

1929 Mythology of Southern Puget Sound. University of Washington Publications in Anthropology 3 (2): 31-150.

1935 Southern Puget Sound Salish Kinship Terms. *American Anthropologist* 37 (1), 111-116.

1950 Calendric Terms of the Southern Puget Sound Salish. *Southwestern Journal of Anthropology* 6 (1): 79-99.

1951 Deposition on Oral Examination of Arthur Condict Ballard. November 26, 27, 28. Testimony before the Indian Claims Commission of the United States, Docket 98. Carolyn Taylor, court reporter. 2 volumes.

1957 The Salmon-Weir on Green River in Western Washington. *Davidson Journal of Anthropology* 3: 37-53.

Barnett, Homer

1955 *The Coast Salish* of British Columbia. Studies in Anthropology 4. Eugene: University of Oregon Press.

1957 *Indian Shakers*, A Messianic Cult of the Pacific Northwest. Carbondale: Southern Illinois University Press.

Bartlett, see Downey-Bartlett.

Bates, Dawn, Thom Hess, and Vi Hilbert 1994 *Lushootseed Dictionary.* Seattle: University of Washington Press.

Berkes, Fikret 1999 *Sacred Ecology. Traditional Ecological Knowledge and Resource Management.* Philadelphia: Taylor and Francis.

Bierwert, Crisca

1986 Tracery in the Mistlines: Semeiotic Readings of Sto:lo Culture. Seattle: UW Ph.D. Dissertation.

1999 *Brushed by Cedar, Living by the River.* Tucson: University of Arizona Press.

Bierwert, Crisca, ed. 1996 Lushootseed Texts. An Introduction to Puget Salish Aesthetics. Translated by Crisca Bierwert, Vi Hilbert, Thomas M. Hess; Annotations by Toby C. S. Langen. Lincoln: University of Nebraska Press.

Binns, Archie

1941 *Northwest Gateway.* The Story of the Port of Seattle. Garden City, NY: Doubleday, Doran & Company.

1942 *The Roaring Land.* New York: Robert M McBride & Co.

1947 *You Rolling River*, Life on the Columbia – 1880. NY: Ballantine Books, 1971.

Bishop, Thomas

1915 An Appeal to the Government to Fulfill Sacred Promised Made 61 Years Ago. Tacoma.

1916 Applications For Enrollment and Allotment, 1911-17. Records Relating to Enrollment of Washington Indians. Special Agent Charles E. Roblin. DC: National Archives.

Black, Anne, and Adam Liljeblad

2006 *Guide to Methods Used for Developing, Analyzing, and Preparing Social Data Related to Attachment to Place*. Missoula: Aldo Leopold Wilderness Research Institute and Joint Fire Science Program.

Blackhawk, Ned 2006 *Violence over the Land ~ Indians and Empires in the Early American West.* Cambridge: Harvard University Press.

BLM 1996 Celebrate BLM's 50th Anniversary, 1946-1996, Brochure.

Boxberger, Daniel 1984 The Introduction of Horses to the Southern Puget Sound Salish, 103-119. *Western Washington Indian Socio-Economics*: Papers in Honor of Angelo Anastasio. Herbert Taylor and Garland Grabert, eds. Bellingham: Western Washington University.

Boyd, Robert

1996 *People of the Dalles.* The Indians of Wascopam Mission. Lincoln: University of Nebraska Press.

1999 *The Coming of the Spirit of Pestilence*: Introduced Infectious Diseases and Population Decline among Northwest Coast Indians, 1774-1874. Seattle: University of Washington Press.

Boyd, Robert, ed. 1999 *Indians, Fire, and the Land in the Pacific Northwest.* Corvallis: Oregon State University Press.

Brooks, James 2002 *Captives and Cousins, Slavery, Kinship, and Community in the Southwest Borderlands.* Chapel Hill: University of North Carolina Press.

Buerge, David, and Junius Rochester 1988 *Roots and Branches.* The Religious Heritage of Washington State. Seattle: Church Council of Greater Seattle.

Burns, Robert 1985 The Shape and Form of Puget Sound. Seattle: Puget Sound Books.

Cammon, Betsey Johnson 1969 *Island Memoir. A Personal History of Anderson and McNeil Islands.* Puyallup, Wa: The Valley Press.

Carranco, Lynwood, and Estle Beard 1981 *Genocide and Vendetta. The Round Valley Wars of Northern California.* Norman: University of Oklahoma Press.

Carlson, Barry, and Thom Hess 1971 Canoe Names in the Northwest, An Areal Study. *Anthropological Linguistics* 12 (1): 17-24.

Carlson, Keith Thor, ed.

1997 *You are Asked to Witness*: The Sto:lō in Canada's Pacific Coast History. Chilliwack, BC: Stolo Heritage Trust.

2001 *A Sto:lō and Coast Salish Historical Atlas.* Vancouver: Douglas and McIntyre.

2007a Innovation, Tradition, Colonialism, and Aboriginal Fishing Conflicts in the Lower Fraser Canyon. *New Histories for Old.* Festschrift for AJ Ray: 145-175. Ted Binnema and Susan Neylan, ed. Vancouver: UBC Press.

2007b Events, Migrations, and the Formation of 'Post-Contact' Coast Salish Collective Identities. *Be Of Good Mind*: Essays on the Coast Salish, Bruce Miller, ed. Vancouver: UBC Press.

2007c Reflections on Indigenizing History and Memory: Reconstituting and Reconsidering Contact. *Myth and Memory - Stories of Indigenous – European Contact:* 46-68. John Lutz, ed. Vancouver: UBC Press.

2010 *The Power of Place, The Problem of Time.* Aboriginal Identity and Historical Consciousness in the Cauldron of Colonialism. University of Toronto Press.

Carlson, Roy, and Philip Hobler 1993 The Pender Canal Excavations And The Development Of Coast Salish Culture. *BC Studies* 99: 25-52, Autumn.

Carpenter, Cecelia Svinth

1986 Fort Nisqually. A Documented History of Indian and British Interaction. Tacoma: Tahoma Research Service.

1994 Where the Waters Begin. The Traditional Nisqually Indian History of Mount Rainier. Seattle: Northwest Interpretive Association.

1996 Tears of Internment. The Indian History of Fox Island and the Puget Sound Indian War. Tacoma: Tahoma Research Service.

2002 *The Nisqually, My People.* Tahoma Research Service.

Carson, Charles 2003 Rising from the ashes : the Puyallup Indians : assimilation, culture & self-determination. UW-Tacoma: MA Thesis.

Castile, George 1982 The 'Half-Catholic' Movement: Edwin and Myron Eells and the Rise of the Indian Shaker Church. *Pacific Northwest Quarterly* 73: 165-174.

1990 The Indian Connection: Judge James Wickersham and the Indian Shakers. *Pacific Northwest Quarterly* 81 (Oct): 122-129.

Castile, George, ed. 1985 *The Indians of Puget Sound.* The Notebooks of Myron Eells. Walla Walla: University of Washington Press for Whitman College.

Chalcraft, Edwin 2004 *Assimilation's Agent. My Life as a Superintendent in the Indian Boarding School System.* Cary Collins, ed. Lincoln: University of Nebraska Press.

Chambers, Andrew Jackson 1975 *Recollections.* Fairfield, Wa: Ye Galleon Press.

Clark, Donald Hathaway 1952 An Analysis of Forestry Utilization as a Factor in Colonizing the Pacific Northwest and in Subsequent Population Transitions. Seattle: UW College of Forestry Ph.D,

Clark, Ella 1953 *Indian Legends of the Pacific Northwest.* Illustrations by Robert Bruce Inverarity. Berkeley: University of California Press.

Cohen, Felix 1942 *Handbook of Federal Indian Law.* Albuquerque: University of New Mexico Press. [revised]

Cohen, Lucille

1959 Port Gamble Vanishing Quietly. *Seattle PI,* Sunday 16 August, page 23.

Collins, June

1949 John Fornsby: The Personal Document of a Coast Salish Indian. Marian Smith, *Indians of the Urban Northwest,* 287-341.

1950a Growth of Class Distinctions and Political Authority Among the Skagit Indians During the Contact Period. *American Anthropologist* 52 (3): 331-342.

1950b The Indian Shaker Church. *Southwestern Journal of Anthropology* 6: 399-411.

1952a An Interpretation of Skagit Intragroup Conflict during Acculturation. *American Anthropologist* 54: 347-355.

1952b The Mythological Basis For Attitudes Toward Animals Among Salish-Speaking Indians. *Journal of American Folklore* 65 (258): 353-359.

1966 Naming, Continuity, and Social Inheritance among the Coast Salish of Western Washington. Papers of the Michigan Academy of Science, Arts, and Letters 51: 425-36.

1974 *Valley Of The Spirits*, The Upper Skagit Indians of Western Washington. Seattle: University of Washington Press.

1979 Multilineal Descent: A Coast Salish Strategy. *Currents in Anthropology, Essays in Honor of Sol Tax*: 243-254. Robert Hinshaw, ed. The Hague: Mouton Publishers.

Colwell-Chanthaphonh, Chip 2007 *Massacre at Camp Grant. Forgetting and Remembering Apache History*. Tucson: University of Arizona Press.

Connolly, Thomas, S.J. 1990 A Coeur D'Alene Indian Story. Fairfield, WA: Ye Galleon Press.

Coman, Edwin, Jr., and Helen Gibbs

1949 *Time, Tide, and Timber: A Century of Pope and Talbot*. Palo Alto: Stanford University Press.

1978 *Time, Tide, and Timber: Over a Century of Pope and Talbot*. Revised, Edited, and Published by Pope and Talbot.

Cope, Leona 1919 Calendars of the Indians North of Mexico. University of California Publications in American Archaeology and Ethnology 16 (4): 119-176.

Cosgrove, Patricia 2001 A Great Diversion. White River Journal, A Newsletter of the White River Valley Museum, Auburn. January.

Costello, Gilbert S. 1906-47 Scrapbooks on Seattle and Indians. Seattle Public Library.

Culin, Stewart 1901 A Summer Trip among the Western Indians (The Wanamaker Expedition). Chapter IV. *Bulletin of the Free Museum of Science and Art of the University of Pennsylvania* III (1): 143-164.

Curtis, Edward 1913 *The North American Indian*, being a series of volumes picturing and describing the Indians of the United States, the Dominion of Canada, and Alaska. Written, Illustrated, and Published By Edward S. Curtis. Frederick Webb Hodge, ed. Volume 9 of 20.

Curtis, Joan, Alice Watson, Bette Bradley 1988 *Town on the Sound. Stories of Steilacoom*. Steilacoom: Steilacoom Historical Museum Association.

Daily Pacific Tribune 1874 Tuesday 14 April, Vol IX # 146: page 3, column 2.

De Laguna, Frederica 1960 The Story of a Tlingit Community. DC: *Bureau of American Ethnology, Bulletin* 172.

*Delaney, Ed, and M.T. Rice 1927 *The Bloodstained Trail*, A History of Militant Labor in the US. Seattle: The Industrial Worker.

Dickey, George, ed. 1989 The Journal of Occurrences at Fort Nisqually, Commencing May 30, 1833, Ending September 27, 1859. Tacoma: Fort Nisqually Association.

Dictionary of Canadian Biography 1982 Volume XI, 1881-1890. Frances Donald Halpenny and Jean Hamelin, eds. University of Toronto Press.

Dixon, Mim, and Pamela Iron 2006 *Strategies for Cultural Competency in Indian Health Care.* DC: American Public health Association.

Dobyns, Henry F. 1983 *Their Number Become Thinned. Native American Population Dynamics in Eastern North America.* Knoxville: University of Tennessee Press.

Donald, Leland 1997 *Aboriginal Slavery on the Northwest Coast of North America.* Berkeley: University of California Press.

Donaldson, Thomas. 1884 *The Public Domain, Its History with Statistics ...* Washington, DC: GPO.

Douglas, James 1853 Private Papers (second series, 1853, 23), census inset after 424, typescript (B/20/1853) and microfilm (737A) in British Columbia Provincial Archives; original in the Bancroft Library at University of California at Berkeley.

Downey-Bartlett, Laura Belle

1898 *The Pure Food – Klondike Cookbook.* Tacoma: Commercial Printing Company. Writing as Mrs LB Ellis and Mrs Geo A Misner.

1914 Chinook-English Songs. Portland: Kubli-Miller Co. June 9.

1915 Wah-Mah-Whah-Lah – Signifying Beautiful Mountains, Lovely Valleys, And Crystal Springs – A Dramatic, Musical Indian Character Play in 5 Acts. May.

1922 *Student's History of the Northwest and State of Washington.* Tacoma: Smith Digby Co.

1924 Dictionary of the Intertribal Indian Language, Commonly Called Chinook. Tacoma: Smith Digby Co.

ms.a *Who's Who of the Washington Pioneer Empire Builders.*

ms.b Indian Stories.

Drucker, Philip

1937 Diffusion In Northwest Coast Culture In The Light Of Some Distributions. University of California at Berkeley: Ph. D. Dissertation.

1940 Kwakiutl Dancing Societies. *Anthropological Records* 6 (6): 201-230.

1951 The Northern And Central Nootkan Tribes. *Bureau of American Ethnology, Bulletin* 141.

Duff, Wilson

1964 The Indian History of British Columbia. Volume 1: The Impact of the White Man. Provincial Museum of British Columbia: *Anthropology in British Columbia*, Memoir 5.

1981 Thoughts on the Nootka Canoe. *The World Is As Sharp As A Knife*, An Anthology in Honour of Wilson Duff: 201-206. Donald Abbott, ed. Victoria: British Columbia Provincial Museum.

Duwamish and Others 1933 Consolidated Petition in the US Court of Claims. DC: Government Printing Office, 2 volumes.

Dyer, James C., Jr. 1985 Historic Houses of Steilacoom. A Sketchbook Guide. The Proverbial Press.

Eells, Edwin ms. Edwin Eells Papers, including Autobiography, Puyallup Agency Records. Tacoma: Washington State Historical Society.

Eells, Myron

1887 The Indians Of Puget Sound (nine parts). *American Antiquarian* 9.

1889 The Twana, Chemakum, and Klallam Indians of Washington Territory. *Smithsonian Annual Report* For 1887: 605-681.

1985 *The Indians of Puget Sound. The Notebooks of Myron Eells.* George Pierre Castille, ed. Seattle: University of Washington Press.

Ellliott, T.C., ed. 1912 Journal of John Work, November and December, 1824. Washington Historical Quarterly 3 (3): 198-229.

Ellis, Mrs L.B., and Mrs Geo A. Misner 1898 *The Pure Food – Klondike Cookbook* Tacoma: Commercial Printing Company.

Elmendorf, William

1935 The Soul - Recovery Ceremony Among The Indians of the Northwest Coast. Master of Arts Thesis. University of Washington.

1946 Twana Kinship Terminology. *Southwestern Journal of Anthropology* 2: 420-432.

1948 The Cultural Setting Of The Twana Secret Society. *American Anthropologist* 50: 625-633.

1960 *The Structure of Twana Culture.* Pullman: Washington State Research Studies, Monographic Supplement 2. (with Comparative Notes on the Structure of Yurok by Alfred Kroeber).

1961a Skokomish and Other Coast Salish Tales. Washington State University Research Studies 29 (1): 1-37; (2): 84-117; (3): 119-150.

1961b System Change in Salish Kinship Terminologies. *Southwestern Journal of Anthropology* 17 (4); 365-382.

1970a Skokomish Sorcery, Ethics, and Society. *Systems of North American Witchcraft And Sorcery.* Deward Walker, ed. Anthropological Monographs of the University of Idaho 1, Chapter VI: 147-182.

1970b Word Tabu and Change Rates: Tests of a Hypothesis. *Languages and Cultures of Western North America: Essays in Honor of Sven S. Liljeblad*: 74-85. Earl Swanson, ed. Pocatello: Idaho State University Press.

1971 Coast Salish Status Ranking and Intergroup Ties. *Southwestern Journal of Anthropology* 27: 353-381.

1993 *Twana Narratives.* Native Historical Accounts of a Coast Salish People. Seattle: University of Washington Press.

Fitzpatrick, Darlene 1968 The 'Shake': The Indian Shaker Curing Ritual among the Yakima. University of Washington: MA Thesis, Anthropology.

*Fort Steilacoom Newsletter

1999 Fort Steilacoom becomes Western State Hospital. By Hilda Skott. XVI (4): 1, 2-3 (Winter).

2000 Glittering Misery. The Army Life of the Kautz and Summerhayes Families. By Carol Neufeld. XVII (1): 1, 3 (Spring).

2001 Reconstruction of Fort Steilacoom 1857-58. By Carol Neufeld. XVIII (1): 1, 4 (Spring).

Franchere, Gabriel 1968 *A Voyage [1810-14] to the Norwest Coast of America.* Milo Milton Quaife, ed. NY: Citadel Press (French 1820, English 1854).

Frank, Willy. 1980. The Recollections of Ernest White and Willy Frank. Metrocenter YMCA, Seattle. *Voices of Washington State*, Discussion Guide 7.

Frykman, George A. 1998 *Seattle's Historian and Promoter*, The Life of Edmond Stephen Meany. Pullman: Washington State University Press.

Galbraith, John S. 1954 The Early History of the Puget's Sound Agricultural Company, 1838-1843. *Washington Historical Quarterly* 55: 234-259.

Gallaghan, Deanie 1976 Minter, in Peninsula Community Histories, Peninsula Historical Society, compiled from the Key Peninsula Civic Center Newsletter Bicentennial Issue, Summer, filed at Pierce County, Key Center Library.

Gallay, Alan 2002 *The Indian Slave Trade. The Rise of the English Empire in the American South, 1670-1717.* New Haven: Yale University Press.

Gates, Paul W.

1968 *History of Public Land Law Development.* Washington, DC: GPO.

1996 *The Jeffersonian Dream, Studies in the History of American land Policy and Development.* Allan and Margaret Beattie Bogue, eds. Albuquerque, NM: University of New Mexico Press for the Center for the American West.

Gibbs, George

1853 Indian Nomenclature of Localities in Washington and Oregon Territories [West of the Cascades]. 14pp. ms # 714. [SI 248] DC: National Anthropological Archives.

1855 Report on the Indian Tribes of Washington Territory. *Pacific Railroad Report* 1: 402-36.

1877 Tribes of Western Washington and Northwestern Oregon. Washington: Department of the Interior, United States Geographical and Geological Survey of the Rocky Mountain Region, Part II: 157-241.

1970 Dictionary of the Niskwalli (Nisqually) Indian Language - Western Washington. Extract from 1877 *Contributions to North American Ethnology* 1, 285-361. Seattle: The Shorey Book Store Facsimile Reproduction.

Goble, Dale D., and Paul W. Hirt, eds. 1999 *Northwest Lands, Northwest Peoples. Readings in Environmental History*. Seattle: University of Washington Press.

Goodman Middle School 1979 *Along the Waterfront*. A History of the Gig Harbor and Key Peninsula Areas. Compiled and Written by 1974-75 Students. Tacoma: Clinton-Hull Publishing.

Gormly, Mary 1977 Early Culture Contact on the Northwest Coast, 1774-1795: Analysis of Spanish Sources. *Northwest Anthropological Research Notes* 11 (1): 1-80.

Green, Frank 1972 A Guide to the Thomas M. Chambers Collection. Tacoma: Washington State Historical Society.

Guilmet, George, and David Whited 1989 The People Who Give More: Health and Mental Health among the Contemporary Puyallup Indian Tribal Community. American Indian and Alaska Native Mental Health Research Journal. Volume 2 (Winter), Monograph 2: 1-141.

Guilmet, George, Robert Boyd, David Whited, and Nile Thompson 1991 The Legacy of Introduced Diseases. *American Indian Culture and Research Journal* 15 (4): 1-32.

Gunther, Erna

1925 Klallam Folk Tales. *University of Washington Publications in Anthropology* 1 (4): 113-170.

1927 Klallam Ethnography. *University of Washington Publications in Anthropology* 1 (5): 171-310.

1928 A Further Analysis of the First Salmon Ceremony. *University of Washington Publications in Anthropology* 2 (5): 129-173.

ms. Culture Element Distributions: Puget Sound (Duwamish, Skokomish, Klallam, Makah). Berkeley: Bancroft Library.

1949 The Shaker Religion of the Northwest. Marian Smith, ed. *Indians of the Urban Northwest*, 37-76.

1973 *Ethnobotany of Western Washington*. The Knowledge and Use of Indigenous Plants by Native Americans. Seattle: University of Washington Press. [1945]

Haeberlin, Herman

1916-17 Puget Salish, 42 Notebooks. DC: National Anthropological Archives. # 2965.

1918 SbEtEtda'q, A Shamanic Performance of the Coast Salish. *American Anthropologist* 20 (3): 249-257.

1924 Mythology of Puget Sound. *Journal of American Folklore* 37 (143-144): 371-438.

Haeberlin, Herman, and Erna Gunther 1930 The Indians of Puget Sound. University of Washington Publications in Anthropology 4 (1): 1-84.

Hagan, William 1980 *Indian Police and Judges*. Lincoln: University of Nebraska Press. [Reprint of 1966 by Yale]

Harkin, Michael 1997 *The Heiltsuks. Dialogues of Culture and History on the Northwest Coast*. Lincoln: University of Nebraska Press.

Harmon, Alexandra

1996 Different Kind of Indians. Negotiating the Meanings of "Indian" and "Tribe" in the Puget Sound Region, 1820s-1970s. University of Washington: History Ph.D. I - 1-365, II - 366-741.

1998 *Indians in the Making.* Ethnic Relations and Indian Identities around Puget Sound. American Crossroads Series. Berkeley: University of California Press.

Hawkins, Kenneth 1998 Research in the Land Entry Files of the General Land Office. DC: NARA.

HBC 1968 A Brief History of the Hudson's Bay Company. Winnipeg: HBC Archives.

Heath, Joseph 1979 *Memoirs of Nisqually.* Lucille McDonald, ed. Fairfield, Wa: Ye Galleon Press.

Heckman, Hazel

1967 *Island in the Sound.* Seattle: University of Washington Press.

1972 *Island Year.* Seattle: University of Washington Press.

Heritage League of Pierce County 1990 A History of Pierce County, Washington. Dallas: Taylor Publishing Co.

Hess, Thom

1971 Prefix Constituent With /xʷ/. *Studies in Northwest Indian Languages.* James Hoard and Thom Hess, eds. Sacramento Anthropological Society, Paper 11: 43-69.

1976 *Dictionary of Puget Salish.* Seattle: University of Washington Press.

1977 Lushootseed Dialects. *Anthropological Linguistics* 19 (9): 403-419.

Hilbert, Vi (*taqʷšəblu*)

1976 Recording in the Native Language. *Sound Heritage* IV (3-4): 39-42.

1979 Yehaw. Privately Printed.

1980a Huboo. Privately Printed.

1980b Ways of the Lushootseed People: Ceremonies and Traditions of the Northern Puget Sound Indians. Seattle: United Indians of All Tribes Foundation, Daybreak Star Press.

1985 *Haboo. Native American Stories from Puget Sound.* Seattle: University of Washington Press.

Hilbert, Vi, Jay Miller, and Zalmai Zahir 2001 *Puget Sound Geography.* sdaʔdaʔ gʷəɬ dibəɬ ləšucid ʔacaciɬtalbixʷ. Original Manuscript from TT Waterman, Edited with Additional Material. Seattle: Lushootseed Press.

Hilbert, Vi, and Jay Miller 2004 "That Salish Feeling ..." *Studies in Salish Linguistics in Honor of M. Dale Kinkade.* Donna B. Gerdts and Lisa Mathewson, eds. Missoula: University of Montana, Occasional Papers in Linguistics 17: 197-210.

Heizer, Robert 1988 Indian Servitude in California. *History of Indian – White Relations*. Wilcomb Washburn, ed. Handbook of North American Indians, Volume 4, 414-416.

Hodge, Frederick, ed. 1910 Handbook of American Indians North of Mexico. Smithsonian: *BAE-B* 30.

Holbrook, Stewart

1943 *Burning an Empire. The Story of American Forest Fires*. New York: The Macmillan Co.

1945 Green Commonwealth. A Narrative of the Past and a Look at the Future of One Forest Products Community. Published for their friends by the Simpson Logging Company, Shelton, Washington, 1895-1945. Seattle: Dogwood Press of Frank McCaffrey.

1957 *Dreamers of the American Dream*. New York: Doubleday & Co.

1986 *Far Corner*. Sausalito: Comstock. [1952]

Horr, David Agee 1974 Coast Salish and Western Washington Indians v. Indian Claims Commission. Findings. New York: Garland Publishing, Inc.

Howard, Florence 1949 An Archaeological Site Survey of Southwestern Puget Sound. UW Special Collections.

Hunt, Herbert 1916 *Tacoma. It's History and Its Builders. A Half Century of Activity*. Chicago: The SJ Clarke Publishing Co.

Indian Land Claims Commission 1952 Jerry Meeker Testimony on 13 June.

Jacobs, Melville 1951 Sound Recordings, Tape 30, Box 10, 14773, UW-SC.

Jenness, Diamond

1935 Saanitch fieldnotes. Copy. Victoria, BC: RBCM.

1955 The Faith of a Coast Salish Indian. Victoria: British Columbia Provincial Museum. *Anthropology in British Columbia*, Memoir 3.

Jilek, Wolfgang 1982 *Indian Healing*. Shamanic Ceremonialism in the Pacific Northwest Today. Surrey, British Columbia: Hancock House Publishers, Ltd.

Jordan, Ray 1974 *Ray's Writin's*. Yarns of the Skagit Country. Everett: The Printers.

Juvonen, Helmi 2000 Religious Background of Salish Aesthetics. Jay Miller, ed. *Northwest Anthropological Research Notes* (*NARN*) 34 (1): 17-48.

Kappler, Charles 1904 *Indians Treaties*. DC: Government Printing Office.

Kennedy, Dorothy

1993 Looking For The Tribe In The Wrong Places: An Examination Of The Central Coast Salish Social Network. University Of Victoria: MA Thesis.

2000 Threads To The Past: The Construction and Transformation of Kinship in the Coast Salish Social Network. Oxford University, Exeter College: Anthropology D. Phil.

Kennedy, Hal, Robert Thomas, and Jerry Jermann 1976 A Cultural Resource Assessment of the Chambers - Clover Creeks Drainage, Pierce County, Washington. Seattle: University of Washington, Institute of Environmental Studies, Office of Public Archaeology.

Kenyon, Susan 1980 The Kyuquot Way: A Study of a West Coast (Nootkan) Community. National Museums of Canada, Canadian Ethnology Service, *Mercury Series*, Paper 61.

King, Thomas 2003 *Places That Count. Traditional Cultural Properties in Cultural Resource Management*. Walnut Creek, CA: AltaMira Press.

Knapp, Douglas 1985 A History of Peninsula Lutheran Church, 1904-1979. Clinton-Hull Publishing Co.

Kowrach, Edward 1992 *Mie Charles Pandosy, O.M.I.* A Missionary of the Northwest. Fairfield, Wa: Ye Galleon Press.

Krieger, Judith 1989 Aboriginal Coast Salish Food Resources: A Compilation of Sources. *Northwest Anthropological Research Notes* 23 (2): 217-231.

Kroeber, Alfred

1925 *Handbook of Indians of California.* BAE B 78.

1939 *Natural and Cultural Areas of Native North America.* Berkeley: University of California Press.

Kroeber, Theodora 1961 *Ishi in Two Worlds.* Berkeley: University of California Press.

Kuiper, Aert 2002 *Salish Etymological Dictionary.* University of Montana, Occasional Papers in Linguistics 16.

Kawashima, Yasuhide 1988 Indian Servitude in the Northeast. *History of Indian – White Relations.* Wilcomb Washburn, ed. Handbook of North American Indians, Volume 4, 404-406.

Lambert [Vincent], Mary Ann

1961 Dungeness Massacre and Other Regional Tales. Port Angeles: Privately Printed.

1960 The House of the Seven Brothers + Trees, Roots and Branches of the House of Ste-tee-thlum. A Genealogical Story of the Olympic Peninsula Clallam Indians. Port Angeles: Privately Printed.

Lane, Barbara

1972 Anthropological Report on the Identity, Treaty Status, and Fisheries of the Squaxin Tribe of Indians. 6 October.

1970s Anthropological Report on the Identity, Treaty Status, and Fisheries of the Puyallup Tribe of Indians.

Lang, William L. 1999 From Where We Are Standing: The Sense Of Place and Environmental History *Northwest Lands, Northwest Peoples. Readings in Environmental History.* Goble and Hirt, eds. Chapter4: 79-94.

Lerman, Norman 1976 *Legends of the River People.* Betty Keller, ed. Vancouver: November House.

Lesy, Michael 1973 *Wisconsin Death Trip.* NY: Pantheon Books.

LeWarne, Charles Pierce 1975 *Utopias on Puget Sound, 1885-1915.* Seattle: University of Washington Press.

Lewis, Peter 1982 2 indicted for arson, linked to Satiacum. *The Seattle Times*, Thursday, 16 September.

Lincoln, Leslie 1991 *Coast Salish Canoes.* Seattle: The Center for Wooden Boats.

Lynden Tribune 1975 Sindick' Jimmy's Memories Legacy from Indian Past. By Liz May. 19 February.

Luttrell, Charles 2006 Archaeology for Young Diggers: Douglas and Carolyn Osborne, the Seattle Young Archaeologists' Society, and the Washington Archaeological Society. *Archaeology in Washington* 12, - .

McDonald, Evelyn Ward 1972 The History of Port Blakely. *Sea Chest* 6 (1): 21-34, September.

McGinnis, Dale, and Jim Forrest 1976 Minter Site, in Peninsula Community Histories, Peninsula Historical Society, compiled from the Key Peninsula Civic Center Newsletter Bicentennial Issue, Summer, filed at Pierce County, Key Center Library.

Maclachlan, Morag, ed. 1998 *The Fort Langley Journals, 1827-30.* Vancouver: University of British Columbia Press.

Mapes, Lynda 2009 *Breaking Ground. The Lower Elwa Klallam Tribe and the Unearthing of Tse-whit-zen Village.* Seattle: University of Washington Press.

Martin, Ken and Vida 2013 *The Ballards ~ Architects or Pioneer Towns, Roads, and Major Gold Mines.* Stanwood: Golden Treasures Publishing

Mattina, Anthony, and Timothy Montler 1993 American Indian Linguistics and Ethnography in Honor of Laurence C Thompson. Missoula: University of Montana, Occasional Papers in Linguistics 10.

Mauze, Marie, Michael Harkin, and Sergei Kan 2004 *Coming to Shore.* Northwest Coast Ethnology, Traditions, and Visions. Lincoln: University of Nebraska Press.

Michaud, Ellen 1977 Women of the Puget Sound Coast Salish Indians. An Inquiry into their traditional role in socialization, religion, and economics. University of Washington: BA Thesis.

Meany, Edmond 1957 *Vancouver's Discovery of Puget Sound.* Portraits and Biographies of the Men Honored in the Naming of Geographical Features of Northwestern America. Portland: Binford & Mort. [1907]

Meeker, Ezra

1870 Washington Territory West of the Cascade Mountains. Olympia: Transcript Office.

1890 Indian Jim Was True. *The Daily Ledger*, 30 June: p3.

1905 *Pioneer Reminiscences of Puget Sound*, and *The Tragedy of Leschi.* Seattle: Lowman and Hanford. [1980]

1916 *Busy Life of Eighty-Five Years.* Ventures and Adventures. Seattle: by the author.

1921 *Seventy Years of Progress in Washington.* Seattle & Tacoma: Allstrum Printing Co.

Ezra Meeker Historical Society 1972 Ezra Meeker, A brief resume of his life and adventures. Puyallup, WA.

Meeker, Jerry 1948 Notebooks by Al Smith. Seattle: UW Special Collections, # 362 A B C.

Miles, Charles, & O. B. Sperlin, eds. 1940 *Building a State, 1889-1939.* Tacoma: Washington State Historical Society.

Miles, George 2003 *James Swan Cha-tic of the Northwest Coast.* Seattle: University of Washington Press for Beinecke Rare Book and Manuscript Library at Yale.

Miller, Bruce 2001 *The Problem of Justice. Tradition and Law in the Coast Salish World.* Lincoln: University of Nebraska Press.

Miller, Jay

1976 The Northwest Coast Of What? Final Address at Conference on Northwest Coast Studies. Simon Fraser University and Canadian National Museum of Man. 12-16 May.

1979a A Strucon Model of Delaware Culture and the Positioning of Mediators. *American Ethnologist* 6 (4): 791-802.

1980 High-Minded High Gods in North America. *Anthropos* 75: 916-919.

1981 The Matter of the (Thoughtful) Heart: Centrality, Focality, or Overlap. *Journal of Anthropological Research* 36 (3): 338-342.

1982 People, Berdaches, and Left-Handed Bears: Human Variation in Native North America. *Journal of Anthropological Research* 38 (3): 274-287.

1985a Salish Kinship: Why Decedence? pp. 213-222. 20th International Conference on Salish and Neighboring Languages. August 15-17. University of British Columbia, Vancouver.

1985b Art and Souls: The Puget Sound Salish Journey to the Land of the Dead. 5th Conference of the National Native American Art Studies Association. Ann Arbor and Detroit.

1988 *Shamanic Odyssey.* The Lushootseed Salish Journey to the Land of the Dead, in terms of Death, Potency, and Cooperating Shamans in North America. Menlo Park, CA: Ballena Press Anthropological Papers 32.

1992a Native Healing in Puget Sound. Portrayal of Native American Health and Healing. *Caduceus* - A Museum Journal for the Health Sciences, 1-15.

1992b A Kinship of Spirit. Society in the Americas in 1492. *America in 1492*: 305-337. New York: Alfred Knopf.

1992c North Pacific Ethno-Astronomy: Tsimshian and Others. *Earth and Sky: Visions of the Cosmos in Native American Folklore*: 193-206. Claire Farrer and Ray Williamson, eds. Albuquerque: University of New Mexico Press.

1992d Society in America in 1492. *America In 1492*: Selected Lectures from the Quincentenary Program, The Newberry Library: 151-169. D'Arcy McNickle Center for the History of the American Indian. Occasional Papers in Curriculum Series 15. Harvey Markowitz, ed. Chicago.

1997 *Tsimshian Culture. A Light Through the Ages*. Lincoln: University of Nebraska Press.

1997a Back to Basics: Chiefdoms in Puget Sound. *Ethnohistory* 44 (2): 375-387.

1999 *Lushootseed Culture and the Shamanic Odyssey*: An Anchored Radiance. Lincoln: University of Nebraska Press.

1999a Suquamish Traditions. *Northwest Anthropological Research Notes* (*NARN*) 33 (1): 105-175.

2000 Inflamed History: Violence Against Homesteading Indiens in Washington Territory. *North Dakota Quarterly* 67 (3/4): 162-173.

2000a Religious Background of Salish Aesthetics by Helmi Juvonen. Jay Miller, ed. *Northwest Anthropological Research Notes* (NARN) 34 (1): 17-48.

2001 Ashes Ethereal: Cremation in the Americas. *American Indian Culture and Research Journal* 25 (1): 121-137.

2002 Dr. Simon: A Snohomish Slave at Fort Nisqually and Puyallup. *Journal of Northwest Anthropology* (*JONA*) 36 (2): 145-154.

2004 Winds, Waterways, and Weirs. Ethnographic Study of the Central Link Light Rail Corridor. Seattle: Sound Transit, Contract RTA/LR 69-00. BOAS Project No 20005.D (Astrida Blukis Onat).

2005 Dibble Cultivating Prairies to Beaches: The Real All Terrain Vehicle. *Journal of Northwest Anthropology ~ JONA* 39 (1): 33-39.

2011 First Nations Forts, Refuges, and War Lord Champions around the Salish Sea. *Journal of Northwest Anthropology ~ JONA* 45 (1): 71-87. Spring.

Miller, Jay, ed.

1990 *Mourning Dove ~ A Salishan Autobiography*. Lincoln: University of Nebraska Press.

2004 Regaining Dr. Herman Haeberlin. Early Anthropology and Museology in Puget Sound, 1916-1917. On Line @ osu.edu library/knowledge bank.

2015 Suquamish Traditions. *Evergreen Ethnographies*. Amazon. JONA 33 (1) 1999.

Miller, Jay, and Vi Hilbert

1993 Caring for Control: A Pivot of Salishan Language and Culture. *American Indian Linguistics and Ethnography in Honor of Laurence C. Thompson*. Missoula: University of Montana, Occasional Papers in Linguistics 10: 237-239.

1996 Lushootseed Animal People: Mediation and Transformation from Myth to History. *Monsters, Tricksters, and Sacred Cows*: *Animal Tales and American Identities*: 138-156. A. James Arnold, ed. New World Studies. Charlottesville: University of Virginia Press.

Morgan, Murray

1971 *Skid Road. An Informal Portrait of Seattle.* New York: Ballantine Books.

1979 *Puget's Sound. A Narrative of Early Tacoma and the Southern Sound.* Seattle: University of Washington Press.

Morse, Eldridge 1880 Notes on the history & resources of Washington Territory furnished to HH Bancroft. BANC MSS P-B #30-53.

Nabokov, Peter 2002 *A Forest of Time. American Indian Ways of History.* Cambridge University Press.

NARA –NW (Seattle)

Records of the Puget Sound District Agency (microfilm P2011).

Tract Books, Plat Books, GLO Public Lands.

Neufeld, Carol 1993 The Ships of Layfayette Balch. *Sea Chest* 26 (3, March): 116-120.

Nelson, Charles 1990 Prehistory of the Puget Sound Region. Handbook of North American Indians, *Northwest Coast*, Volume 7: 481-484.

Newcombe, C.F. 1923 Menzies' Journal of Vancouver's Voyage, April to October, 1792. Victoria: WH Cullin.

Norton, Helen H.

1980 Evidence for Bracken Fern as a food for Aboriginal Peoples of Western Washington. *Economic Botany* 33 (4): 384-396.

1990 Fort Nisqually: A Little Known Historical Treasure, Index for 1833-1849. Seattle Genealogical Society Bulletin 39 (3, Spring): 103-118.

1990a Fort Nisqually: A Little Known Historical Treasure: Part Two. Seattle Genealogical Society Bulletin 39 (4, Summer): 161-177.

1990b Fort Nisqually Index, Part Two, Index for 1849-1859. Seattle Genealogical Society Bulletin 39 (5, Autumn): 7-14.

1990/1 Fort Nisqually Index, Part Three – Settlers' Accounts of 1841-1879. Seattle Genealogical Society Bulletin 39 (3, Winter): 59-67.

1991a Index IV: Fort Nisqually Servants' Accounts 1836-1867. Seattle Genealogical Society Bulletin 39 (3, Spring): 111-115.

1991b Fort Nisqually Index 5: Women and the Frontier – 1840-1872. Seattle Genealogical Society Bulletin 39 (5, Autumn): 5-10;

ms. Huntington Microfilm, misframed inventory. (Norton 1990-91).

Oles, Floyd Hall c1986 *Glen Cove*, Scenes from a Puget Sound Boyhood. Tacoma: Privately Printed.

Oliver, R.C.B. 1978 Captain Peter Puget. *Sea Chest* 12 (1, September): 12-19.

Onat, Astrida Blukis 1984 The Interaction of Kin, Class, Marriage, Property Ownership and Residences with Respect to Resource Locations among Coast Salish of the Puget Sound Lowland. *Northwest Anthropological Research Notes* (*NARN*) 18: 86-96.

Pacific Daily Tribune

1872 Wednesday 16 October Vol VII # 2 page column 1 bottom, with the same text in *Washington Daily Standard*, 19 October 1872, page 3, column 2.

1874 Tuesday 14 April. IX (146), page 3, column 2.

Pierce County

1888 Auditor, Index to Deeds, 1859-1888, Grantor I-P. Tacoma.

1982 Cultural Resource Inventory, Volume IV, Peninsular Planning Area. Department of Planning and Community Development. November.

1988 Burley/Minter Drainage Basin Water Quality Plan. January.

Pethick Derek 1970 *SS Beaver, The ship that saved the West.* Vancouver: Mitchell Press Limited.

Porter, Joy 2001 *To Be Indian. The Life of Iroquois-Seneca Arthur Caswell Parker.* Norman: University of Oklahoma Press.

Post Intelligencer 1955 Tuesday April 5, page 1. [Jerry aged 74 (sic)]

Price, Andrew, Jr. 1989 *Port Blakely, The Community Captain Renton Built.* Seattle: Port Blakely Books.

Puyallup Land Commission Report 1903 Seattle: Puyallup Agency, National Archives and Records Administration, Sand Point Way.

Raibmon, Paige

2005 *Authentic Indians. Episodes of Encounter from the Late-nineteenth-Century Northwest Coast.* Durham: Duke University Press.

2008 Unmaking Native Space: A Genealogy of Indian Policy, Settler Practice, and the Microtechniques of Dispossession:, 56-85. *The Power of Promises ~ Rethinking Indian Treaties in the Pacific Northwest.* Alexandra Harmon, ed. Seattle: University of Washington Press.

Ray, Arthur J. 1988 The Hudson's Bay Company and Native People. Winnipeg: HBC.

Reddick, SuAnn 1996 Chemawa Indian Boarding School ~ The First Chapter. ms. on file, Seattle NARA Federal Archives.

Reece, Gary Fuller 1989 Origins of Pierce County Place Names. Tacoma: R&M Press.

Reid, Robie 1942 How One Slave Became Free, An Episode of the Old Days in Victoria. *British Columbia Historical Quarterly* 6 (4): 251-256.

Retherfod, Sylvia (Stella) 1997 History of Home, Washington, copies and clippings in four binders, filed at Peninsula Historical Society, Vaughan, and Key Center Library.

Reynolds, Nathan 2012 email of Dec 15, 11am, re: sweet acorns.

Robins, Mardel, Alice Rushton, and Louise Koehler Anderson 1987 *Ms. Guided Adventures.* Orting Valley, Yesterday and Today. Orting: Heritage Quest.

Rodman, Margaret 1992 Empowering Place: Multilocality and Multivocality. *American Anthropologist* 94 (3): 640-656.

Roe, JoAnne 1980 *The North Cascadians.* Seattle: Madrona Publishers.

Ross, John Alan 2011 *The Spokan Indians.* Spokane: Michael Ross.

Ruby, Robert, and John Brown

1992 *A Guide to the Indian Tribes of the Pacific Northwest.* Norman: University of Oklahoma Press.

1996 *John Slocum and the Indian Shaker Church.* Norman: University of Oklahoma Press.

Rygg, Lawrence Daniel 1977 The Continuation of Upper Class Snohomish Coast Salish Attitudes and Deportment as seen through the Life History of a Snohomish Coast Salish Woman. Bellingham: Western Washington University, MA Thesis.

Sale, Roger 1976 *Seattle Past to Present.* Seattle: University of Washington Press.

Sampson, Chief Martin 1972 Indians of Skagit County. La Conner: Skagit County Historical Society Historical Series 2.

Sanders, George 2012 *Honne ~ The Spirit of the Chehalis. The Indian Interpretation of the Origin of the People and Animals.* Collected and Arranged by Katherine Van Winkle Palmer. Introduction by Jay Miller. Lincoln: Bison Books.

SASSI (see Washington Department of Fish and Wildlife and Western Washington Treaty Indian Tribes, 1994).

Schaefer, Kurt Kim 2010 A Bitter Pill: Indian Reform Policy, Indian Acculturation, and the Puyallup Act of 1893. *Pacific Northwest Quarterly*, 102 (1): 14-28. (Winter ~ 2010-2011).

Schroeder, Albert, and Omer Steward 1988 Indian Servitude in the Southwest History of Indian – White Relations. Wilcomb Washburn, ed. Handbook of North American Indians, Volume 4, 410-413.

Schwantes, Carlos 1996 *The Pacific Northwest. An Interpretive History.* Revised and Enlarged. Lincoln: University of Nebraska Press.

Seattle Post Intelligencer

1940 Indians Moved When Old Homes Destroyed [Little Boston], Sunday, 27 October: p15.

1952 Brown's Point Gets Forecast. June.

Seattle Times 1946 13 January.

Seaburg, William 1999 Whatever Became of Thelma Adamson? A Footnote in the History of Northwest Anthropological Research. *Northwest Anthropological Research Notes* (*NARN*) 33 (1): 73-83.

Shackleford Newspaper Clippings. Tacoma: Washington State Historical Society.

Shackleford, Charlotte 1940 XVI. Donation Land Claims, *Building A State, Washington, 1889-1939*: 403-452. O. B. Sperlin, ed. Tacoma: Washington State Historical Society.

Shakleford, Elizabeth 1918 A History of the Puyallup Indian Reservation. Tacoma: College of Puget Sound, BA in History.

Sharp, Paul 1973 *Whoop-Up Country, The Canadian-American West, 1865-1885.* Norman: University of Oklahoma Press. [1955, 1960]

Shelton, Ruth Sehome 1995 "Gram" siastənu. The Wisdom of a Tulalip Elder. Recorded by Leon Metcalf, Translated by Vi Hilbert and Jay Miller. Seattle: Lushootseed Press.

Sicade, Henry 1940 The Indians' Side of the Story. *Building A State, Washington, 1889-1939*, XIX, 490-503. Charles Mills and O.B. Sperlin, eds. Tacoma: Washington State Historical Society.

Skahan, Elmer 1997 Early Days of Minter and Elgin. Talk to Key Peninsula Historical Society, 27 March.

Slauson, Morda C. 1976 *Renton* – From Coal to Jets. Renton Historical Society.

Smith, Marian

1940a *The Puyallup-Nisqually.* Columbia University Contributions to Anthropology 32.

1940b The Puyallup of Washington. *Acculturation in Seven American Indian Tribes*, Chapter 1, 3-36. Ralph Linton, ed. NY: D Appleton-Century Co.

1941 The Coast Salish of Puget Sound. *American Anthropologist* 43: 197-211.

Smith, Marian, ed.

1949 *Indians of the Urban Northwest.* Columbia University Contributions to Anthropology 36.

Snyder, Warren

1956 "Old Man House" on Puget Sound. *Washington State University Studies* 24: 17-37.

1968 *Southern Puget Sound Salish: Texts, Place Names, and Dictionary. Sacramento Anthropological Society*, Paper 9.

South Sound Spring Chinook Technical Committee

1996 Recovery Plan for White River Spring Chinook Salmon. July. Washington Department of Fish and Wildlife, Puyallup Tribe, Muckleshoot Tribe. July.

Stegner ,Wallace 1992 *Beyond the Hundredth Meridian*, John Wesley Powell and the Second Opening of the West. NY: Viking Penguin. [1954]

Stewart, Hilary

1982 *Indian Fishing. Early Methods on the Northwest Coast.* Seattle: University of Washington Press.

1984 *Cedar. Tree of Life to the Northwest Coast Indians.* Seattle: University of Washington Press.

Sturm, Circe

2002 *Blood Politics ~ Race, Culture, and Identity in the Cherokee Nation of Oklahoma.* Berkeley: University of California Press.

Suttles, Wayne

1987 *Coast Salish Essays*. Vancouver, BC: Talonbooks.

1987a The Plateau Prophet Dance among the Coast Salish, *Coast Salish Essays*, Chapter 9, 152-198. Vancouver, BC: Talonbooks.

1991 The Shed-Roof House *A Time of Gathering*: 212-222. Wright, ed.

Suttles, Wayne, ed. 1990 Handbook of North American Indians, *Northwest Coast*, Volume 7. Smithsonian Institution Press.

Suttles, Wayne, and William Elmendorf 1963 Linguistic Evidence For Salish Prehistory. pp. 41-52 in *Symposium on Language and Culture.* Edited by Viola E. Garfield and Wallace Chafe. Proceedings of the 1962 Annual Spring Meeting of the American Ethnological Society. Seattle: University of Washington Press.

Suttles, Wayne, and Aldona Jonaitis 1990 History of Research, *Northwest Coast.* Handbook of North American Indians, Volume 7: 73-87. DC: Smithsonian Institution Press.

Suttles, Wayne, and Barbara Lane 1990 Southern Coast Salish, *Northwest Coast*, Volume 7: 485-502. DC: Smithsonian Institution Press.

Tacoma Daily Ledger 1900 3 July.

Tacoma News Tribune

1878 24 September.

1938 15 April.

1955 April 4, Front page, Jerry Meeker Obituary, aged 93.

Tacoma Public Library (TPL)

Puyallup Cemetery Record (PCR).

Murray Morgan Collection (MMC).

Tacoma Times

1937 15 January.

1944 6 April.

Tacoma Sunday News Tribune and Ledger 1900 John McDonald, How Pierce County Took Part of King Co. [date missing at TPL, 1900 from other sources]

Taylor, Herbert 1974 Anthropological Investigation of the Medicine Creek Tribes Relative to Tribal Identity and Aboriginal Possession of Lands Docket 234, Defendants Exhibit 129, 1974: 401-473, *Coast Salish and Western Washington Indians* II: 475-694. David Agee Horr, ed. NY: Garland Publishing, Inc.

Thom, Brian 2005 Coast Salish Senses of Place: Dwelling, Meaning, Power, Property and Territory in the Coast Salish World. Montreal: McGill Anthropology PhD.

Tolmie, William Fraser 1963 *The Journals of William Fraser Tolmie: Physician and Fur Trader.* Vancouver: Mitchell Press, Ltd.

Tollefson, Kenneth 1995 Snoqualmie Indians as Hop Pickers. *Columbia* Winter 8 (4): 39-44.

Tollefson, Rodika 2009 Historians record nearly forgotten WA cemeteries. *Kitsap Sun*, August 1.

Tuan, Yi-Fu 1977 *Space and Place. The Perspective of Experience.* Minneapolis: University of Minnesota Press.

Turner, Nancy J 1975 *Food Plants of British Columbia Indians.* Part 1/ Coastal Peoples. Victoria: British Columbia Provincial Museum, Handbook 34.

Tweddell, Colin

1950 The Snoqualmie-Duwamish Dialects of Puget Sound Salish. *University of Washington Publications in Anthropology* 12.

1974 A Historical and Ethnological Study of the Snohomish Indian People. *Coast Salish And Western Washington Indians* V. David Agee Horr, ed. Indian Claims Commission, Findings 120: 475-694. New York: Garland Publishing, Inc.

UW – SC Special Collections [formerly UW – MSCUA = University of Washington, Manuscripts, Special Collections, and University Archives], Seattle.

Biography File (Meany Pioneers),

Sound Recordings (Melville Jacobs).

Back to the Farm (Ezra Meeker).

Viola, Herman, and Carolyn Margolis 1985 *Magnificent Voyagers, The US Exploring Expedition, 1838-1842.* Smithsonian Institution Press.

Walkinshaw, Robert 1929 *On Puget Sound.* NY: G. P. Putnam's Sons.

Walls, Robert 2000 E-mails to Jay Miller, Tuesday 03, Wednesday 04, October.

Walters, Raymond, Jr. 1957 *Albert Gallatin, Jeffersonian Financier and Diplomat.* NY: Macmillan Co.

Washington Department of Fish and Wildlife and Western Washington Treaty Indian Tribes. 1994 The 1992 Washington State Salmon and Steelhead Stock Inventory (SASSI). Appendix One, Puget Sound Stocks, North Puget Sound (NPS) Volume - 418pp, South Puget Sound (SPS) Volume - 371pp.

Washington Geology, 28 (3, May): 1-60, Nisqually Earthquake Issue 2001.

Washington State Historical Society (WSHS, Tacoma)

Puyallup Newspaper Clippings File

Edwin Eells Papers.

Washington Standard

1874 19 December, Olympia, Saturday Morning, Vol XV # 4: page 3, column 2.

1894 16 February, Olympia, Friday Evening, Vol XXXIV # 13: page 3, column 5.

Waterman, Thomas Talbot, and Geraldine Coffin 1920 Types of Canoes on Puget Sound. New York: Museum of the American Indian, Heye Foundation, *Indian Notes and Monographs.*

Waterman, Thomas, and Ruth Greiner 1921 Indian Houses of Puget Sound. New York: New York: Museum of the American Indian, Heye Foundation, *Indian Notes and Monographs*, Miscellaneous Series 5.

Waterman, Thomas, and Collaborators 1921 Native Houses of Western North America. New York: Museum of the American Indian, Heye Foundation, *Indian Notes and Monographs*, Miscellaneous Series 11.

Waterman, Thomas

1920 The Whaling Equipment of the Makah Indians. *University of Washington Publications in Anthropology* 1 (2).

1922 The Geographical Names Used by the Indians of the Pacific Coast. *The Geographical Review* 12 (2): 175-194.

1924 The Shake Religion of Puget Sound. *Smithsonian Report* for 1922: 499-507.

1930 The Paraphernalia of the Duwamish 'Spirit-Canoe' Ceremony. New York: Museum of the American Indian, Heye Foundation, *Indian Notes* 7 (2): 129-148, 295-312, 535-561.

1973 Notes on the Ethnology of the Indians of Puget Sound. New York: Museum of the American Indian, Heye Foundation, *Indian Notes and Monographs*, Miscellaneous Series 59.

2001 See Hilbert, Miller, and Zahir.

White River Historical Society, Auburn

Arthur Condit Ballard Interview.

Charles H Ballard, Pioneer Experiences of the Ballard Family on White River.

Wickersham, James

1892 A Boston Tillicum ~ A Plea for the Puyallups. Tacoma: Daily News Print.

1896 Pueblos on the Northwest Coast. *American Antiquarian* 18: 21-24.

1898 Nisqually Mythology, Studies of the Washington Indians. *Overland Monthly* 32: 345-51.

1899 Notes on the Indians of Washington. *American Antiquarian* 21: 269-375.

Wihr, William 1995 "You Toad Sucking Fool": An Inquiry into the Possible Use of Bufoteninie by Northern Northwest Coast Shamans. *Northwest Anthropological Research Notes* (*NARN*) 29 (1): 51-59.

Wike, Joyce

1941 Modern Spirit Dancing of Northern Puget Sound. University of Washington: M.A. Thesis.

1952 The Role of the Dead in Northwest Coast Culture. *Indian Tribes of Aboriginal America*, Proceedings of the 29th International Congress of Americanists: 97-103. Sol Tax, ed.

Williams, Judith 2006 *Clam Gardens ~ Aboriginal Mariculture on Canada's West Coast*. Vancouver: New Star Books, Transmontanus 15.

Willoughby, Charles 1969 Indians of the Quinaielt Agency, Washington Territory. Seattle: Shorey Book Store Facsimile Reproduction of 1886 *Smithsonian Institution Annual Report*, 1889: 267-282.

Wing, Robert, with Gordon Newell 1979 *Peter Puget*. Seattle: Gray Beard Publishing.

Winthrop, Theordore 1862 *Canoe and Saddle*. Boston: Ticknor & Fields. Reprinted Portland: Binfords and Mort, 1955.

Winterhouse, John 1948 A Report of an Archaeological Survey of Lower Puget Sound. Seattle: UW Office of Public Archaeology.

Wood, Peter 1988 Indian Servitude in the Southeast History of Indian – White Relations. Wilcomb Washburn, ed. Handbook of North American Indians, Volume 4: 407-409.

Wright, Robin, ed. 1991 *A Time of Gathering, Native Heritage of Washington State*. Seattle: University of Washington Press.

Yonce, Fred

1969 Public Land Disposal in Washington. UW History PhD.

1972 The Public Land Surveys in Washington. *Pacific Northwest Quarterly* 64 (4): 129-141, October.

York, Annie, Richard Daly, and Chris Arnett 1994 *They Write Their Dreams on the Rock Forever: Rock Writings of the Stein River Valley of British Colombia*. Vancouver, BC: Talon Books.

Index

E

F

G

H

I

J

K

Q

R

S

T

* # = footnote + number

Please Help Banish Typo Gnomes!

Sold @ Amazon.com

Jay Miller's books & E-books @ Amazon.com

ACCULTURATING AMELIA ~ Round Valley 1937 California
ALASKA EDGE ISLAND ~ Siberian Yupiks of St Lawrence Island
ALLIED MOUNDS ~ Touching the Earth, Modeling the World, Reaching the Sky
ANIMAL PEOPLE ADVENTURES ~ Native North American Tribal Stories
AT BAY ~ Cultures Converging through Southwest Washington
BALLARD BULWARK ~
CHACO ECHOES ~ Pervasive Keresan Priesthoods
CHACOKIA ~ Chaco, Cahokia, Cities & Ceremonies ~ Bundles & Blood Lines Centuries Ago
CHINOOK CONCERNS ~ Emma Millett Luscier, Isabella Bertrand, Verne Ray
CIRCLING FOUR CORNERS ~ Re-Viewing Native American Indiens
CROSSING ~ LINES: An Educational Memoir of Native North America
DEL-AWARE ~ Lenape Legacies
DELAWARE INTEGRITY ~ Rituals, Removals, Reforms by Lenape Indiens
DISCLAIMING TREATIES I ~ Puget Tribes 1927 Testimonies
DISCLAIMING TREATIES II ~ Puget Tribes 1927 Testimonies
ELDERS' DIALOG ~ Ed Davis & Vi Hilbert Discuss Native Puget Sound Language, Culture, & Heritage
EVERGREEN ETHNOGRAPHIES ~ Hoh, Chehalis, Suquamish, and Snoqualmi of Western Washington
FEDERAL FISH FILES ~ Swindell 1942 Treaty Rights Report
GEORGE GIBBS NORTHWEST ARRAY ~ Full Reports, Place Names, Word List, Artifact Names, and Guide
GRASSROOTS JANET ~ Advancing Salish and Traditional Cultures
HERMAN HAEBERLIN REGAINED ~ Anthropology and Artifacts of Puget Sound 1916-17
HERSTORY NW ~ Women Upholding Native Traditions
INDIEN ~ ETHNOGRAPHY: Cultural Traditions of Native North America
INDIEN ~ ETHNOLOGY: Grounded, Gendered, Meaningful Cultural Traditions
LESCHI IN LOVE ~ A Novel of Native Puget Sound > x2
MARCO MUCK MASKS ~ Frank Cushing on Marshes and Mounds
MINTER BAY ~ Land, Lore, Loss, and Lucre in the South Salish Sea
NATIVE MET HOW ~ Improving Posterity
OLD LUKH ~ A Novel of Native Puget Sound Daily Life, Places, and Stories
OVER THE FALLS ~ Sdoqwalbixw Survivance Surrounding Seattle
PACIFIC PLATEAU PORTRAYALS ~ People Places Ponderings
RAY'S ARRAY ~ Raymond D Fogelson's Works
RIGHTING NATIVE PLACES ~ Adventures in Northwest Geography
SAHAPTINS STUDIES ~ Columbia River Plateau, Cora Du Bois, Homer Garner Barnett, Gerald Raymond Desmond
SDOQWALBIXW
SOUND SALISH STRAITS ~ Central Salish Sea Cultures
UNSETTLING SEATTLE ~ Arresting Local Talent and Academic Illiteracy
WRITING WORDS IN WARY WORLDS ~ World Wide Improved Spellings of Native America Languages

JONA Memoirs

RESCUES, RANTS, & RESEARCHES ~ A Re-View of Jay Miller's Writings on Northwest Indien Cultures ~ #9
TRIBAL TRIO of the Northwest Coast by Kenneth D Tollefson ~ #10
INTERWEAVING COAST SALISH CULTURAL SYSTEMS ~ Collected Works of Pamela Thorsen Amoss ~ #14

University of Nebraska Press

ANCESTRAL MOUNDS ~ Vitality and Volatility Crossing Native North America 2015
HONNE ~ The Spirit of the Chehalis 2015